THE ART OF STYLING PARAGRAPHS

THE ART OF STYLING PARAGRAPHS

ROBERT M. ESCH

ROBERTA R. WALKER

THE UNIVERSITY OF TEXAS AT EL PASO

MACMILLAN PUBLISHING COMPANY
NEW YORK

Editor: Barbara A. Heinssen
Production Supervisor: Katherine Evancie
Production Manager: Richard C. Fischer
Text and Cover Designer: Patrice Fodero
Cover Illustration: Istvan Nyari

This book was set in Bembo by V & M Graphics, Inc., and
printed and bound by R. R. Donnelley & Sons Company.
The cover was printed by Phoenix Color Corp.

Macmillan Publishing Company
866 Third Avenue, New York, New York 10022

LIBRARY OF CONGRESS CATALOGING-IN-PUBLICATION DATA

Esch, Robert M.
    The art of styling paragraphs / Robert M. Esch, Roberta R. Walker.
        p.   cm.
    ISBN 0-02-334310-9
    1. English language — Paragraphs.   2. English language — Rhetoric.
3. English language — Style.   I. Walker, Roberta R.   II. Title.
PE1439.E83   1990   89-37762
428.2 — dc20   CIP

Acknowledgments

  Copland, Aaron, "What to Listen for in Music." Copyright © 1957 by
McGraw-Hill Book Company. Reprinted by permission of McGraw-Hill Book
Company.

  Faulkner, William, excerpt from "William Faulkner's Speech of Acceptance
upon the Award of the Nobel Prize for Literature." Reprinted from *The Faulkner
Reader* by William Faulkner, by permission of Random House, Inc.

  Lessard, Suzannah, excerpt from "Notes and Comment," from *The Talk of the
Town.* Reprinted by permission; © 1977, The New Yorker Magazine, Inc.

  Levy, Norman, "The Camera Eye." Copyright © 1952 by Norman Levy as
first published in *The Atlantic Monthly.* Reprinted by permission.

  MacKaye, William R., "The Way We Wrote." Originally appeared in *The
Washington Post Magazine,* July 28, 1988. Reprinted by permission of the author.

  McGinley, Phyllis, "Are Children People?" Reprinted with permission of
Macmillan Publishing Company from *Sixpence in Her Shoe* by Phyllis McGinley.
Copyright © 1963, 1964 by Phyllis McGinley.

Printing: 1 2 3 4 5 6 7   Year: 0 1 2 3 4 5 6

In Memory of
Marie
and
Philip

Contents

Chapter 3   THE MATERIAL THAT DEVELOPS THE PARAGRAPH   50

Preface

The philosophy underlying this book is that writers learn by imitating patterns, both written and visual. When the ability to analyze patterns is coupled with an understanding of the writing process, effective composition results. Writing by pattern is a long-standing tradition in the world of letters, going back to classical rhetoricians and the Renaissance. Based on this tradition, *The Art of Styling Paragraphs* presents boxed visual diagrams of paragraph patterns, explanations, and analyses of different types of paragraphs, with examples from students and professional writers. The text integrates an on-going discussion of the writing process within explanations of the patterns. Numerous checklists, activities, writing assignments, and exercises appear throughout that serve to reinforce instruction.

This book integrates its coverage of the writing process and its analysis of the final product to provide a balanced approach to composition. *The Art of Styling Paragraphs* is designed for multiple audiences both inside and outside the classroom: the puzzled first-year college student wanting to improve essay exam writing skills; the adult learner returning to college; and the career person interested in learning strategies for more effective communication. Composition teachers will find the explanations, examples, diagrams, and exercises appropriate for development and first-year level English courses. Students will discover easy ways to master paragraph style, content, and structure. The accompanying *Instructor's Manual* stimulates the new teacher to develop creative approaches for introducing the text to students.

Overall Goals

Both students and teachers will find the text comprehensive, presenting all that anyone ever wanted to know about paragraphs. The completeness of the treatment challenges teachers to select what is appropriate for a particular class. The text challenges readers to organize their thoughts logically, to establish goals and plans, to write with more impressive style, and to gain greater respect for their work. Knowledge of these patterns provides a vast pool of resources, which, in the long run, will free writers to create their own unique style.

Organization

Chapter 1 defines the paragraph with its parts and presents a complete discussion of the writing process. In addition to analysis of prewriting, brainstorming, clustering, drafting, revising, and editing, the chapter explores six journalistic questions and Kenneth Burke's "Pentad" as aids to stimulate ideas for writers. Process-oriented exercises and writing assignments, together with readers and writer commentary guides, encourage students to explore new strategies for composing.

Chapter 2 introduces the topic sentence (its parts and placement), the subtopic sentence (its parts and number), and the final clincher sentence. The chapter encourages students to experiment with a variety of techniques for developing each of these organizational sentences for writing paragraphs. Simple outlines of paragraphs and an eight-point editing checklist act as composing aids for revising.

Chapter 3 describes in substantial detail supporting materials, including invention strategies for locating them and drafting techniques for using more than ten different types. The chapter also illustrates how specific details function within paragraphs.

Chapter 4 introduces bridge building within paragraphs and devices for achieving coherence and transition through coordination, subordination, repetition, and selective use of pronouns. The chapter also includes a detailed chart of transitional words and phrases as well as one on coordinators, each with numerous examples for analysis and exercises for reinforcement. The goal of the chapter is to help writers internalize knowledge of transitional elements and how to use them to create effective, unified writing. The chapter concludes with a discussion of sexist pronouns and strategies to avoid them.

Chapter 5 introduces six familiar patterns and the rationale for using each. These patterns include the chronological pattern, the spatial pattern for descriptive writing, the kite pattern with a delayed topic sentence, the circular pattern with the topic sentence omitted, and the sandwich pattern with the topic sentence repeated in two key positions. Inductive ordering of ideas, with important information withheld from the reader, is the final pattern discussed. Additionally, this chapter introduces detailed audience analysis, rhetorical stance, and arranging ideas based on order of importance. Example paragraphs motivate students to learn how professional writers use the skills; many student paragraphs illustrate the successful ways students adapt the techniques to their own composing methods. These examples are analyzed and discussed within the context of writing as a process.

Chapter 6 continues the presentation of patterns by focusing on the most common structure in English prose—the general-to-particular structure and its variations. In addition to the basic deductive pattern, this chapter includes more complicated structures: the question-to-answer pattern, causal analysis, and the problem-to-solution pattern. Many illustrative paragraphs show how writers use novel structures to present ideas more effectively.

Chapter 7 focuses on five deductive patterns that are in some manner analytical. They are presented from the simplest to the most complex, from comparison–contrast, process analysis, enumeration, and classification, to the more technical and difficult argumentative pattern. The chapter carefully analyzes the parts of an argument, including its premise and the various appeals and psychological strategies that argument requires. Links between speaking and writing, such as the "motivated sequence," alert students to techniques shared by speakers and writers. A checklist for effective argument concludes the chapter.

Chapter 8 discusses very special, essential paragraphs for the whole essay—the introductory, concluding, and transitional paragraphs. The chapter also explores minor paragraphs for expansion of examples, and other supporting details. A sketch helps students visualize possible placement of major transitions. Also included are rarely treated paragraph conventions: using special indentations, citing verbatim material, poetic indentations, and eccentric forms such as those used by John Dos Passos and others. The chapter also shows how to paragraph conversation, dialogue, and interview, as well as special gimmicks commercial writers use for emphatic paragraphing in advertising script.

Chapter 9 forms the bridge between a paragraph and a multiparagraph theme. Numerous student examples (complete with multiple drafts and peer editing sheets) supplement the discussion, which covers selecting titles; structuring the thesis; outlining short essays; and creating introductions, conclusions, and body paragraphs with essential transitions. The aim of the chapter is to bolster student confidence in writing a larger essay and to prepare college students for handling more complicated writing skills demanded by upper-division courses. The chapter concludes with a final checklist, student themes complete with drafts, and a short professional essay for analysis.

Chapter 10 concludes *The Art of Styling Paragraphs* with techniques for adapting paragraphing skills to writing essay examinations. The chapter contains several "secrets" that will help students raise test grades at least ten points. An important portion focuses exclusively on reading and analyzing test questions. Definitions of key terms frequently appearing in examination questions supplement the discussion. The chapter includes both poor and satisfactory examination answers for students to analyze. A final goal is to show students the meanings and implications behind test grades.

Acknowledgments

We owe a considerable debt to our late colleague, Philip J. Gallagher, who read and annotated early drafts of the manuscript with great care and insight. We never won all of our battles with him.

Our special thanks to other friends and colleagues for their help and encouragement: Tommy Boley, Betty Manriquez, Shireen McIntyre, Gail Mortimer, Maureen Potts, Donna Reardon, Cindy Reza, Agnes Robinson, Gladys Shaw, Marjorie Thurston, and Pat Withers. We also wish to acknowledge those El Paso students whose work appears throughout the book. We are grateful to our typists, Jean Hocking and Florence Dick, who worked with patience, care, and diligence.

We are particularly indebted to Jennifer Crewe, former editor at Macmillan, who first expressed enthusiasm about the manuscript, and to Barbara Heinssen, who sustained that enthusiasm and encouraged us in carrying the project to its completion. The following reviewers offered numerous helpful comments, and we thank them for their insights and guidance: Donald Cruickshank, University of Illinois; Martha French, Fairmont State College; Walter Klarner, Johnson County Community College; Beatrice Tignor, Prince George's Community College; Evelyn Webb, Mississippi Coast Community College; Warren Westcott, Francis Marion College; and Beverly Wickersham, Central Texas College.

R.M.E.
R.R.W.

The Paragraph	CHAPTER 1

One of the things we hear so often is that ours is a visual age. Billboards present wildly extravagant lures for us to buy a product, plan a vacation in Hawaii, or trust a friendly bank downtown. Colors and popular models beckon us to specific products advertised in the pages of *Time, Playboy, Vogue,* and other popular magazines. In supermarkets we often reach for products that were not on our shopping list simply because attractive packaging has made them so appealing. At home we watch television so often that we have become accustomed to communicating without words. When we do communicate, we telephone, telegraph, or speak our messages; less frequently do we write them down. Even universal logos communicate through symbols, not words. What messages do these logos convey?

This is a book about communicating, but we will be talking about written communication. And in a special form for arranging thoughts — the paragraph.

What exactly is a paragraph? And what does one look like? In her book *Paragraph Practice*, Kathleen Sullivan suggests through a cluster of *x*'s a pattern that you will recognize as the paragraph (New York: Macmillan, 1989, p. 21).

Xxxx xxxx xxxxxxxxxx xxxx xxx. Xx xx xxxxx xxxxx xxxxxxxx xxxx, xxx xxxx xxxxx xxxxx? Xxxxxx xxxxx xxx; xxxxx xxxxx xx xxxx xxxxxxxx, xxx xxxxx xxxxx xxxx xxx. Xxxx! Xxxx xxxxx, xxx xxx, xxx, xxx. X xxx xxxxx xxxx xxxxx xxxxx xx xxxxxxx xxx. Xxx xxxxx xxxxx xxxxx xxxxx xxx xx xxxxx, xxxxx xxxxx xx xxx xxxx xxxxx. Xxx xxxx xxxx xx xxxx, xxx xxx xxxxxxxx xxx xxx xxxxxx xx.

You can see in this brief diagram some of its characteristics:

1. The first line of a paragraph is indented.
2. Sentences within begin with a capital letter.
3. Some sentences have internal punctuation, and all have special end markers.
4. A paragraph appears to have several sentences, not just one or two. (We will learn about special, brief paragraphs later. See Chapter 8.)

If you were to look at a thirteenth-century manuscript (see page 3), you probably would be surprised to find no clearly identifiable paragraphing.

Definition

The word *paragraph* derives from two Greek word parts — *para*, meaning "beside," and *graphein*, meaning "to write." Early writers put a mark (something similar to ¶) or a pointing finger to signal where a new unit (or paragraph) in their writing was to begin. Indentation was an aid to a reader, not necessarily an indication of a new thought unit. A little later we will learn even more about the history of paragraphing and special signals writers have relied on to indicate new paragraphs. (See Chapter 8.)

oïa:quî ſe ſaüp cogitat effe moꝛîtuꝛ
Jncipit plogus in paritharcucū moïſi
Eſîderiĵ mei deſideratas
accepi lꝛãs·quî quodam
pſagio futuroꝛ·cū Danii
le ſoꝛtitus ē nomen:obſi
cꝛãtis ut tranſſatū ī latinā linguā ʒ
hebreo ſermone penthateucū noſtroꝛ
auribꝫ tradece. Pericloſū opus certe
ʒ obtrectatoꝛ meoꝫ latratibꝫ patens
quî me aſſerūt ī ſeptuaginta interpti

Why Write in Paragraphs?

Paragraphing gives readers time to think about what you have said. The paragraph conveniently allows them to take "intellectual breaths," as Fred Bergmann calls them in *Paragraph Rhetoric*, by breaking up the monotony of the printed page. By giving readers time to think about ideas, you make the message easier to understand. The paragraph is a package for an important idea that you hope others will be eager to read about.

Paragraph Length

How often have you wanted to ask about the length of an assignment? How many pages should it be? How many words? Have you ever thought about the length of a paragraph in this same way?

There is no ideal length for a paragraph. Don't believe anybody who tells you there is! Some paragraphs may be only one word; others are 250 words or more. Length depends entirely on the writer's purpose. Is there a brief message that can be communicated rapidly? Is the message longer, and does it demand greater development? Open a few books — your history text, for example — and see how long the paragraphs are. You'll probably find from one to three paragraphs on each page. Sometimes, even more. You might want to go further and count sentences or lines to get a rough idea of average paragraph lengths. Just be certain to say enough so that the subject is clearly and fully explained.

Christy's teacher has remarked about her paper, "Short, choppy paragraphs; can't you combine them?" How might Christy revise these three short paragraphs at the beginning of her research paper?

No More Lies

"Pilferage, theft, and embezzlement by employees has increased to a problem of major proportions," Nevil Coghil said in a recent <u>Newsweek</u> article. The polygraph, better known as the "lie detector," is not the solution to these problems.

Key issues have been brought up concerning the use of polygraph testing in employment. They are (1) test accuracy, (2) individual privacy, and (3) operator ability, according to Nicolas and Elaine Fry in the February 1988 issue of <u>Personnel</u>.

The accuracy of these polygraph tests has been questioned for years. The accuracy of results, the Frys say, range from 60% to 90%, according to opponents, and from 90% to 100%, according to polygraph operators. Even so, these polygraph tests should be banned because they foster discrimination against employees, invade the privacy of workers tested, and may lead to many unreliable interpretations that affect innocent people applying for jobs.

What Is a Developmental Paragraph?

This book explains in considerable detail the *developmental paragraph* — a composition in miniature, part of a larger essay. All of the sentences in this developmental structure are interwoven and develop a single idea that is either stated or implied.

Definition Let's define the developmental pargraph because it is our major concern. <u>It is a group of interrelated sentences that together support or prove one single idea.</u> It should be complete with (1) precise examples and other specific details, (2) sufficient transitional elements or other devices for achieving coherence, (3) some predetermined order or pattern, and (4) <u>development of only one main thought</u>.

Other terms used to describe this sort of paragraph are *major paragraph, main paragraph,* or *complete paragraph.* But whatever the terminology, it is important to recognize the characteristics of this paragraph structure and to imitate its pattern in your writing. Here are some developmental paragraph checkpoints:

1. It has a clearly identifiable beginning.
2. It develops only a single idea.
3. It has a *topic sentence* that states the central or controlling idea. (See Chapter 2.)
4. It has a middle, with supporting sentences full of details related to the central idea.
5. It has several subtopic sentences that enlarge upon the topic sentence. (See Chapter 2.)
6. It has supporting material for explaining these subtopics. (See Chapter 3.)
7. It usually has a "clincher sentence" that concludes the argument on a strong, forceful note. (See Chapter 2).

A diagram of a developing paragraph follows. Notice where each of the parts belongs:

TOPIC SENTENCE: THE START

SUBTOPIC SENTENCE 1: THE MIDDLE

SUBTOPIC SENTENCE 2: THE MIDDLE

SUBTOPIC SENTENCE 3: THE MIDDLE

THE CLINCHER SENTENCE: THE FINISH

Following is a more detailed diagram of a paragraph.

BEGINNING

Introduction — the big idea
The Topic Sentence

MIDDLE

Point One — the smaller, narrowed topic
Subtopic Sentence 1

MIDDLE

Point Two — the smaller, narrowed topic
Subtopic Sentence 2

MIDDLE

Point Three — the smaller, narrowed topic
Subtopic Sentence 3

END

Conclusion — restatement of big idea
Ending on the Clincher Sentence

The following diagram illustrates the detailed structure of the whole paragraph. Each developmental paragraph roughly follows this form, with sentences alternating in levels of generality from the general (topic sentence), to the specific (subtopic sentence), to the highly specific (explanatory sentence), and back to the general (clincher sentence).

TOPIC SENTENCE

Explanatory sentences

SUBTOPIC SENTENCE 1

Explanatory sentences plus supporting detail

characterization   facts
comparisons   instances
contrasts   statistics
definitions   testimony
examples

SUBTOPIC SENTENCE 2

Explanatory sentences plus supporting detail

SUBTOPIC SENTENCE 3

Explanatory sentences plus supporting detail

CLINCHER SENTENCE

What Is a Minor Paragraph?

Definition

A *minor paragraph* is a very short one that does not fully develop an idea. But despite its length, it is extremely important. It has no topic sentence. It even may be only a few sentences long, whereas a developmental paragraph can have numerous sentences. There are four kinds of minor paragraphs (discussed in more detail in Chapter 8):

Introductory paragraph

An *introductory paragraph* arouses reader curiosity about your idea and forecasts what you will say.

Transitional paragraph

A *transitional paragraph* is the most common type of minor paragraph. It "pre-outlines" what will follow in the next paragraph or serves as a summary of material discussed previously.

Extension paragraph

Occasionally, you might want to use an *extension paragraph* that helps link thoughts among larger paragraphs. It may have only one or two words. "But how" might serve as an extension between two paragraphs—the first identifying the nature of a problem, the second enumerating ways to achieve a solution.

Concluding paragraph

Similarly, at the end of a long theme, a *concluding paragraph* may draw inferences from all you have said and brings the paper to a meaningful close.

CHECKLIST

What follows are some checkpoints for a minor paragraph:

1. It is succinct.
2. It has a special function.
3. Its length is dependent on this function, but normally it is relatively short.
4. It does not develop an idea or contain supporting material that belongs in a development paragraph.

The Writing Process

Once challenged by a writing assignment, no matter whether it is from a teacher at school or a supervisor in the workplace, you have to find a starting point. You may already have a topic assigned, such as "Write a three-paragraph theme on handwriting analysis." Or you may have to invent an idea to write about, such as a paper describing a phase you went through during adolescence. Or you may simply have some idea of a task, such as a résumé or proposal, that you need to complete. But where do you go from this point? Writing itself is a process that moves through several recognizable stages. To simplify, let's discuss five stages: prewriting, drafting, revising, editing, and proofreading. You need to recognize, however, that these steps necessarily overlap.

Prewriting

You usually start prewriting by listing all the things you know about the topic, probing your mind to recall personal experience, seeking new ideas. Doing so may take a few minutes or several weeks, depending upon your recall ability or the magnitude of the task. Once you have the list, you need to move beyond personal experience, inventing new ideas. Magazines, books, pamphlets, and newspapers might provide you with new insights. The more you read, the more knowledgeable you become. You may even get information from radio or television to help find a subject. Then by a process called "clustering" (grouping related ideas under a single category of knowledge), you move during prewriting to narrow the topic from something too broad to handle to a really manageable size.

On a sheet of paper, make a large circle in the center and in it write your proposed subject. Around this center circle, quickly jot down ideas related to the main subject. Circle each and connect with linking lines to the subject circle to show relationships and order of importance. Do this clustering rapidly; spend only seconds doing it. The purpose behind this technique is to get you to narrow your subject. For instance, the example of the clustering around a topic such as financing a college education should generate many ideas — more than you'll be able to cover, except in a book. You'd be wise to decide upon one small phrase, one of the small circles. Consider, possibly, a topic based upon National Guard scholarships or the advantages and disadvantages of a part-time job at Wendy's.

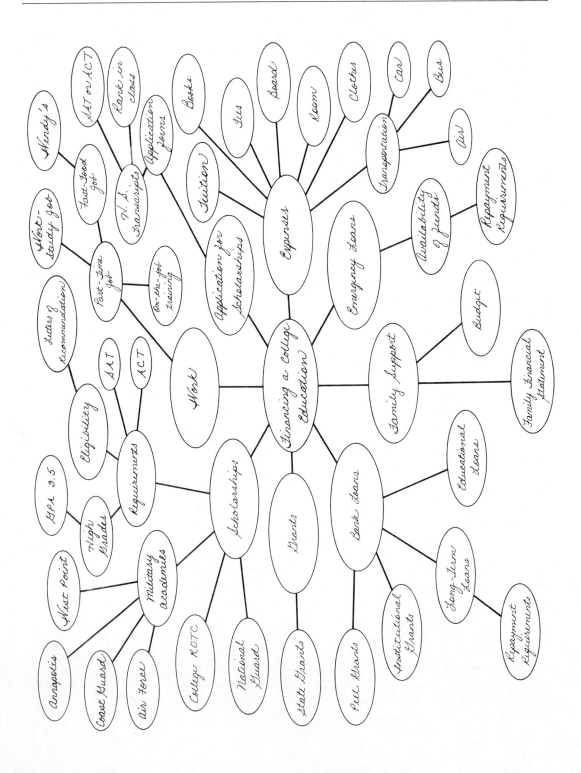

```
Exercise 1–1
```

Create a cluster using one of the following topics or select a topic of your choice.

1. Communication satellites
2. Unusual birthday gifts
3. Health spas
4. Planning a costume party
5. The car of the future
6. Role models
7. Job hunting
8. Strategies for getting promoted
9. Quitting a job
10. Budgeting

Another strategy of prewriting is brainstorming with others, tossing ideas around. Talking with friends, fellow employees, or other informed individuals provides you with a useful invention resource.

Or you might try freewriting (writing nonstop for several minutes). It is an excellent start because you don't worry about getting everything right. When writing nonstop, don't pause to edit, change spelling, or alter structure; write breathlessly.

Even after brainstorming and freewriting, you may experience writer's block and feel you have nothing more to say. Begin by asking the journalistic questions of *who, what, when, where, why* and *how* to stimulate yourself.

```
Writing Assignment
```

Recall an important event that had special meaning to you. Write a paragraph in which you incorporate answers to *six* basic questions. Use as many specific details as you can.

Example: A baby's christening

Who	Who is being christened? How old is the baby? What is the baby's age and name? Who are the parents and godparents? Who was the minister?
What	What took place during the ceremony? What rituals did you observe? What did the baby do at the ceremony? What did the baby wear?
When	When did the ceremony take place? What time of day, month, year?
Where	Where did the ceremony take place? Can you describe the setting?
Why	Why did the ceremony occur? Why did some in the audience cry?
How	How was the ceremony conducted?

Or analyze the topic further by identifying Act, Scene, Agent, Agency, and Purpose as Kenneth Burke describes them in his Pentad in *A Grammar of Motives*. Give your material a dramatic approach by thinking of it in stage terms of the following:

Act	Names what took place, the deed, what was done or said
Scene	The situation in which the deed occurred, when or where it was done, the backgrounds or setting for the Act
Agent	The person/persons who perform the Act
Agency	The means by which the person/persons performed the Act: how it was done, including words and behavior
Purpose	The reason/reasons for the action, why it was done, the end sought by the Agent

The Pentad will help you determine what strategies to use to clarify relationships; it will help you avoid ambiguity, and you'll gain new ways of looking at your topic. The following is a sentence analyzed by the Pentad questions:

Example: In "Hills Like White Elephants" at a
scene   *agent*
small bar in the train station, the American and the
agency   *act*
girl Jig discuss her "awfully simple operation" (an
purpose
abortion) as a way to achieve greater happiness in

their relationship.

The Pentad: Prewriting Activity

The Pentad is an intensive prewriting technique. Using it will help you explore in depth your subject matter and help you think about it before you begin writing. The Pentad will help you recall what you already know about a subject; it may guide you in library research. Select to analyze an important event (marriage customs, bar mitzvahs, quinceañeras) in your life or within your family, then ask the Pentad questions that apply to the event. Write out in list form the questions and your answers. Using five separate sheets of paper, head each one with a Pentad question. Then list as many specific details as you can for each question.

1. *The Action*
    What is the action? When did it occur?

2. *The Scene*
    Where did the action happen? What was the scene like?

3. *The Actors*
    Who or what was responsible for the action? Who were the persons (actors) who caused the action?

4. *The Agency*
    What method was used to create the action? What occurred?

5. *The Purpose*
    What was the purpose of the action? How did purpose affect the actors? What else influenced purpose?

At this point in the invention stage, you should consider a few preliminary questions about audience. How much can you assume your readers know? How informed are they? Do they share a particular bias? (For a more complete discussion of audience analysis see Chapter 5.)

You might also begin to think about your emotional stance. Will irony be understood? Should the paper sound humorous? Or is the topic serious, requiring you to reflect this seriousness?

Drafting

Even though **prewriting, drafting,** and **revising** are discussed separately here, they are not independent activities. Instead, they overlap in the writing process because when writing, you take steps backward in order to take others forward. That is, write, then rewrite. You may pause in the middle of one draft to do some additional brainstorming. You may want to do more research that may make you reconsider ideas already developed. You may decide to omit—or include—additional explanations. The point is, writing is not a linear (straight-line) process. Rather, it is like a series of loops.

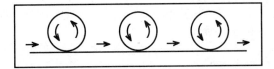

During drafting, you should analyze, more precisely than before, the intended audience. If you're writing just for yourself, as in notes and diaries or journal entries, it's unlikely that another person would understand either the notes or the entries. Purely personal writing is sometimes called writer-based prose. But more often than not, you have to reach out to others. When writing to communicate with them, you are developing reader-based prose for a specific audience.

There is no single way to draft a paper. Are you comfortable writing on legal-sized paper? Or are you already composing in front of a microprocessor? It will be helpful in revising if you write each paragraph on a single sheet, using only one side of the paper. This format allows you to "cut and paste," adding, deleting, and rearranging.

From brainstorming, you have decided upon a central idea. Now begin to narrow and focus the writing by discarding irrelevancies. Next think about shaping your paper. Will ideas fall naturally into a chronological order? If so, you can move from past to present. Or perhaps from present to future. You might even consider writing in retrospect.

Are you telling someone how to do something? If so, outline the steps, making sure that their order is correct. Think for a moment about a recipe. How important is it to give instructions to follow steps in a specific order?

Are you establishing cause–effect relationships? It's important to list effects first. Imagine the first thing that happened in an accident you have just observed. Was someone injured? Was someone's new Corvette dented or destroyed? Relate these effects, then, to their specific causes. What caused one car to hit the other? List the causes and write about each.

Are you trying to define, deduce, compare, or contrast? When writing a lengthy paper, you will have to decide what the basic structure will be. (You might say to yourself, "Basically, my main structure is telling a story," or "Here I'm going to argue a point.") Afterward, you can begin thinking about some of the "mini-structures" of individual paragraphs. In paragraphing, if you have an intention such as comparing or contrasting, you can quickly review and follow the specific patterns of organization illustrated in Chapters 5, 6, and 7.

In Chapter 8, you'll learn about strategies for writing introductions and conclusions. Right now, you only need to realize that introductions set out specific promises to readers and establish limits. The thesis statement, which helps establish these limits, usually appears in the introduction. The thesis is generally not firmly established before you begin a paper. When you write, it may be subject to modifications as you learn more about the topic. Normally, you will write introductions and conclusions last. You can't introduce until there is a content to introduce. Nor can you conclude until you know what you've said in the whole paper.

With early drafts of concluding paragraphs, make certain that the paper comes to a meaningful close and avoids a "That's all folks!" type of ending. An abrupt ending may confuse readers or leave them hanging, wondering whether part of the paper is missing. Conclusions may look ahead to the future. Or they may look back at what precedes, possibly even drawing inferences from the whole paper. Usually there is some word in the final paragraph that helps indicate closure.

One crazy-sounding principle about drafting is valid: let the first draft be bad. Make it your sloppy copy! Don't be inhibited by thinking everything must be perfect. But be careful: this sloppy copy is your first draft; it's not the copy you turn in to your teacher or present to the public as a final draft. Your first draft might resemble the following example:

The absence of logical connections among
~~One of the most disturbing characteristics of poor writ~~ing *sentences* *and*
~~ing is that sentences and thoughts do not flow logically~~ *thought*
When ideas neither
~~into the sentences that follow. Ideas neither~~ grow natur-
neither
ally out of ^those that have preceded nor anticipate those *is characteristic of poor writing.*
that ~~are to~~ ^follow. Poorly constructed paragraphs often

have inadequate "bridges" between sentences because the

writer was not conscious of <u>coherence</u>.

no ¶ Coherence *t* ~~is a characteristic of~~ writing ~~that~~ holds to-
its
gether; that is, ^thoughts flow smoothly and naturally *or*
because they are held together by devices that guarantee

continuity. ✗ [by natural, logical connections that are a

part of the writer's thinking process.] A writer who thinks
a *composing*
through ~~his~~ composition n before ~~he writes it~~ will create ~~a~~

~~piece of writing with~~ natural coherence.

(See Chapter 4 for the final version.)

Revising

After completing the first draft, set it aside with the intention of returning to it later (at least several hours, preferably for a day) when it is no longer fresh in your mind. Revising, the third step in the writing process, is important because it forces you to take a global look at the whole piece of writing. "Revising" means taking another look at content—literally "reseeing" your paper. The reason for delaying the revising process is that now you will possibly see gaps in ideas not obvious before. Read aloud with a fresh, critical eye. Read with feeling, not in a monotone. Read your paper to someone else. You might even discover that what you thought was so clear is vague and incomplete, possibly not really developing the ideas you had in mind.

Whether you or a peer editor is looking over the paper, the focus should be to examine content critically. Does the paper develop the thesis? (This is a concept you will learn about in Chapter 9.) Is there sufficient supporting material? (Supporting material is covered in Chapter 3.)

If you have addressed too many ideas, you have violated one of the major principles of clear writing—unity. In a single paragraph the topic sentence controls this unit. In a longer paper the thesis statement limits the paper to one idea. Chapter 2 will help you distinguish the topic sentence from a thesis statement.

Let's follow a student trying to create a topic sentence for a paragraph about computers. Nadia first wrote, "In my opinion a computer has a lot of advantages and disadvantages." One of the criticisms she received in her peer editing circle was, "That's too broad. You'll have to narrow it." So Nadia tried again: "Not only does the computer have advantages in everyday life, but also the computer can provide jobs such as a computer programmer, a computer engineer, a computer salesman, and a computer repairman." Has Nadia made progress, or has she created a monster?

Well, she has narrowed the general idea—advantages and disadvantages—to a series of advantages—kinds of computer jobs. But can she write about all these jobs in just one paragraph? Let's help her try again. "The most unique job computers have created is that of computer engineer." Although the sentence still needs further refining,

Nadia has limited her focus to a single aspect — the computer engineer.

You may also discover that your thoughts seem jumbled, disorganized. They simply do not flow logically from one to another. Occasionally, transitional words may give the paper coherence. At other times, you may simply have to rewrite, as your paper betrays gaps in thinking.

A final point about the revising stage: have you made yourself clear? Will your audience understand your position? If you are trying to write informatively, will the audience *be* informed? Reading your paper aloud at this stage may be useful, but only if you read slowly and objectively. You must not allow your closeness to the paper to be deceiving. Be critical and open minded; don't be afraid to discard sections of the paper that you thought profound when you wrote them. Although answering questions about unity, coherence, and clarity is often difficult, it is best now to share your paper with others and get their thoughts about what you have written.

In a classroom your instructor might want you to share your paper with others who can give advice about specific development of ideas. The instructor might even have a list of detailed questions to guide the "peer editor" in evaluating your paper.

Reader Commentary on Draft

1. What do you like best about this piece of writing? Why?

    _____

    _____

2. What do you find troublesome about this paper? Why?

    _____

    _____

3. What do you think the writer wants to accomplish?

_____

_____

4. What do you think is the main idea of this piece of
    writing? Can you locate a single sentence that states
    this main idea? (If so, copy it down.)

    _____

    _____

5. What parts of this draft do you think need further
    attention?

    _____

    _____

Outside the classroom, share your paper with friends or
family, possibly even with tutors in a writing center.
Whether you or a peer editor is looking over your paper,
the focus should be to examine content critically. Does the
paper develop the thesis? Is there sufficient supporting material? For some assignments, you may need to write a
formal outline or a table of contents. You might even want
to test how well your rough draft is by writing an outline
of it, looking for flaws in organization and thinking. Ide-
ally, outlines are written _before_ you ever write your paper.
If you write them after you have completed the final draft,
you are writing the outline for the instructor, not as a
guide to help you develop your thoughts. Doing so pretty
well defeats the purpose of an outline: to map out your
paper. Other more formal documents, such as business reports, will need a transmittal letter rather than an outline.
In addition to drafting these at the conclusion of the revising stage, you begin to make decisions about the final copy
of your paper, such as what format will be needed. But
you have a couple of more steps to follow before you are
ready to "go public" with your paper.

Some teachers may ask you to write a critique of your
own paper and attach it to the final draft. For some questions you might consider, look over the following self-
analysis sheet for a critical book review:

Writer Commentary on Draft

1. Can you describe the intended audience? Be specific. Be certain that both peer editors and your professor understand your intended audience.

    _____

    _____

2. What was the most *difficult* challenge to writing this critical book review? Why? How were you able to overcome this challenge — or weren't you? Explain.

    _____

    _____

3. What was the most helpful comment a peer editor made? Repeat that comment as you remember it.

    _____

    _____

4. What do you like best about your paper? Why?

    _____

    _____

5. If you had more time to work on this book review, what, specifically, would you wish to change? to improve on? expand? eliminate?

    _____

    _____

Here is another example of a reader commentary sheet that your instructor might use for an in-class activity:

Peer Editing Sheet

1. Comment on the *clarity* and *organization* of this first draft. Do you understand all sections of this draft?

2. Does the writer need to add more supporting materi-
    als? If so, where? Which sections need more work?
    Why?

_____

_____

3. Does the writer need to work on sentence structure?
    on paragraphing? Mark examples of this on the copy
    of the writer's draft.

_____

_____

4. What would you advise this writer to work on to
    make the draft significantly *stronger*? Be specific.

_____

_____

Editing

At the editing stage you should look at your paper on
three levels: word, sentence, and paragraph. We weren't
primarily concerned with these "parts" of the paper when
we were revising. "Editing" is the act of seeking out and
correcting specific errors on these three levels. For the first,
a recently edited dictionary or thesaurus will list appropriate synonyms for some of your worn-out words, such as
good, nice, big, things, and *interesting*. Select vivid and precise words that create mental pictures appealing to the
senses, but don't go out of your way to use a strange or
unfamiliar word. Also, be careful to check for misspelled
words. If you notice some strange spellings, check them
carefully with your dictionary. (Even the experts do!) If
English is not your native language, focus on three problem areas: verbs, articles, and idioms. If, for instance, you
know that your instructor has repeatedly corrected your
use of prepositions, examine each one in your paper, pro-

nounce it, and try again to determine if your choice is the correct one. Again, the dictionary will help.

Read your paper aloud once more, listening for short, choppy sentences that could be combined to form mature structures. Possibly some can be rearranged in imaginative patterns. A few might start with different participial openers, such as *-ing, -ed,* or *-en* words; others might begin with prepositional phrases or dependent structures. If you want to learn about new patterns, you might consult a sentence pattern manual where you will be introduced to a variety of structures.

Next, take a final look at your developmental paragraphs. Do they develop a single idea clearly? Is there a topic sentence? If not, is the idea easily understood without one? Look also at the supporting material. Is it adequate? Have you used a variety of types? (See Chapter 3.) How coherently are ideas linked? Chapter 4 outlines strategies for creating effective coherence.

The editing stage is a crucial step with two primary goals. First, read your paper carefully several times, searching for mechanical errors with the help of a handbook. It takes tremendous patience to do this. It is difficult to read the whole paper looking simultaneously for all types of errors. Your focus is confined to one type of error, such as subject–verb agreement. In a subsequent reading, check the diction of the whole paper. In still another reading, focus exclusively on punctuation. The major purpose in editing is to force you to correct surface errors. The second goal of editing is to produce a legible copy, getting it ready for your reader. Now you are ready to proofread if you are satisfied that the content of your paper is clear and your message complete.

Proofreading

The final step before submitting your writing to your intended audience is proofreading. It is important at this stage to read what you have *actually* written rather than what you *think* you have written. Missing letters might leap out at you during this final stage of the composing process.

The "point and lift" method of proofreading might be useful. Find a sharp pencil. Point at each word with the pencil and, simultaneously, follow the pencil with your eye. Lift the pencil, following it with your eye as you point to a new word. Carefully examine each word, checking for spelling, word form, and proper use. But be careful. This method draws your attention only to surface errors.

Some like to proofread by reading the paper backwards, word by word. This process eliminates context, forcing you to concentrate. You read each word slowly, checking for accuracy. Sound out each pause indicated by punctuation marks. Be particularly alert for fragments and comma splices. Or cover up the lines with a blank sheet of paper. Read the material from start to finish, a line at a time, moving the blank page from top to bottom.

Once you have completed proofreading, you have accepted full responsibility for your paper and are now ready to give it to your reader. Remember, the way a paper looks makes a dramatic statement about you.

Exercise 1–2

Find and circle the careless errors students have made in the following paragraphs; look, in particular, for the following errors, and then rewrite the paragraph in more acceptable form:

Punctuation errors (missing quotation marks, fused sentences, comma splices, missing commas and semicolons)
Wordiness
Spelling errors
Word choice
Reference problems
Agreement errors

1.   There are several holidays celebrated in America throughout the year, among the most celebrated is Halloween. which may seem unusual and strange to a foreign visiting student. For example, Halloween which is celebrated on October 31st every year has some bizarre and wacky traditions attached to it. However, today, Halloween is commonly referred to as a children's holiday. They dress up in customs. Wiches and goblins are among the favorites however there are some princess, cartoon-characters &

monsters too. Usually the children go on from house to house asking for candy. They say treat or trick & the owner of the house gives them a candies. Others have parties with food, candies and everything else that goes with parties.

2.   I went to make an application for a job at an elementary school. The experience I had was being as a substitute in a classroom. My job is being a clerk but when teachers have an emergency I go in and stay in their classrooms. One day I went in a classroom and the student were looking at me. It is a very nervous situation that the one hour I stayed there was like hours. After awhile, I said to myself I have to do it. The students were very understanding so it sure helped alot. I looked in the teacher's plan book and everything looked so difficult. I read everything for that date and eventually I made it. After all this happened I decided to be a teacher.

<table>
<tr><td>

The Parts
of the Paragraph

</td><td>

CHAPTER

2

</td></tr>
</table>

The Topic Sentence

Perhaps the most important part of a developmental paragraph is the topic sentence. A *topic sentence* is the single sentence within a paragraph that states the central idea to be developed. It must be a suggestive statement that can be enlarged upon, not a factual statement that no one would dispute.

Definition

Suggestive Statement: It was Christopher Columbus' sense of curiosity that led to his discovery of America.

Factual Statement: The date commonly associated with the discovery of America is 1492.

Also, it should be a *simple sentence* (a single idea that can stand alone). It normally should not be a *compound sentence* (two or more ideas that can stand alone, with at least two subjects and two verbs) because a topic sentence has the special function of limiting the subject matter to a single idea. If you have more than one main thought in the topic sentence, as you have in a compound sentence, you may confuse your readers, sending them off in multiple directions uncertain about which idea you really want to develop.

And finally, it must be carefully and precisely worded. Precise wording means that each word in the topic sentence performs a specific function; each has been selected with care for clarity and exactness. All nonworking, nonessential, ambiguous words have been eliminated. For example, a topic sentence that begins with a transitional element—"On the other hand, the death penalty imposed without restriction on drug dealers in Singapore has greatly descreased drug traffic in that city"—implies that preceding paragraphs have presented contradictions or alternate views. A revision with even fewer words would be: "Singapore has decreased drug traffic by imposing without restriction the death penalty on all drug dealers."

Why is the topic sentence so important? First, it creates a clear and single focus. Also, it controls thoughts and sets limits for discussion. In fact, it acts as a fence to corral writers and prevent them from straying off into unmarked territories. All other sentences in the paragraph will be related to it, will support and clarify it.

Idea Word

Definition

Because a paragraph talks about an idea, a key part of the topic sentence is the *idea word*. This word identifies the subject matter—what the paragraph will argue, prove, explain, define, or illustrate. It will be easier to construct a topic sentence if you make the idea word a noun, because a noun will explicitly name what your subject is. Let's look at a topic sentence and identify the idea word:

Aerosol sprays damage the ozone layer in the earth's atmosphere.

If you were to identify the idea word, you might choose from a number of recognizable words: *atmosphere, ozone, damage, layer,* and *sprays.* Careful examination of this topic sentence should help you eliminate some of these choices and isolate the idea word. Is this paragraph going to be chiefly about the ozone layer? Will it talk primarily about the earth's atmosphere? Or will it discuss aerosol sprays? In the sentence itself, the subject is *sprays.* To identify an idea word, look for the subject in the topic sentence. It usually will be a noun—a name of a person, place, thing, animal, idea, action, state of existence, or color. It may be a common noun, ordinarily not capitalized (*cattle, geometry, gloves*); a proper noun, singular or distinctive enough to require capitalization (*German, Roman Catholic Church,* the *Beatles*); or a compound noun with two or more words acting as a unit (*sergeant at arms, General Motors Corporation, well-being*).

The topic sentence above suggests that the paragraph will concentrate on aerosol sprays; it will discuss the damage they do to the ozone layer. Even though there will be discussion about the earth's atmosphere, the central focus will be on the damage caused by aerosol sprays.

CAUTION

Your reader should be able to recognize the central idea of your paragraph by the idea word in the topic sentence. Occasionally, your "idea" will appear in a short word group rather than in a single word. Having an idea word helps focus your reader's attention on a single subject matter that you plan to develop.

Attitude Words

In addition to the idea word, the topic sentence will have an *attitude word*, which Harvey Wiener calls the "opinion word" in *Creating Compositions*. The attitude word will establish the tone for your paragraph—that is, the writer's feelings about the subject. Your feelings might range from fear and anxiety to confusion and anger. It's crucial to find the exact word that captures your emotions. For instance, in the topic sentence on aerosol sprays, the verb *damage* suggests the writer's feelings about this attitude of "damage." If you suddenly begin to talk about the advantages of aerosol sprays, such as their convenience or cost, your reader will be confused about what your attitude really is. Attitude words may be suggested in the verb or may be explicitly stated elsewhere, perhaps in modifying words or phrases. Here is a slight revision in the example, using the attitude word in another position: "Aerosol sprays pose a serious threat to the ozone layer of the earth's atmosphere." The word *threat* expresses the attitude. Sometimes more than one word will express the writer's attitude, but usually you will detect it by one key word.

Definition

CAUTION

Some words that we rely on too often are poor choices to express attitudes. These all-purpose words may be misinterpreted. Such words as *nice, good, interesting, boring, dull, exciting, terrific, pleasant, bad, great,* or *fantastic* are just a few that are too broad or too vague. They are convenience words that we return to when we really don't want to think clearly. What specific meaning does a word like *interesting* have? Can you pin it down precisely? Contrast *interesting* with *provocative, stimulating,* or other, livelier synonyms. Two precise words to express contempt are *scornful* and *disdainful*; reading them, you know exactly how the writer feels. Have you ever felt frustrated when a paper was returned to you marked B+ with the teacher's comment, "A very interesting treatment of a very difficult subject"? Perhaps the teacher means, "You have a fairly good discussion, but your evidence on page 2 is too general. You need concrete details and specific examples." You don't want a teacher to say your paper is "wretched," but if the teacher did, you would know exactly how he or she felt, wouldn't you? Choose definite, precise, vivid attitude words for your topic sentence.

Another caution about attitude words: don't have too many! You can overuse them (especially if you have two or three), confusing your readers, making them wonder precisely what your attitude is. In a topic sentence this precision is necessary because you do not want to seem ambivalent or wishy-washy. Limit yourself to one attitude, as more may shift your point of view or become contradictory.

Here is the example topic sentence with two attitude words, neither of which could be adequately developed in a short paragraph: "Aerosol spray cans are convenient for people but can be destructive to the ozone layer." Consider another topic sentence about an audience at a speech: "Everyone in the audience at the graduation ceremony seemed restless and attentive." The writer uses contradictory attitude words; how could a group simultaneously be "restless" and "attentive"?

Exercise 2—1

The following sentences need to have a word that helps identify the writer's attitude (feeling, emotional engagement) toward the subject. Rewrite the sentence inserting an *adjective*, an *adverb*, or a *noun* that makes the writer's attitude clear.

Example: The auctioneer began the bidding for the vase.

Revision: The auctioneer enthusiastically began the bidding for the rare oriental vase.

1.   The boy on the fifth floor is in a hypnotic trance.

   _____

   _____

2.   The farmers had a reaction to the new soil conservation plan the Department of Agriculture advocated.

   _____

   _____

3.   The oil spill damaged the wildlife refuge along the Maryland coast.

   _____

   _____

4.   The alligator is no longer on the endangered species list.

   _____

   _____

5.   I dialed the number of the call-in radio show.

   _____

   _____

Exercise 2–2

The following topic sentences are poorly structured. They contain a number of errors that you should try to find. First, circle the idea and attitude word in each; if you don't find either, add an idea or attitude word. Second, on the lines provided, answer one or both of the following questions: Is the sentence too broad to be developed in a paragraph? Is it so narrow that very little else can be said about the topic?

1. The trade of the quarterback to the Washington Redskins was a strategic move.

    _____

    _____

2. My cruise was really hectic.

    _____

    _____

3. The gun-control law is bad.

    _____

    _____

4. Humans were very independent in previous centuries.

    _____

    _____

5. Giving birth to a tiny little thing called a "baby" is not as easy a job as it seems.

    _____

    _____

6. Andrew Jackson and Ronald Reagan were two of the four presidents who married divorced women.

_____

_____

7. In 1963, Lyndon Johnson was an appointed, rather than an elected President, but he was an effective leader at times.

_____

_____

Indicator Words

In addition to idea and attitude words, a topic sentence should also have a number of *indicator words*. An indicator word is a response to a question that you might ask yourself silently as you compose your topic sentence. Let's look at the example about aerosol cans again:

Definition

> Aerosol sprays damage the ozone layer in the earth's atmosphere.

You might want to have an indicator word answering the question, *Which* aerosol spray? It is reasonable to say that you will not be talking about *all* aerosol sprays, but rather specific ones. Mentioning a brand name or a specific type of can would add a "which" word to your topic sentence.

General: Aerosol deodorant sprays damage . . . .
Specific: Right Guard spray damages . . . .

Here is another topic sentence with different types of indicator words.

> My aunt's kitchen is always a mess after Thanksgiving dinner.

The indicator words here answer the questions *who*, *where*, and *when*. *Whose* kitchen? My aunt's. *When?* In November when we are having Thanksgiving dinner. *Where* is the mess? In the kitchen. Such indicator words create a vivid impression for readers, orienting them so that they know where they are and what specifically you are describing.

Exercise 2–3

Here are some topic sentences that might lead to an effective paragraph. (*Might* is an important word because a paragraph does not rest on its topic sentence alone; it relies on its supporting materials to make the point clear.) Examine each of these sentences, circling the idea and attitude words. What do you think is effective about these examples? How could you improve them further? Write a brief analysis on the lines provided.

1. Wiretapping is a legal way to abuse power.

    _____

    _____

2. Some of the skiers at Vail prefer the new, shorter skis.

    _____

    _____

3. A bilingual medical technician can command a lucrative salary.

    _____

    _____

4. Horror films featuring ghouls and monsters outdraw the traditional Western at theater box offices.

    _____

    _____

5. Unsightly billboards destroy the natural roadside beauty of our main streets.

    _____

    _____

6. Despite a serious physical handicap, an athlete may often succeed in his sport.

_____

_____

7. The Chinese herb ginseng has valuable medicinal
    properties.

_____

_____

8. Lawyers may abuse the privilege of advertising.

_____

_____

Exercise 2–4

The following topic sentences are poorly structured.
They contain a number of errors that you should try to
spot. Can you identify the idea and attitude words? Is the
topic sentence too broad or too narrow? Is it a compound
sentence? Does it refer to the title of the paper? Give
reasons why these are poor examples.

Last night's basketball game was quite lucky for our team.

My vacation was really fun.

Capital punishment is bad.

Abraham Lincoln was a great president.

Douglas MacArthur was an arrogant general whom President Truman dismissed, but he was an effective leader at
times in the Philippines.

From the 1960s through the 1980s rock music developed
in a number of ways as its sounds changed from that of
the Beatles, to the Rolling Stones, and finally to Michael
Jackson.

This is the place where I grew up in the mid-sixties.

The topic sentence has two parts, then, each having specific duties to perform. A topic sentence itself is crucial, but its functions are limited. It cannot, for instance, serve as the title for your paper, even though it may contain ideas that inspired the title. (If you need to have a title, invent one appropriate for your theme — one that arouses your reader's interest, echoes or alludes to your central idea, and is something fresh and original rather than an overworked cliché.) The topic sentence limits your paragraph to one idea; by doing so, it also indicates what your paragraph is *not* about. You may imply what you are not discussing, or you may designate areas of a broad issue that you will not address. Thus, your topic sentence gives the paragraph focus, direction, and clarity.

Unity in the Topic Sentence

One of the major tasks of the topic sentence is to ensure "oneness," to unify the paragraph under a single idea. When constructing your topic sentence, remember this: it must be a simple sentence, expressing only one complete thought and ensuring unity. If you construct your topic sentence as a compound, you imply two ideas. Let's look at one that has this major flaw, two ideas instead of one:

Large suburban shopping malls have destroyed inner-city stores, and city planners should be more cautious in designing them.

There are two ideas here: first, the malls have destroyed inner-city stores; and second, city planners must be aware of this impact when designing them. Having these two ideas destroys the unity of the topic sentence. This weak example suggests too large an idea to cover in one paragraph. Yes, there are topic and attitude words; there is potential for a paragraph about the impact of malls on inner-city stores. But the compound sentence with its two ideas suggests that the writer needs to rethink what he has written. Here is a revised version:

Large surburban shopping malls have affected the profits of two inner-city stores in my town.

This revision has a unified focus because the reader knows you will talk about two specific stores in the inner city of your town and how the appearance of large shopping malls in the suburbs affected them.

Tone

Another way your topic sentence suggests unity is by the *tone* it sets. If it is sarcastic, solemn, funny, or ironic, all of the sentences must sustain this tone. If you shift tones, your readers will be confused and will not know where you stand; they might ask, "What exactly is this writer's position on this issue?"

Placement of the Topic Sentence

At the Beginning

Where does the topic sentence belong? There are no set rules about placement just as there are no set rules about paragraph length. Beginning writers, however, are encouraged to write the topic sentence first. If it is the first sentence of the paragraph or very near the beginning, it is easier to remember as the paragraph develops. And it immediately establishes the format for the entire paragraph.

For early writing assignments, place the topic sentence first. This placement alerts your reader at once to your subject. Also, you can keep your subject in mind and refer to it often as you write. Later, as you become more experienced, you will want to vary the position. Doing so will help you create appeal, variety, and a different emphasis.

In the Middle

Let's assume you want to stress a contrast between two approaches to a subject. It might be useful to place the topic sentence in the middle instead of near the start of the paragraph. The focus shifts from one side of your topic to another side — probably the more important one. This shift in emphasis comes with the sudden appearance of the topic sentence in the middle. Look at this paragraph, which has its topic sentence in the middle. The writer sweeps you toward the central idea, then away from it:

Nineteenth-century schoolboys knew who Homer, Dante and Virgil were. And they weren't chums down the block. Latin and Greek were a standard part of the language curriculum, and nearly every student was expected to recite in classical languages. Contests for best poem written in Latin or Greek were fiercely waged both at Oxford and Cambridge and in public schools like Eton. Even in America at Harvard such prizes were awarded at graduation. Educators and intellectuals believed that studying these languages added to the student elegance, polish, and style. Today's teachers need to convey the importance of studying classics and developing a familiarity with mythology among twentieth-century students. A gifted teacher will help students see a connection between their lives and those of classical heroes and warriors, thereby realizing the importance of classical myth to their own lives. The heroic deeds of Odysseus and Jason, the quests of even medieval figures like Arthur's for the Holy Grail or the brave adventures of Joan of Arc, the exploits of more contemporary heroic figures like the Indian warrior Geronimo, Charles Lindbergh, or today's astronauts — once students study the deeds and lives of these figures, they come to respect both the heroic characters and will find models whose lives are worthy for them to imitate. Also, a teacher who can relate such film characters as Dirty Harry, or such comic book figures as Wonder Woman, Superman, or even Tarzan, or possibly detective figures like Sam Spade or Mike Hammer, to the exploits of mythic figures can awaken an interest in the contemporary student for the more classical figures found in ancient myths.

On the lines below, write out what you think is the topic sentence for this paragraph.

_____

_____

_____

At the End

To create suspense, however, you might delay the topic sentence until the end of your paragraph. Readers will have gained a sense of what you are talking about, but the major point will remain partly hidden until the end. A turnabout effect might be created, if this is your purpose; you can provide a surprise ending in the style of O. Henry!

The topic sentence at the end stresses an emphatic generalization. The writer has built up the point by creating suspense. Now, by introducing the topic sentence at the end, he establishes a bold climax. The reader does not think, "So this was what he was talking about!" Rather, after reading a paragraph developed in this manner, the reader says, "Yes, this is a valid point that has been well supported throughout this paragraph," as Monica's paragraph illustrates:

If you enjoy a challenge, try one of the popular board games like Parcheesi or Monopoly. Parcheesi, developed in India centuries ago, and Monopoly, invented during the Depression by the Parker brothers, both depend upon the throw of the dice. Each is an extremely popular board game; in fact, there is an annual international Monopoly playoff. Or perhaps you prefer one of the tile games — dominoes, triominoes, or Mah-jongg, all of which require a keen mind and a sharp eye. Players have been fascinated by dominoes since the eighteenth century when they were introduced in Europe, and domino parlors are still a part of rural America. Triominoes, however, a more recent invention, require even more astute skills. The mesmerizing tiles of Mah-jongg came to us through ancient China, where it still is played avidly. The object of these three tile games is to build combinations or sets by drawing, discarding, or exchanging tiles. These games, too, are designed for several players, many of whom have regularly scheduled weekly games or all-night contests. Other compulsive games require two players. Checkers, backgammon, and chess, using especially designed markers and boards, present provocative mental challenges and demand intense concentration. You should be cautioned, though, that if you take any of these games too seriously, becoming an ardent devotee, you take a chance of becoming glassy-eyed and absent-minded. You'll join, perhaps unwillingly, a fanatical games cult. Be warned! These games are addictive.   Topic sentence

The Implied Topic Sentence

Not all paragraphs have topic sentences. Occasionally, the topic sentence is implied (suggested) rather than stated. You might try to analyze a paragraph in *Time, Reader's Digest*, a textbook for a history course, or an editorial and determine whether the writer has actually used a topic sentence. Look for idea and attitude words. Possibly, you will find a paragraph that only implies an idea. Although you may know the point the writer made and be confident about the emotional stance, you cannot find a single sentence that might be classified as a genuine topic sentence. If such is the case, make up one that the writer might have used.

Exercise 2–5

Read the following paragraph carefully. Then, on the lines provided, answer each of the questions.

The first tedious task is to give the passengers instructions for securing their seat belts. I have to lift up a demonstration belt and show how the clasp works; it would be difficult to find someone who couldn't figure this out alone! Then I must hold up a model oxygen mask and show people how to breathe. After that, it's time to take drink orders, being careful not to mix up the Bloody Mary for 15E with the V-8 juice for 15D. While making drinks, I have to dodge the hefty lady on her way to the lavatory. After serving them, I have to pick up "empties" and get the passengers ready for dinner. As they sit comfortably, some reading, others sleeping, I take orders for chicken with cherry sauce or beef tips in wine and sometimes search out those who ordered special meals. And even before I've finished, the captain announces that the plane will be landing in fifteen minutes.

1. What is the central idea of this whole paragraph?

   _____

   _____

2. What are three key details that the writer used to support the central point?

   _____

   _____

3. What type of person might have written this paragraph? How can you tell by the writer's language?

   _____

   _____

4. Who is the audience being addressed?

   _____

   _____

5. The paragraph lacks a topic sentence. Can you write one for it here?

   _____

   _____

As you practice writing topic sentences, keep in mind this simple caution: When you are satisfied that you have a single focus, an idea word, and a clearly stated attitude word, review the following checklist.

CHECKLIST

1. Is the topic sentence short, concise, clear, and specific?
2. Is it a simple sentence?
3. Is there a clearly stated idea word?
4. Does the sentence indicate who, what, where, and/or when? Is this identification appropriate?

5. Is there a word expressing an attitude toward the subject?

6. Are the words vivid and precise? Are they trite? Is the sentence merely a cliché?

7. Will the topic develop one point fully, or is it so limited or factual that it will dead-end after the first three sentences?

The Subtopic Sentence

The Parts

After writing your topic sentence, you might find it useful to write a few sentences of explanation to make your reader more fully aware of your task. A key word might be defined; a concept might be explained through synonyms that relate to the idea or attitude words. After these preliminaries, you are ready to start the central task of the paragraph: to present an idea to a reader.

A paragraph breaks down the topic sentence so that its thought is carefully and completely developed. These parts are subordinate; they are subdivisions of the whole idea embodied in the topic sentence. There probably will be three or four of these major subdivisions that help develop separate portions of the topic sentence. What is important to remember is that each subtopic sentence is a part of the whole supporting proof.

Subtopic sentences remind readers what your opinion is by echoing the attitude word. Subtopic sentences also sharpen the focus of a section by concentrating on one portion of the supporting evidence advanced to prove the idea. They remind the writer to provide necessary supporting materials—such as instances, cases, expert testimony, or statistics—to make the point clear. In addition, they further remind the writer to establish clear relationships between the supporting material and the central idea.

Since it is important that readers recognize these subtopic sentences, try using a few techniques that introduce them. Enumeration devices, for example, will call attention to the subtopic sentences. Words such as *first, second,* and *third* are useful indicators for beginning subtopic sentences. Also, you might want to have a series of sentences with the same structure (parallel sentences). Rhetorical questions might serve as subtopic sentences, too. Even repetition of key words or phrases from the topic sentence might identify subtopic sentences. When you phrase sentences in the same structure, readers will remember the similar pattern and be alert to a key supporting example, which the subtopic sentence will introduce. There are other techniques that you will invent yourself as you master paragraph structure, but these three are useful starters.

How Many?

It is difficult to establish rigid rules for the number of subtopic sentences. That number will depend on your intent, your audience, the amount of detail you need, and many other variables. If you have four subtopic sentences, you will not provide much supporting material for each of them. By contrast, if you have only two subtopic sentences, you will elaborate on each more fully. You must make these decisions as you structure your paragraph and consider the type of evidence you need.

Exercise 2–6

Let's try to predict two subtopic sentences for the following topic sentences.

Example: One of the major differences between primitive and modern medical treatment is the type of healer people can choose from.

a. *The villager called upon the witch doctor, whereas today's urban dweller uses medical specialists.*

b. *The witch doctor learned from his forebears, not from modern medical educators.*

1. An abused spouse bears many emotional scars.

_____

_____

2. It is often logical to grant custody of children to the father rather than the mother.

    _____

    _____

3. One of the chief characteristics of the extended family is separation by geographical distance.

    _____

    _____

The Topic and Subtopic Sentences Contrasted

For purposes of clarity, let's establish a contrast between the topic and the subtopic sentence. Imagine that the paragraph is a block structure that looks something like this diagram:

TOPIC SENTENCE: THE START

Subtopic Sentence 1: The Middle

Subtopic Sentence 2: The Middle

Subtopic Sentence 3: The Middle

THE CLINCHER SENTENCE: THE FINISH

This diagram illustrates the relationship between the subtopic and topic sentences. Each subtopic sentence is subordinate to the topic sentence. But let's recall the subject of shopping centers and see how we might use two subtopic sentences to support it:

Large suburban shopping malls offer conveniences unavailable in the two inner-city department stores in my town.	Topic sentence
They provide convenient parking unavailable in the downtown area.	Subtopic sentence 1
And they offer a larger variety of shops with greater selection of merchandise than what is available in the two downtown stores.	Subtopic sentence 2

These two subtopic sentences will support and help prove the point made in the topic sentence. After each will come illustrative material that reveals the various types of parking alternatives or the numerous types of large and small shops—from small specialty shops for luggage or furs to larger variety shops where you could purchase a hairpin or a refrigerator. Each illustration, however, is subordinate to the subtopic sentence which, in turn, is directly connected to the idea word of the topic sentence.

Let's imagine inserting a few sentences after the first subtopic sentence to show how convenient parking in the suburbs provides an advantage unavailable for stores downtown. Often suburban stores have free parking within walking distance of the stores themselves. Have you ever seen the parking available at Tyson's Corner in Vienna, Virginia, or at the Ala Moana in Honolulu, or at the Galleria in Houston, Texas? By describing the convenience of such excellent parking facilities at these complexes—or the similar convenience of a suburban center in your town—you illustrate what your subtopic sentence implies. You might continue by describing the enclosed or underground parking facilities at the suburban center or point out how the downtown stores do not offer such convenience. Indeed, you might want to stress how this characteristic of the suburban shopping center has precipitated a flight of consumers from downtown.

Now notice the second subtopic sentence. Suburban shopping malls have many specialty stores with a large variety of merchandise. You can often find "just what you were looking for" in shops near each other. You might want to illustrate your frustration in walking several blocks downtown in your city to find items you wanted to purchase and then set up a contrast with more convenient shopping in the suburban mall. The large variety of easy-to-find merchandise made shoppers in your city abandon the downtown stores and seek out those in suburban malls.

A different approach for this subtopic sentence might be to describe the consumers at a suburban mall. Point out how young people swarm in on Saturday to windowshop, ride the escalator, play records or videogames, meet friends, and possibly even make purchases. Suburban malls often have The Limited, The Gap, Miller's Outpost, and other shops specially designed for the younger consumer, the teenaged trend setter. Consumer demand for comfort and informality has made designers of malls provide shops specializing in jeans, inexpensive casual clothes, and "separates" or "mix and match" items. There are countless ways to develop your subtopic sentence. Can you think of other supporting material you might include to amplify these two subtopic sentences?

The Paragraph: A Simple Outline

Once you have clarified your intention, you need to construct a topic sentence and search for the subtopic sentences that will support it. With these tasks complete, it's time to outline your thoughts. An *outline* is a guide for your organization. What follows is a simple diagram with a topic sentence, several subtopics and explanatory sentences, and a clincher.

Definition

This diagram distinguishes topic and subtopic sentences. But it also introduces *explanatory sentences*. They provide the concrete detail that helps the reader understand the intent of the subtopic. Therefore, they are the most specific sentences. Imagine that the following portion of a paragraph is the one you are considering for a theme about health-care facilities on campus:

Definition

Topic sentence   A completely equipped facility would provide better health service for students on the campus of this university.

Explanatory sentence   At present, all laboratory work must be sent to either a local hospital or a pathologist.

Topic Sentence
(Brief explanatory sentences — no more than two
or three)

Subtopic Sentence 1

    Explanatory Sentence 1
    Explanatory Sentence 2
    Explanatory Sentence 3

Subtopic Sentence 2

    Explanatory Sentence 1
    Explanatory Sentence 2
    Explanatory Sentence 3

Subtopic Sentence 3

    Explanatory Sentence 1
    Explanatory Sentence 2
    Explanatory Sentence 3

Clincher Sentence   (explained on page 47)

Both of these facilities are several miles from campus.	Explanatory sentence
And students must wait several days before learning the results of tests, even simple ones like urinalysis.	Explanatory sentence
A fully equipped laboratory under a trained technician would expedite health services.	Subtopic sentence 1
Important X-rays could be evaluated without any delay.	Explanatory sentence
Results from blood tests, urinalyses, and similar examinations would be available to the campus physician in a few hours to expedite proper diagnosis and begin appropriate treatment. . . .	Explanatory sentence

Subtopic sentences provide the primary support, whereas explanatory sentences give secondary support. Each explanatory sentence will offer concrete details. An alternating pattern of subtopic sentence and explanatory sentences will clarify ideas. As you write, you will have to decide just how many explanatory sentences to have. The number of subtopic and explanatory sentences you need will depend on decisions about how fully and specifically you wish to develop the idea. As you revise early drafts, you may discover additional ideas and supporting material.

A paragraph cannot have merely a topic sentence and three or four subtopic sentences. Explanatory sentences are essential to provide necessary detail. Look at this student's paragraph, keeping in mind the function of explanatory sentences. As you read, identify the topic sentence. Can you locate subtopic and explanatory sentences? Why is this paragraph marginal or incomplete?

A well-balanced meal is essential for the growth of a healthy person. It provides the vitamins needed each day for the growth of bones, muscles, and nerves. It has an impact on the mental growth of the person. And finally, without the well-balanced meal a person is apt to experience fatigue or illness.

Did you observe that the explanatory sentences that would add the completeness are missing? Details about specific vitamins and their relationship to the growth of bones, their impact on one's complexion, and their role in building nerve fibers would make the first subtopic sentence clearer in the reader's mind. Let's flesh out the paragraph by adding supporting material after each of the subtopic sentences:

A well-balanced meal is essential for the growth of a healthy person. It provides the vitamins needed each day for the growth of bones, muscles, and nerves. For example, vitamin D, found in milk and dairy products, contains calcium necessary for building bones, and vitamin E, found chiefly in grains and vegetables, strengthens nerves. Additionally, a well-balanced meal has an impact on the mental growth of a person. Proteins, particularly from fresh fish, help eliminate stress. They also make one more alert, whereas the caffein found in cola products and coffee is more likely to overstimulate. Finally, without a well-balanced meal a person is apt to experience fatigue or illness. Foods high in natural fiber and fiber-rich carbohydrates in whole-grain cereals, plus vitamins C and D, prevent a number of life-threatening diseases. Clearly, one has much to gain from planning a well-balanced meal.

The Clincher Sentence: A Strong Finish

The beginning and end of your paragraph are two extremely important positions. Why? At the first you announce your topic. Each of the sentences that follows will echo the topic sentence and develop your point. But the last words you write are the ones that will linger in your reader's memory. They must be stated effectively or they'll be forgotten.

There are a number of techniques helpful in ending a paragraph. One is the *clincher sentence*. It includes a few specific parts that can be quickly identified. There should *Definition* be some word in it that indicates you are ending your paragraph—a concluding term, such as *thus, in brief, finally, ultimately*. This term will say to your reader, "Hey, this paragraph is ending." If you simply stop without a clincher, the reader will be left dangling. It helps finish your paragraph because your entire thought is decisively settled—*clinched*—in this last sentence. Inferences from the whole discussion may be drawn in this clincher sentence. Examine your paragraph and draw a conclusion from all you have said. Does your paragraph develop a thought that perhaps has universal application? If so, possibly suggest this universality in the clincher sentence.

If you are writing several paragraphs for a long composition, you may find another characteristic helpful. Allow the clincher to do two things: conclude the thought that you have developed and anticipate what lies ahead. You might not want to use this technique in every paragraph, but practice will show you its usefulness. Look at the following example of a clincher sentence that both concludes and anticipates:

Clearly, then, these recommendations about academic performance from the NCAA committee are vital to improving the image of college athletics, but the NCAA must also address important financial issues mutually beneficial to both the university and the athlete.

The clincher should be vigorous and succinct. A strong finish will impress your reader. Be forceful so that your paragraph will be memorable rather than easily forgotten.

Illustrating clincher sentences here is difficult because they must be isolated in this discussion from the whole of the paragraph. Examine the following clinchers and imagine a paragraph they might conclude:

Even so, the Haitian republic is still not totally liberated from tyranny.

Whatever its degree, whatever its name, human bondage is still reviled in a contemporary society.

ONE LAST WORD...

Not all paragraphs need a clincher. More experienced writers manipulate the paragraph formula, molding it to suit their style, purpose, and subject matter. They may not use a clincher sentence, concluding instead with an example, an anecdote, or a question to ponder. Following is a paragraph that ends with an example:

Earthquakes kill indirectly. A person would be quite safe in an open field, for example, during even a great earthquake. Fissures rarely open up on the surface. People are killed and injured by buildings collapsing on them, or by flying glass, falling objects, flooding from broken dams, fires or explosions from broken gas and electric lines, landslides, or tsunamis, the deadly ocean waves sometimes produced by earthquakes. (Such waves killed most of the dozens of people who died in the quake that struck northern Japan in late May. That earthquake, the strongest to hit Japan in 15 years, was centered about 100 miles offshore in the Sea of Japan.)

Richard L. Williams, "Science Tries to Break
New Ground in Predicting Great Earthquakes"

CHECKLIST

After writing your paragraph, evaluate it by the following checklist. It is not definitive, but it will help you recognize some of the important features of a paragraph. If you find deficiencies, revise with these eight points in mind.

1. Do I have a clearly stated topic sentence that focuses on a single idea?

2. Does my topic sentence have an idea and attitude word?

3. Is my paragraph structured according to a clear pattern? (See Chapter 5.)

4. Have I unified my paragraph by using transitional words and phrases judiciously? (See Chapter 4.)

5. Have I provided sufficient supporting material and details to make my points clear? (See Chapter 3.)

6. Have I proofread for grammatical, spelling, and punctuation errors?

7. Have I developed a clearly stated clincher sentence that effectively sums up my paragraph?

8. Have I written my paragraph conscious of a specific audience?

<table>
<tr><td>CHAPTER
3</td><td># The Material
That Develops
the Paragraph</td></tr>
</table>

To make paragraphs complete, writers must have supporting material to help develop their thoughts. Let's look at this paragraph to see whether it fully expands a single thought.

> It looks as if it might rain today. There is a large rain cloud in the east. All morning it has been windy and cold. In fact, there is even a slight mist outside. I guess I better wear my raincoat this morning.

Are any of the ideas fully developed? No. In fact, all you receive is a general impression about the possibility of rain. This paragraph lacks the texture that supporting material would give it. Now contrast this skimpy paragraph with the following revision:

> Oh, look at those heavy black clouds building up in the east against Crazy Cat mountain. **It looks as if it might rain today.** In fact, the weatherman on Channel 6 predicts we'll have heavy rain; outside, **there is a large rain cloud in the east.** The weather bureau has just posted a storm warning. Low-pressure areas building up off Baja California may bring violent weather to our area. **All morning it has been windy and cold.** The north wind has been blowing a gale with gusts as high as 55 miles per hour, and the barometer has fallen

three degrees in the last six hours. Through the windows I can see **there is even a slight mist outside;** it's still dewlike, but later in the day this mist may turn into a cloudburst. **I guess I better wear my raincoat this morning**, or better still, take an umbrella or galoshes. Who knows, it's possible we may even have a few snow flurries by nightfall.

Supporting Material

Supporting materials function in several ways. Certainly the primary one is to clarify, support, and prove the idea stated in the topic sentence. *Supporting material* is the specific detail one uses to amplify an idea. All of it must be related to the central idea; if not, then it is unnecessary and should be omitted. But even as it helps inform, amplify, or prove thoughts, supporting material may well be amusing, entertaining, or surprising. In addition to proving and entertaining, it also may set limits or qualify. For example, if you were writing about children, you might focus your investigation only on preschool children ages three to five. This limiting thus sharpens the focal point, as all of your supporting material must then concentrate only on three- to five-year-olds.

Definition

Supporting material may also arouse emotions. Readers may be stirred to anger or joy or whatever other emotion you want to awaken. Vivid supporting materials also make points memorable. Excite readers, then overwhelm them with a memorable idea by using vivid details. This vividness builds your own trustworthiness in the minds of readers, who will recognize you as knowledgeable and reliable. As Aristotle might have said, you have built up ethos! The persuasiveness of your presentation will help readers respect you and sympathize with your point of view; you will have greater rapport and empathy because the persuasive nature of your character emerges through the details you select and your way of presenting them.

Another function of supporting material is to define important terms. Foreign words, vague abstractions, and special jargon—*kitsch, truth, put and call, couch potato, floppy disk, handler, kissy-face, Kirlian photography*—all need defining. For example, in his famous article on *kitsch*, Gilbert Highet goes beyond a simple definition of the term as a vulgar showoff or anything requiring much labor to make and looking quite hideous. He uses examples to define the term, illustrating the wide range of *kitsch* in art, literature, sculpture, music, and the decorative arts. He finds *kitsch* in Italian majolica vases, in the statue of Atlas in Rockefeller Center, New York, and in the bad poetry of nineteenth-century imitators of Wordsworth.

Finally, if you want your paragraph to have impact, it must paint lively pictures readers will remember. Use descriptive words economically and effectively to paint word images. Appeal specifically to your readers' sense of sight, hearing, and smell. Carefully choose nouns, active-voice verbs, and colorful modifiers that will create these images as you write. Omit anything unclear or undefined; strive for a vivid paragraph. A bewildering thought will become clear if you use vivid supporting details.

FUNCTIONS OF SUPPORTING MATERIAL

1. Clarify ideas. (Make them memorable or create emotion.)
2. Support and prove ideas.
3. Arouse interest or amuse or entertain.
4. Supply texture to a composition (ideas plus supporting material plus transitions).
5. Emphasize a point.
6. Enlarge upon a statement (amplify) in order to create understanding.
7. Qualify or set limits.
8. Create ethos (trustworthiness).
9. Create empathy and rapport.
10. Above all, be specific.

Supporting Materials: How to Find Them

Looking   Listening   Reading

You are probably your own best source for supporting materials. Your experiences and the inferences drawn from them will provide you with needed details.

Brainstorming

Here is a helpful technique to use once you have formulated your topic sentence. Sit back and think about all the particulars relating precisely to this sentence. Practice the same elementary brainstorming you engaged in when you were selecting your subject and your approach. Jot down quickly and briefly all the specifics that come to mind. From this list select or reject those that fit your subject and suit your needs. Memories can become convincing supporting material because they will help personalize what you say and reveal your direct involvement. When you add details, you will write more convincingly, and this conviction will be evident.

Inner Sources

Continue meditating about the topic sentence. Close your eyes and think of instances and illustrations. Now open your eyes. What do you see around you? Observe closely — even something in the room might remind you of a useful detail. When you are describing a person or an object, this technique of close observation will be helpful.

Outer Sources

The world around you has vast resources that will be useful. Going outside yourself will open up new vistas. But where? A gallery or museum, a trip to the zoo or a movie, a journey to a special place or an event like a circus or hockey game or rock concert or play — all of these are experiences where you can gather material. You might even enjoy people-watching in an arcade, a supermarket, or a suburban mall. From each experience you will gain insight and find specific details useful in making your paper more persuasive. In brief, by recalling memories from your past and through observing, you broaden your resource pool.

The following brief narrative points up the importance of having observant eyes.

The Camera Eye

We were seated in the lobby of the hotel as she walked swiftly by us, turned a corner sharply, and was gone.

"That's an uncommonly good-looking girl," I said to my wife, who was deep in a crossword puzzle.

"Do you mean the one in that imitation blue taffeta dress with the green and red flowered design?"

"The girl that just walked by."

"Yes," said my wife, "with that dowdy rayon dress on. It's a copy of the one I saw at Hattie Carnegie's, and a poor copy at that. You'd think, though, that she'd have better taste than to wear a chartreuse hat with it, especially with her bleached hair."

"Bleached? I didn't notice her hair was bleached."

"Good heavens you could almost smell the peroxide. I don't mind a bit of make-up provided it looks fairly natural. But you could scrape that rouge off with a knife. They ought to add a course in make-up to the curriculum at Smith."

"Smith? Why Smith?"

"From her class pin, of course. You must have noticed it hanging from her charm bracelet."

"I wasn't looking at her wrist."

"I'll bet you weren't. Nor at those fat legs of hers, either. A woman with legs like that shouldn't wear high-heeled patent-leather shoes."

"I thought she was a very pretty girl," I said apologetically.

"Well, you may be right," said my wife. "I was busy with my puzzle and I didn't notice her particularly. What's the name of a President of the United States in six letters, beginning with *T*?"

Norman Levy, *The Atlantic Monthly*

Interviews

Talking formally with others is another useful resource. A novel approach to your subject might emerge in a conversation, which may perhaps convince you to take a "second look" at your subject or rethink your approach. An interview with an expert in the field may offer insights richer than those you derive from conversation with a friend. But interviews with both will give you fresh perspectives and perhaps provide some "expert testimony."

Besides these conversations and interviews, you can also learn more about your subject by listening to radio and television or by attending lectures. To enrich your resource pool even further, become an active listener, absorbing and distilling what you hear, simultaneously analyzing (breaking down a whole conversation into its parts) and synthesizing it (putting the parts together again).

Printed Sources

The resources just mentioned have all been those you could experience directly, but printed sources will also be a major source of information. Books, magazines, government documents, unpublished theses, pamphlets, monographs, and other printed matter provide a useful variety of supporting material. A visit to the library will open up a vast area for details — newspapers (local or foreign), periodicals, indexes, abstracts, encyclopedias, and books on nearly all subjects. Details you find in what you read will add breadth to your writing and provide convincing evidence that you understand your topic well.

Process Questions

Before deciding what types of supporting material will be appropriate, however, take another quick look at your topic. Approach it with a questioning mind. Here are some questions you might consider. Answering them will help you discover what types of supporting material you need.

1. What is the topic?
2. Do I need to define it?
3. Do I need to describe it?
4. Do I need to measure or explain?
5. Do I need to locate it specifically (time and place)?
6. Do I need to state whether it is real or imaginary?
7. Do I need to compare or contrast it?
8. Do I need to consult an expert about it?
9. Do I need to state causes, effects, or both?
10. Do I need to defend or attack it?

Types of Supporting Material

Examples

Definition

The most common type of supporting material is the *example*. An example is an elaboration of a specific detail; it focuses on one of a kind. For instance, there are many details you might observe about a salad, such as the greens. As you sharpen your focus, you notice specific greens, such as different kinds of lettuce. Romaine is an example of one type; bibb and iceberg are two others. As you refine your observations, you move from general categories to specific types, from tiny details toward more elaborate examples, from greens to lettuce, from lettuce to romaine or bibb or red-tipped.

A person's name is another type of vivid detail. For instance, a paragraph about athletes will become more meaningful if the supporting material includes specific examples with athletes named — Babe Ruth, Boris Becker, Arnold Palmer, Muhammad Ali, Steffi Graf. The power of an example is in its ability to represent an entire group of details.

Real examples

Real examples describe things that still exist or events that have happened. Names of people who are alive or once lived are real examples. Or a corporation in a quarterly earnings statement might provide its stockholders with some real examples of recent acquisitions, such as these sentences illustrate:

General

Specific

You might be interested in knowing your firm has recently purchased another large main-frame for our data processing division, in this case a second IBM 3083. This new computer will not only give us another big 20 megabytes of capacity, but will help us process clear and accurate transactions with incredible speed and efficiency.

Imaginary examples

But if the real world does not provide the precise type of example you want, you might need to create a hypothetical one. *Imaginary* examples spring from your creativity; they are imagined by-products of your ingenuity. A composite picture of the ideal man or woman might be completely fictional — what you imagine him or her to be. Here is an entire paragraph that develops a hypothetical example similar to one you might find in a prospectus for an imaginary mutual fund:

> Let's assume that in 1960 you invested $10,000 in the XYZ Mutual Fund and reinvested all capital gains distributions. The purchase of these additional shares has kept the original investment intact as dividends have steadily increased over the past 25 years. In 1962, dividends totaled $464. By 1974, they had more than doubled; by 1980, they had more than doubled again — to $2,143. Between 1980 and 1987, they increased by another 47 percent. And in 1988 (the last year for which we have data), they amounted to $3,147. Some years extra dividends were paid as a result of heavy investment by XYZ in government instruments that were providing unusually high yields. Through this Fund you will continue to have broad diversification and professional management, as well as a sound protection against inflation.

Characterizations

Characterizations are a special type of supporting details   Definition
that catalog the impression of a person — facial expressions, features, movements. Characterizations might even become caricatures (like Scrooge) in which you wildly exaggerate the character, as Dickens did in *A Christmas Carol*. In deciding whether a characterization would be an appropriate supporting example, ask yourself whether the audience will be able to identify with the character. Here is a short example:

> The actor plays the part of a washed-up country-western singer appearing weather-beaten and worn, chewing now and then on a piece of straw, pausing sometimes to rub his stubbled chin. . . .

Cases

Your reader will nearly always enjoy reading about real people and significant events in their lives. For source material you may want to develop a *case*, a highly factual   Definition
study of a real person, cataloging details about birth, home situation, employment, education, civic involvement, club or fraternal participation, or other similar factual evidence.

A doctor keeps a record of cases; large organizations use "case studies," which may involve detailed descriptions pertinent to the organization's business. Notice in this paragraph from *Forbes* how Norman Pearlstine chooses personal experience from Kim Yung Gee's life to describe the economic situation of a "typical South Korean." The details become a case study in the life of the young man.

> Does the typical South Korean have an easy or affluent life? Not yet — perhaps he *never* will. Kim Yung Gee, a 27-year-old auto assembler at the Hyundai Motor Co., in Ulsan, 200 miles south of Seoul, heads for the factory gate at 7 a.m., leaving his wife and two small children behind in a cramped, company-subsidized two-room apartment. Forty minutes later he is at his post on the assembly line, ready to endure noise, dust and fumes that would keep an OSHA inspector busy writing reports for a month. Kim works 10 to 12 hours a day, six and sometimes seven days a week. In return, he makes about $3,500 a year. That's above average for Korean workers but much less than auto workers around the world typically make. Kim knows that compared with most citizens of the Third World, he is fairly well off. Considering the economic depths from which the country emerged, he is fortunate indeed.
>
> Norman Pearlstine, "How South Korea Surprised the World."

Pearlstine implies that Kim Yung Gee is a typical South Korean. His routines, his salary, his work hours, and his schedule — all of these are presented as representative of the South Korean worker. Veiled hints of the author's judgment about poor work standards in South Korea and the living conditions of the South Korean worker emerge explicitly in details about Kim's house and work area. Notice how the author's feelings about the case are implied in the second sentence, a fragmentary answer with an italicized word emphasizing the author's doubt. Also, note how Pearlstine inserts some dry humor by the reference to an OSHA (Office of Safety and Health Administration) inspector. OSHA inspections, which simply do not exist in South Korea, suggest a burden an American worker might have to endure. Even though Pearlstine recognizes a lack of quality control in Korea, the work of OSHA inspectors is nevertheless dismissed, almost off-handedly, as report writing. In such ways does the skillful writer manipulate the language and the case to present a point of view, which we can discover only with careful, painstaking analysis of the prose.

Instances

Instances are another form of supporting example; they are very brief, undetailed, condensed. They remind readers of what they already know, acting as "ticklers," merely suggesting what might be more fully developed. Writing about college registration, a student might voice his complaints: long lines, too many forms, inadequate directions, the "run-around." These instances might appear in the introductory part of a paragraph. A useful structure for presenting them is a series pattern with three or more items: A, B, and C. Yet instances will not fully support a topic sentence because they are not developed; they only suggest, providing reminders to your reader of what they already know and making them feel comfortable with a familiar subject.

If you are still puzzled about instances, try thinking about names, for a name is an instance. Have you ever thought what stereotypes a name conveys to others? Some names have specific connotations — that is, they suggest instances of personalities or traits. For instance, Patricia and Jane may suggest pleasant, plain people, whereas Sara is sensual and Maureen, sultry. Rogers may be plodders; Edwards, thoughtful; Donalds, smooth and charming; Simons, introverted.

Now let's look at another way of using names as instances. In her book about the Patty Hearst trial, Shana Alexander uses an image of the flipping back and forth of white hats and black hats, worn by well-known personalities, to suggest shifts in celebrity status between the sixties and seventies. It's use of these names themselves that creates the instances illustrating Alexander's point:

In the period between the death of President Kennedy and the fall of President Nixon, just to set out some rough markers, white hats and black hats flipped back and forth like a troop of Arabian tumblers. Malcolm X flipped from pimp to prophet; Robert Kennedy, from Joe McCarthy stooge to golden boy; Daniel Ellsberg, from traitor to Paul Revere; Eldridge Cleaver, from rapist to literary lion to political exile — and now to born-again Christian; Anita Bryant flipped from Mary Sunshine to Mrs. Grundy; Eugene McCarthy, from hero of the cause to betrayer of the cause; George Wallace, from narrow racist to broad-appeal populist; Betty Friedan, from national joke to founding mother. Teddy Kennedy sprang upward like a backward movie from the waters of Chappaquiddick to the heights of elder statesmanhood. But no mythic transformation surpassed Patty's own.

Shana Alexander, "Anyone's Daughter."

| Exercise 3–1 |

On the lines provided list instances that might appear in a paragraph with the indicated general topic.

1. Washington political disgraces.

    _____

    _____

2. Heroes of the 1990s.

    _____

    _____

3. Chinese dishes.

    _____

    _____

4. Specially designed cars.

    _____

    _____

5. Items of popular women's fashion.

_____

_____

_____

Illustrations

If you are reading a magazine article, one of the things accompanying it might be a photograph illustrating the author's point. Similarly, in a paragraph you might want to rely on *word illustration*—an extended example that tells a story. Illustrations narrate an incident, often creating suspense, laughter, panic, or tears. Some include bits of dialogue. Historical events, jokes, and fables are other types you might want to use. A striking feature of them is that they usually follow a chronological sequence (time order), creating interest in your writing and drawing readers into your thoughts.

Definition

As the years slip by, it seems that I lose touch more than I wish with old friends from the past. Some of them come to mind as I look through an old scrapbook or laugh about photographs I pasted in an album from college. One of my favorite friends is Bob Dierdorff who was once arrested as the "mad bomber" on the campus of the University of Wisconsin. He had arrived only the day before, but had been spotted by someone who thought he was Karlton Armstrong, one of the fellows who wound up in the pen for the crime. Bob was walking across the quadrangle near Witte Hall, the graduate students' dorm, when he was stopped by a plainclothesman who demanded identification. Bob was taken into the police station on the campus where he used his broad southern drawl to help him get out of the situation. "Why, I'm a graduate student," I can recall Bob saying. "I teach at the University of Texas, out in El Paso. Oh, I was playing cards at the Holiday Inn in Lubbock when that explosion took place. Surely you guys don't think Karlton Armstrong is still around Madison when he knows everyone is looking for him." I can re-member Bob's stories well, and wish I hadn't lost touch with him over the years.

General Versus Specific Examples

Combining both general and specific examples will help clarify points. In a paragraph about choices you might have when you go to buy a new car, you might enumerate the general types, such as Ford, Porsche, Cadillac. But within each of these general categories there is a specific model; Cadillac makes De Ville, Fleetwood, and El Dorado. Your paragraph might want to focus on the specific model rather than the general. A paper becomes livelier as you move away from general examples toward specific ones, from tennis players to Jimmy Connors, from golfers to Arnold Palmer or Tom Watson. The following chart illustrates through various levels movement from something general (food) to something quite specific (peaches and cream). Communication improves as your examples become more specific.

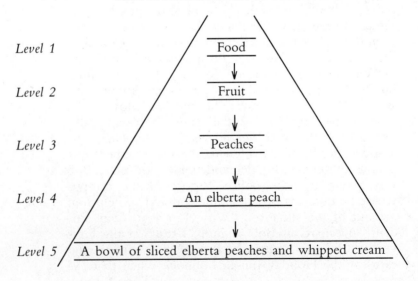

**FROM THE GENERAL TO THE CONCRETE
AND SPECIFIC LEVELS OF SPECIFICITY**

Level 1 — Food

Level 2 — Fruit

Level 3 — Peaches

Level 4 — An elberta peach

Level 5 — A bowl of sliced elberta peaches and whipped cream

Exercise 3–2

Look at the example on peaches. Try making up a similar series of levels for these topics. If possible, write out five levels — or more if you can think them up.

1. Sports
2. Dates
3. Wedding customs
4. Teachers
5. Experiments

Statistics

Have you ever turned on the television, only to be confronted with commercials using numbers? Gas mileages, numbers of people who participated in a poll, lengths golf balls can be hit — these and other types of comparative statistics are supporting evidence the advertiser relies on to persuade the viewer. *Statistics* are numerical examples — Definition facts, figures, percentages, measurements — all of which support an argument and persuade.

Consider the impact of these two statements.

The sides of the Great Pyramid of Cheops at Giza are about 755 feet long.

The sides of the Great Pyramid of Cheops at Giza are roughly 2½ times as long as a soccer field.

Which has the greater impact on you? Why does the writer use a soccer field to present length in the second sentence?

Dramatizing   We must be cautious, however, when we consider certain comparative statistics. Dramatic figures impress a reader. If a used-car advertisement promises you 1,000 gallons of gasoline or a $500 rebate, you might be lured to the dealership to examine the offer. Such statistics are supporting evidence for the advertiser and may give misleading figures that help sell cars. Statistics in a composition or a letter may also have similar impact. Judiciously used, however, they can reinforce your argument; but if you burden your readers with too many, they may forget your point.

Let's look at a part of a paragraph from *The College Board Review* in which Marcia Sharp presents a number of statistics to suggest the fine record women's colleges have in complying with affirmative action guidelines:

> Studies conducted by the Women's College Coalition show, for example, that in 1976, women made up 55 percent of all faculty at women's colleges, 42 percent of all full professors, and 71 percent of all academic deans. More recent figures on presidents show that more than 60 percent of all chief executive officers at women's colleges are women. In comparison, the national figures for all colleges and universities show that women constitute less than 25 percent of faculties and, more important perhaps, only 10 to 12 percent of tenured professors, about 15 percent of academic deans, and about 6 percent of presidents.

> Marcia Sharp, "Women's Colleges: Equity and Optimum"

Exercise 3–3

1. What detail in the paragraph do you find particularly startling?

    _____

    _____

2. What is the source the author identifies for these statistics? Does the source seem a biased or reasonable source? How can you tell?

    _____

    _____

3. An *inference* is an opinion you draw from a source. What is the inference you draw about the opportunities for women in university teaching and administration?

4. Does your college have an affirmative action officer? Can you find these statistics: number of women working at your university, number of female full professors, number of female administrators (department heads, deans, vice-presidents)? Now that you have collected these statistics, write a paragraph that includes some of the statistics and conclusions you derive from them about the opportunity for women in your university.

Statistics and numerical analogies can be particularly dramatic. Do you remember the commercial using such an analogy to compare a super oil tanker to the Empire State Building lying on its side? Once readers imagine the building lying on top of the Pacific Ocean, sailing to the Orient, they conjure up in their heads the probable length the writer or advertiser had in mind.

Both when we read statistics and when we use them, we must be careful about interpretation. Clearly, some statistics are being manipulated in advertising. As writers, we may be guilty of similar abuse. When using statistics or listening to someone quote numerical evidence, we must ask certain questions: How reliable and accurate are these statistics? Can they be verified? How dependable is the source? Occasionally, we may not be able to answer each of these questions, but we must be able to defend any statistics we use.

One point to keep in mind when using statistical data is that they alone are not conclusive proof. Writers often advance them for self-serving reasons. Americans in particular love numbers. For instance, tobacco lobbyists rely on statistical information presented by the U.S. Tobacco Institute in the public smoking controversy to advance their cause; however, counterclaims, supported by equally convincing, seemingly reliable statistical data, could be used by other lobbyists who are opposed to smoking in public places and who advocate laws prohibiting smoking in airplanes, elevators, restaurants, and other public areas. One must always consider the reliability of statistics, the type of sampling that generated them, and other such relevant variables. Maintain your integrity when you use statistics.

Testimony

Definition   After completing several interviews or surveys, you might have gathered data appropriate for supporting a topic sentence. Such information is called *testimony* — reliable evidence from either the expert or the nonexpert. Mere testimony is the opinion of a source other than yourself; for example, conversation with a relative or friend — a man-on-the-street interview — is simple testimony. But expert testimony introduces the opinions of well-known authorities to make your ideas more impressive and convincing. A government expert, an academic authority, an entertainment figure, or a sports hero — any of these individuals might be recognized immediately as an expert whose testimony will enhance your proof. You can find expert testimony in books, news reports, journals, lectures, and interviews you conduct or listen to on talk shows. In some of these sources you will encounter real professionals who know crucial facts about your subject. They have studied it thoroughly and can communicate their knowledge in an articulate manner.

Reliability   The value of testimony depends on the reliability of your source. Is the source trustworthy? A handwriting authority, a ballistics expert, a layman with special training are all reliable sources. A quick test for evaluating evidence is asking a simple question: who said that? Once you have identified your source, you may use other clues to determine reliability. The education of the expert, his ability to reveal his familiarity with the subject, and his performance (as before a jury, a television audience, or an interviewer) may be useful clues for determining whether you can trust your expert.

Television advertising constantly deluges us with expert

testimony about why we should purchase one product instead of another. Some advocates are experts; others are
people on the street who are lured into testing a product,
later discovering that the "whitest white" clothes were
washed in Brand X, *the* product. As you compose, you
can make a convincing case by citing experts advocating
your point. You will be even more convincing if your expert is reliable and trustworthy.

Let's say that in writing about UFOs you have discovered an outdated 1974 Gallup Poll that reported over 15
million Americans believed they had seen an unidentified
flying object. But you might be even more convincing if
you presented some current expert testimony. Can you
find a quotation from an astronaut who reported a sight-
ing? What have some famous astronomers said about
UFOs? Carl Sagan and Frank Drake are prominent astronomers who have written and spoken about them. Testimony from either might strengthen your report. Also,
you might consult some government documents for quotations from officials at NASA, the National Radio Astron-
omy Observatory, the National Security Agency, the
Ames Research Center in California, or other reputable
government agencies. Although your readers might enjoy
a quotation from a science fiction writer, such as the English author H. G. Wells, they would probably be skeptical
about an eyewitness report he might present.

Citing Experts

If you decide it would be appropriate to quote an expert's exact words, whether they are opinions or assumptions, how do your introduce them into your paper? First,
you must identify the source. Give the expert's name. Then
identify the place where you found the quotation. Was it
in a magazine, book, newspaper article? Finally, you must
put the exact borrowed words in quotation marks. (Check
your citation form for accuracy in a reputable handbook.)
Here are two examples from Dick Russell's "They Fly in
the Face of Logic" that appeared in *TV Guide*:

In response to Freedom of Information requests filed   Citing an expert
by National Security Agency communications specialist   in summary form
Todd Zechel, the CIA released approximately 125
documents about UFOs.

Citing a direct quote from an expert and identifying the source

Another student of the subject, Phillip J. Klass (senior avionics editor of *Aviation Week* and *Space Technology*) states, "After twelve years of investigating some of the most famous UFO reports, I am convinced that all UFO reports have prosaic/terrestrial explanations."

Personal Opinion Versus Assumption

Opinions and assumptions are two types of testimony needing careful handling. A *personal opinion* is an emotionally laden judgment. Since it is not based on fact, "I feel," "I believe," and "I think" often identify statements of opinion. "I think all drugs are dangerous" is an example of one person's opinion, a conclusion possibly arrived at after some research or from personal experience, but having no factual evidence to support it. "William Shakespeare wrote both comedies and tragedies," however, is a statement of fact because it can be proved. An opinion can't be proved or disproved, nor can one place much faith in it. Because of its subjectivity, an opinion may mean something quite different to different people. By contrast, an expert's opinion may be valid. When using opinions, one should be careful to test for accuracy; when identifying opinions of others, one should consider whose opinion is being advanced and how accurate it might be.

Definition

A *value judgment* is an individual's opinion expressing the worth or worthlessness of a thing or an idea — whether it is good or bad. Some scented words involve value judgments, such as those in statements like "he's a liar" or "she's a real dog." Each of these implies values; neither affirms the truth.

Definition

Assumptions, on the other hand, are based even more on emotions than opinions, because when one assumes, he takes something for granted. An assumption is a personal guess, a conclusion based not on facts but on hopes and emotional involvement with the subject. For practice, take a well-known fact and create an opinion and a faulty assumption about it.

Fact: The moon affects the movement of the tides.

Opinion: The moon is yellow.

Assumption: The moon is a source of mineral wealth.

Plagiarism

You must be careful to avoid *plagiarism*, the misappropriation of another writer's ideas or words. Intentional plagiarism is academic theft. Be certain to identify the source, to use quotation marks to indicate you've borrowed exact words, and to use either an in-text citation, a footnote, or an end note. Formats for identifying sources vary among academic disciplines. Be clear about whether the format of the American Psychological Association (APA), the Modern Language Association (MLA), *The Chicago Manual of Style*, or some other style manual is appropriate for your paper in terms of audiences and their expectations. Be certain there is a marked separation between your opinions and those of your sources. Even if you borrow ideas or paraphrase them, you must tell your reader where they come from.

Definition

Exercise 3–4

Now that you have reviewed opinions, assumptions, and value judgments, let's try identifying what the following statements are and then give the reason for your particular classification.

Example: The morning call to prayer in Moslem countries is annoying to members of other religions. This is a value judgment because the writer finds, according to his value system, a custom annoying that wouldn't bother members of a particular religious group.

1.   It looks like it might rain this afternoon.

   _____

   _____

2.   I never thought that a girl her size should wear polka dots.

   _____

   _____

3. John Irving's novel *Cider House Rules* has many situations similar to those in *The World According to Garp*.

_____

_____

4. The paper would be better if you expanded the conclusion and included a prediction about the future.

_____

_____

5. My pastor's advice about the death of my friend John gave me so much comfort.

_____

_____

Facts

A particularly convincing type of supporting material is factual evidence. Facts are unalterable truths. They *are*—that is, they exist and do not change. They remain constant because they have been verified, proved. A date is a fact. For example, if you mention the date of someone's birth, that fact is impersonal and objective; it cannot be altered by someone else. Yet a special type of fact, such as Chaucer's birthdate, might be illustrated by following it with a question mark (1340?), thereby indicating an unverifiable date.

Facts are particularly useful as persuasive evidence. Imagine you are writing a persuasive paragraph about your favorite sport, tennis. You have decided to focus on three pros on the touring circuit: John McEnroe, Ivan Lendl, and Jimmy Connors. A fact about each of these pros would be his height: McEnroe, 5'10"; Lendl, 6'2"; Connors, 5'10". McEnroe and Connors are both left-handed; Lendl is right-handed. No one can dispute these facts, and you might want to use these supporting details. If you did some research, however, you might find some other facts (such as the relationship between physical characteristics and performance) helpful in determining which of the three should head the list of top international players. Useful data could be major wins in international competition, amount of money won, number of opponents defeated, number of tournaments entered, and Association of Tennis Professionals computer points ranking. The facts you finally decide to present will be the persuasive evidence for your choice of top international tennis pro for that particular year.

CAUTION

Occasionally, statements using facts are untrue because the writer has manipulated them dishonestly to support a particular viewpoint. Such slanted facts are really distorted and jumbled, like those in unsubstantiated claims or half-truths we find in advertising, political claims, or government figures. These distortions of fact promote a misleading image. Partially quoted facts or those quoted out of context may create an entirely new impression, something totally alien to the truth.

Comparison and Contrast

Within a paragraph another valuable type of supporting material is comparison or contrast. When you *compare* items, you show how they are similar to each other; when you *contrast*, you describe differences.

Definition

The following paragraph illustrates how Mimi Sheraton, a free-lance writer for *Esquire* and specialist in foods and restaurants, establishes a number of contrasts among Chinese restaurants. Her comments describe restaurants in general — that is, without mentioning any names of specific places. Let's look at one of her paragraphs, noticing the supporting material for her comparisons and contrasts:

> Most Chinese restaurants in New York (and perhaps throughout the country) have a common flaw in that they subscribe to two different standards: one for what is perceived to be the tourist customer hooked on the egg roll–won ton soup, spareribs–subgum routine so blandly served up at third-rate neighorhood restaurants; the other for Chinese and those few Occidentals who have convinced the management that they want the real McCoy. The first

group gets short shrift indeed, with purchased frozen egg rolls, watery soup, greasy precooked spareribs and other dishes, whether from the regions of Canton, Fukien, Hunan, Szechwan, Peking, Shanghai, or wherever. It is, therefore, a good idea to make it plain at all of the following places that you want the food prepared as it would be for Chinese customers, and if you like your hotly-seasoned dishes really hot, say so. Using chopsticks, shunning the fried noodles and mustard, and avoiding the standard neighborhood dishes will go a long way toward convincing the waiter that you rate the kitchen's best effort, something that should not be necessary but that, unfortunately, is, especially at large, "fancy" uptown places.

Mimi Sheraton, "My Favorite New York Restaurants"

Nearly every day we involve ourselves in a similar but rapid mental process of comparing and contrasting. When we shop in the produce section of the market, we compare this avocado with that one, squeezing, pressing, trying to determine which is fresher, riper, tastier. We engage in a private argument trying to convince ourselves whether the Calavo or the black-skinned avocado is the better choice, mixing two thinking modes — contrast and argumentation.

Simultaneously when we compare two objects, we are often apt to contrast them, too — that is, to point out the differences between them. With the avocados, we might point out how the darker skin on one contrasts with the light green skin on the other. We might compare the beauty of a mother and daughter but simultaneously make comments about the "prettier" skin of the mother, the "more golden" hair of the daughter. Although both are alike, each is also unique.

Figurative Comparisons   A special kind of comparison is *figurative language*. A few figures of speech will create an enriching type of supporting material. Figurative language helps words say more and mean more than their literal meanings convey. Figures of speech compare one item from one class with another item from a totally different class. That is, when you say "the sky is like a blue tapestry," you are pointing out the similarities between the natural colors of the sky and man-made fabric. Three common types of figurative language are *simile, metaphor,* and *analogy.*

Simile.   *Simile* is stated comparison between essentially un-   Definition
like things. You must have one of the following connec-
tives in all similes: *like, as, than,* or a verb such as *seems.* A
simile says that two things are similar when they are really
not alike at all. Here is an example: "Trying to pin a
reason on the sudden elopement of those two is *like* trying
to nail Jello to the wall."

Metaphor.   *Metaphor* is an implied comparison between   Definition
two items from different classes. The connectives are omitted; you simply say one thing *is* something else (A is B).
There are two kinds of metaphors: single-word and analogy. Sports writers often exploit such metaphors for colorful descriptions: "The young rookie skyrocketed to fame;
the quarterback blasted through the line; the hockey fans
came unglued."

Analogy.   *Analogy* is an extended simile or metaphor com-   Definition
paring at length two objects from different classes. A classic analogy compares the human heart to a mechanical
pump or the eye to a camera. A simile and a single-word
metaphor are usually only one sentence, whereas analogy
is sustained through several. For example, if you decide to
write an analogy comparing your favorite aunt with her
poodle, you might want to focus on several major points
in four or five sentences. You probably would notice similarities in their eating behavior, their walking mannerisms,
and even their facial expressions. You might begin to recognize how similar the two are!

Such figurative comparisons and contrasts can be valuable supporting materials within paragraphs. They may be
combined with other types of supporting evidence, such as
expert testimony or statistics. Or they may be used by
themselves as ways of developing ideas dramatically.

CAUTION

A careful writer will avoid relying on worn-out clichés
or trite comparisons. Here are just a few to avoid:

White as snow
Fresh as a daisy

Diamond in the rough

Pleased as punch

Tit for tat

Salt of the earth

The straw that broke the camel's back

An ounce of prevention is worth a pound of cure.

A rolling stone gathers no moss.

Definitions

In order to establish communication bridges between writer and audience, you may find it necessary to define and clarify terms. One of the strategic places to do so is in the early paragraphs. If your topic sentence includes obscure words, explain them quickly; otherwise, you are going to baffle everybody. Define key terms and clarify difficult concepts by identifying what they mean. What you interpret as the definition of a key term and what you hope your reader will understand must be completely reconciled if effective communication is to take place. Imagine writing a paper that forces you to rely on a special vocabulary. Let's say that some of the words are *handicap, chipping, full-swing drills, bad lies, downswing,* and *divot.* If your reader is a real outsider, there will be no communication until you make him or her an insider by defining these golf terms. You may provide specific definitions or context clues that help define terms. But if you expect to communicate, you must recognize the limitations of the outsider's vocabulary and overcome the barriers language erects when you (as writer) and your audience (as reader) do not understand each other.

Abstract words like *love* or *failure* have special meanings for each reader; be certain that your particular definition is clear. Otherwise, readers may misinterpret. When in doubt, always define so that your paragraph will be clear and your message convincing.

Special words even more abstract than *love* or *failure* — such as *antisocial, communist, libertine* — have particular connotations even more difficult to contend with than the more familiar abstract terms. You must make your personal interpretation of these terms clear. Your audience must know what limitations or qualifications you give to these words; if they are not clear, you will confuse your reader and obscure your message.

Other special words needing definition are technical terms or unusual words, such as the jargon of a group. If you are discussing ALS disease (amyotrophic lateral sclerosis), you should define its characteristics. Invoking the memory of Lou Gehrig may be enough to define it for some audiences, but others may not recognize the baseball player's name or know of his early death from muscular atrophy. Use the language of the layman to describe the difficult term.

Occasionally, you may want to use light or humorous definitions. Some of Ambrose Bierce's facetious definitions, for example, might add just the right light touch:

Male, n. A member of the unconsidered, or negligible sex. The male of the human race is commonly known (to the female) as Mere Man. The genus has two varieties: good providers and bad providers. *Monday*, n. In Christian countries, the day after the baseball game. *Happiness*, n. An agreeable sensation arising from contemplating the misery of another.

Humor in America, ed. Enid Veron

Another, more contemporary lighthearted definition from *Time* follows:

LIZANDICK ('liz n 'dik) n. pl. [contemporary usage fr. Liz and Dick often followed by exclamation point, *i.e.,* Lizandick!] 1. *Archaic.* Mythic American actress and Welsh actor whose names were eternally coupled despite their celebrated uncoupling(s). 2. Aging and forever expanding histrionic duo whose sum is greater than their individual parts, and whose mutual moves are perpetually played out in public (did you hear that _____ started a limited-run revival of Noel Coward's *Private Lives* in Boston last week?). 3. Any pair of people who come together, split, come together, split, until they seem to make a profession of it or until their acquaintances move past empathy to ennui.

Richard Stengel, "People"

Here is a student's definition in a one-paragraph theme:

Snow

The American Heritage Dictionary defines snow as
"translucent crystals of ice that form from water vapor in
the atmosphere. A falling of snow or snowstorm." The very
mention of snow turns me into a little kid again, yet my
expectations of an accumulation are different from those
of a child. I watch the sky, waiting for the first flake to
fall, and then I am hypnotized by the white fluff falling to
earth. As I watch the storm I envision a white crystallized
winter wonderland; everything is frosted in snow and ice,
clean, perfect and untouched by humans. My illusion is
quickly shattered by the voices of screaming children as
they run across my yard, leaving footprints the size of
Bigfoot's. They just rolled a snowman and left criss-cross
paths in the lawn. What once was perfect is now a horror
scene that can only be surpassed by a wet, cold child entering the house. Snow is packed into the carpet; wet
coats, clothes and gloves lead a path down the hall where
a child is changing into dry gear for the snowball war.
Where will it end? The washer and dryer will run most of
the day, and only God knows how long it really takes for a
pair of boots to dry. I say many prayers during the day, one
for sunshine, one for no frostbite, one for no flu, and yes,
one for school the next day. Yet, with the next weather forecast for snow, my memory short circuits and I anxiously
await the first flake's fall while my mind builds ice castles
in never never land.

Exercise 3–5

Go to the library and look up the name William Safire in
the *New York Times Index*. Safire writes repeatedly about
language, particularly abusive or misused words. Read two
or three of his columns in recent issues of the *Times*. List
below four words that you found that Safire precisely defined for you, and give his definitions. Identify the date
and page number in which you found the definitions.
Then, selecting one of the words, write a definition paragraph expanding upon the information you found.

1. _____

_____

_____

2. _____

_____

_____

3. _____

_____

_____

4. _____

_____

_____

_____

_____

Descriptive Details

Descriptions   Lively descriptions can be exciting supporting material. For papers treating an object in minute detail,
you will need descriptions that appeal to the senses
through painting visual, auditory, olfactory, or tactile images. Let nouns and sensory verbs carry the descriptive
message. Use words telling who, what, where, and when,
but be careful: too many adjectives may clutter up your
writing, making it sound overblown and melodramatic.
Before using any adjective, remember this sound principle
of descriptive writing: *show* your readers, don't *tell* them.
Instead of saying that Laurie is pretty, show your reader

how attractive she is by describing her hazel eyes and blonde curls.

When describing a person, concentrate on facial features— lips, eyes, brows. Observe how John Steinbeck gives precise details about Juan Chicoy's face and gestures; he makes Juan become real for readers of *The Wayward Bus* who can visualize this strong man:

> Juan picked a striped mechanic's cap from his work-bench. He wore Headlight overalls with big brass buttons on the bib and side latches and over this he wore a black horsehide jacket with black knitted wristlets and neck. His shoes were round-toed and hard, with soles so thick that they seemed swollen. An old scar on his cheek beside his large nose showed as a shadow in the overhead light. He ran fingers through his thick, black hair to get it all in the mechanic's cap.
>
> John Steinbeck, *The Wayward Bus*

By presenting a carefully detailed, naturalistic description, Steinbeck gives us another clear picture, this time of the slow-moving turtle in *The Grapes of Wrath*:

> And over the grass at the roadside a land turtle crawled, turning aside for nothing, dragging his high-domed shell over the grass. His hard legs and yellow-nailed feet threshed slowly through the grass, not really walking but boosting and dragging his shell along.
>
> John Steinbeck, *The Grapes of Wrath*

The verbs and verbals— *crawled, threshed, boosting, dragging* —highlight the features of the turtle's actions. Even the meandering sentence structure itself reinforces the slowness of the turtle's movements and has a powerful impact on the reader.

When describing a place, you need to focus on one dominant impression. It would be impossible to reproduce every detail about it, but it is important to make your reader feel the atmosphere of the area. Create with carefully chosen details the sense of "being there." Arturo Vivante makes his readers believe they are really in this restaurant simply by providing precise details of the room:

The place had a glow the chandeliers couldn't account for. It came from a fire—a robust flame that rose from an open burner in full view of the tables. With its wavering light, it lit our faces orange and made the shadows dance. A white-bonneted cook busied himself about it. . . . The tables were beautifully laid with white linen cloths, fine dishes, long-stemmed slender goblets, silver, napkins folded in the shape of cones.

Arturo Vivante, "The Holborn"

Besides describing people or places, you might also enliven your message by describing actions. Choose precise action verbs that create vivid images. For example, in describing a man walking down a street, what are your options for creating a visual image of him? Does he stumble, stagger, shuffle, weave, zig-zag, jog, trip, or skip? Each of these words creates a different impression. Norman Mailer uses a variety of verb forms to suggest Muhammad Ali's movements against George Foreman in their famous fight: "He was almost tender with Foreman's laboring advance, holding him softly and kindly by the neck. Then he stung him with right and left karate shots from the shoulder." (Norman Mailer, *The Fight*).

Another fine description details the movements of the water strider, an insect that has the power to walk on water:

Texans call them "Jesus bugs," whereas in Canada they are skaters. Their slender feet are covered with a short pile of greasy hairs that the water fails to invade. Each foot presses the water surface and makes a dimple there, but the water does not let the foot fall through the surface film as it would if the fine waxy bristles were absent. . . . The strider stands chiefly on its hind and foremost legs, while with the middle pair as oars it sculls along, its body well above the smooth and slippery surface of the pond.

Lorus J. Milne and Margery J. Milne,
A Multitude of Living Things

CHAPTER 4

Bridge Building in the Paragraph: Coherence and Transition

Definition   The absence of logical connections among sentences and thoughts, when ideas neither grow naturally out of those that have preceded nor anticipate those that follow, is a characteristic of poor writing. Poorly constructed paragraphs often have inadequate "bridges" between sentences because the writer was not conscious of *coherence*. Coherent writing holds together; that is, its thoughts flow smoothly and naturally because they are held together by natural, logical connections that are a part of the writer's thinking process, or by skillful use of devices that guarantee continuity. A writer who thinks through a composition before composing will create natural coherence.

yeast
flour
baking powder
sugar
salt

To understand the term *coherence*, let's draw an analogy to cooking. Imagine a large mixing bowl filled with these dry ingredients: yeast, flour, baking powder, sugar, and salt. But if you were to include *only* these ingredients and attempted to stir and stir them, you would not be making dough. What is missing? Cohesive agents—eggs, milk, butter, shortening, or water to mix and hold these dry ingredients together.

This cooking example suggests analogies to the writing process. Within a paragraph all sentences and ideas similarly need to be mixed. Their interrelatedness will help readers move smoothly from topic to subtopic to supporting materials. A writer who thinks solely in terms of the number of sentences in a paragraph often creates isolated sentences that do no have bridges between them. In contrast, a writer who thinks in terms of the whole paragraph will include bridging devices naturally; and just like the cook who remembers the importance of shortening, water, milk, or eggs in mixing, the writer will produce a coherent paragraph—the result of clear, logical thinking. A paragraph develops not because of one or two units working independently, but rather because all of the parts work together to make the whole.

Two Devices for Coherence

Occasionally, experienced writers depend upon certain mechanical devices to help strengthen paragraphs and achieve coherence. Two types of devices, repetition and transition, appear in the following chart, which shows how to create various kinds of bridges within paragraphs:

Repetition Devices	*Transition Devices*	
1. Repetition of key words or phrases (may be different form of the same word)	1. A single word of transition	Minor transitions that show coordination or subordination
	2. A transitional phrase	

Repetition Devices	*Transition Devices*	
2. Repetition of distinctive patterns (or a portion of a particular sentence pattern)	3. A sentence	Major transitions that a. Pre-outline what is to come OR
3. Repetition of pronoun patterns (repeating at least two)	4. A paragraph	b. Provide an internal summary
4. Repetition of parallel sentence patterns throughout a paragraph		

Transitional Elements

Definition   Etymologically, *transition* comes from the Latin *trans* + *ire* + *tion*, a "going across." Transitions are either single words or word groups within a paragraph that help bridge thoughts between sentences. They also connect supporting material and establish clear relationships for the reader. In a way, they are like signposts that dot the highway; in your theme they act as signposts that move your paper along. To speak metaphorically, there are *detour* words, *merge* or *yield* words, *count* words, and other groups that serve specialized functions within the paragraph.

Where do you place transitions? Hide them inconspicuously in the middle of a sentence, but occasionally you will find them near the beginning or end. Usually, they are set off from the rest of the sentence by commas—one before, one after. Note that the same transitional marker, depending on context, may have different functions.

The following chart will be helpful. The words set in capital letters identify the relationship shown by each group. Practice using transitions, and try spotting them in articles you read. Listen for them in lectures. How do they help make logical connections? Finally, try analyzing a piece of writing, appreciating how the writer uses transitional words to make a point clear.

ADDITIONAL ITEMS add something to what has been stated before.

add to this	fourth	likewise
again	further	moreover
also	furthermore	next
and	in addition	second
besides	in fact	third
equally important	in the first place	too
finally	last	yet another
first		

CAUSAL RELATIONS add up the consequences and show the cause–effect relationship.

accordingly	for this reason	so
and yet	hence	still another result
because	if . . . then	therefore
but	it follows that	thus
consequently	since	yet

COMPARISONS show how things are similar.

alike	at the same time	in the same way
another	by the same token	same
resemblance	in like manner	similar
a similarity	in similar fashion	similarly

CONCLUSION OR SUMMATION says the end is near.

all in all	on the whole	to end
finally	thus	to summarize
in brief	to conclude	to sum up
in short		

(Avoid using, *as a conclusion, in conclusion, in summary,* and *to sum up,* as they are overused.)

CONDITIONALS express reservations.

although this may be true	if	though
even so	nevertheless	under these
even though	otherwise	circumstances
	this being	

CONTRAST shows how things are dissimilar.

after all	however	otherwise
and yet	in contrast to this	still
but	in spite of	though
conversely	nevertheless	to the contrary
despite	nonetheless	unalike
dissimilar	on the contrary	whereas
dissimilarity	on the other hand	yet

CONVICTION tries to persuade.

above all	certainly	surely
after all	indeed	to be sure
apparently	it is apparent	undoubtedly
besides	of course	without a doubt
by all means		

ENUMERATION counts.

another	in the beginning	primarily
finally	last of all	primary
first of all	next	still another
first . . . second . . . third, etc.	one . . . two . . . three, etc.	the final point

EXEMPLIFICATION OR ILLUSTRATION indicates that examples will follow.

an illustration	in particular	to be specific
for example	one case	to demonstrate
for instance	specifically	to illustrate
for one thing	such as	

REPEATING terms say it again.

again	namely	to repeat
in brief	on the whole	to restate
in other words	that is	to sum up
in short		

SEQUENCE IN TIME shows the passage of time or chronological order of things.

after that	always	at the same time
after this	at last	before
afterward	at length	by that time

during	never	soon after that
earlier	now	subsequently
formerly	once	then
immediately	presently	this instant
in the meantime	previously	to begin with
later	simultaneously	when
later on	sometimes	while
meanwhile	soon	

Exercise 4–1

Transitions

1. From the list of words that follow this paragraph, select the appropriate transitional element for each blank space.

    Although marijuana and alcohol are similar in many respects, there are several differences. _____, the laws regulating their use differ; they are unequal. _____, marijuana has laws similar to those regulating the use of hard drugs; _____, currently there seems to be a general lessening of harsh penalties for possession. _____, possession of alcohol is legal, _____, its use is very common. _____, unless alcohol is involved in the commission of a felony, _____ drunk driving, the police and the law do not intervene. _____, are differences in physical effects. _____ marijuana has not yet proved to be very destructive with moderate use. _____, heavy alcohol consumption leads to severe medical illnesses, _____ cirrhosis of the liver and adult onset diabetes. _____ both drugs are habit forming; marijuana is psychologically addictive. _____ different, both drugs can impair those who use them.

but however	in contrast	on the other hand
first	likewise	second
for example	moreover	such as
for instance	nevertheless	third
however	nonetheless	whereas

Brainstorming

2. Select an appropriate transitional element for the blank spaces. Use some of the same words listed in question 1, or provide other ones you are familiar with. (See the list of transitional elements on pages 83–85 for suggestions.)

Brainstorming is a useful technique for discovering ideas for writing. Within a small group, toss around a variety of subjects or issues. _____ you'll have a chance to share impressions and thoughts. _____, this sharing of ideas may help you focus on a specific topic for writing. _____, you might _____ find the supporting material you'll need. _____ any questions the group has raised might help you see the questions your readers might have.

_____ let the brainstorming be a testing ground

to shape and direct your ideas. _____ let every-

one say whatever comes to mind. _____ have a

totally frank, open-ended discussion.

Coordinators Some transitions show coordination of ideas. The enumerative coordinators—*first, second, another, next,* and *last*—list points that are equal. Coordinators such as *and, or, but, nor, for, yet,* and *so* also join equals and enhance the logical flow of thoughts, some sending the reader forward (such as *and*), others backward (such as *but*). The following chart lists common coordinators and explains their function and use. Note the important difference, however, between connecting two ideas with *and* or *but*. Recognize also how an inappropriate coordinator might alter the meaning of the message.*

Coordinator	*Function*	*Use*
AND	What follows *and* is in addition to the information given before the *and*, implying continuation of a thought.	The young woman walked in the garden and enjoyed the fragrant flowers. (what the woman did in addition to walking in the garden)
BUT	What follows *but* is something unexpected—a contrast, an exception, or something contrary to the first thought. *But* implies opposition or contrast in a casual way.	The students wanted to go to the movies, but their tour leader led them into another museum.

*We are indebted to Harvey S. Wiener, *Creating Compositions,* 5th ed., for the idea of presenting definitions and explanations of coordinators.

Coordinator	Function	Use
FOR	What follows *for* expresses a condition, why something did or did not occur. There is a causal connection between two thoughts, why something could or could not be.	The puppies were not supposed to eat the mother dog's food, <u>for</u> they needed extra vitamins and nutrients.
NOR	What follows *nor* is a continuation of a previous negative thought.	She never saw John again, <u>nor</u> did she ever regret his absence.
OR	What follows *or* expresses an alternative, another option. *Or* suggests only one alternative at a time.	You must be at the airport by ten o'clock, <u>or</u> you will miss your connection to New York.
SO	The material after *so* implies a consequence, a result, or a reason for something to occur.	Your season tickets for the basketball games are just behind the opponent's bench, <u>so</u> yell your lungs out all season!
YET	What follows *yet* implies a conditional situation; something is true despite apparent obstacles.	The plan for the new condominium is practical, <u>yet</u> it could be improved.
	What follows a semicolon coordinates two short, closely related independent thoughts. The semicolon is like an equal (=) sign.	Caesar, try on this toga; it seems to be your size.

Exercise 4–2

Join the following pairs of sentences with an appropriate coordinator:

1. Rex sprained his ankle playing tennis yesterday. He won't be able to go to tonight's rock festival.
2. Mr. Crane is a paraplegic and is confined to a wheel chair. He never misses musical concerts or most sporting events.
3. I have to do the grocery shopping and cooking at my home. My parents both work late each day.
4. I love to bake and cook. My sister Ellen won't go near the kitchen.
5. Please turn off the air conditioner. I may take cold if you don't.

Subordinators   Another type of transition word, the subordinator, shows inequality of thought. Subordinators (*while, because, if, when*) make one idea less important than the one in the main clause. They help connect supporting material to the main idea and signal the introduction of supplementary detail.

Subordination is particularly important in revision, especially when you discover you have too many short, *choppy* sentences. For example, consider these two short sentences:

Carole wrote Tim a loving four-page letter.
Tim sent only a postcard to Carole.

With subordination, making one sentence a dependent clause and the other the more grammatically important main clause, the two sentences combine like this:

Although she wrote Tim a loving four-page letter,
Tim sent only a postcard to Carole.

Subordination is an invaluable writing technique, as it creates desirable sentence variety. But only you can decide which of the two sentences is to receive the added stress. Also, you must select the appropriate subordinator. Following is a list of common subordinators:

after	because	since	whenever
although	before	so	where
as	how	so that	whereas
as if	if	though	wherever
as long as	in order that	unless	while
as soon as	once	until	
as though	provided	when	

Exercise 4–3

Join the following pairs of sentences subordinating one to the other; make one unequal grammatically.

1. Eric had carefully hidden himself in an abandoned mine. The sheriff wanted to question him.
2. The museum with its magnificent exhibits was totally destroyed. The roof collapsed during last week's blizzard.
3. Television viewing can be relaxing. Too much television viewing often leads to apathy.
4. At last, the curtains parted and the actors appeared on the stage. The audience became still.
5. Mavis always begins the newspaper by reading her horoscope. She sets her goals for the new day.

Repetition Devices

Repetition of Key Words   Repeating a key word throughout a speech helps a speaker emphasize a key point for the audience. Similarly, when you compose paragraphs, you

Key words   can stress a main point by repeating a key word that you consider important enough to keep before the reader's eyes. A meaningless word, such as *good*, *nice*, or *interesting*, is unworthy of repetition. But in a paragraph about human rights for an oppressed minority, the word *freedom* might be repeated a number of times to emphasize the writer's urgency. It remains the writer's decision, however, which word is the important one, worthy of repetition.

What does this repetition help you achieve? It provides an echo of an important idea that you want remembered. But does such repetition create monotony? It can, if the writer is not careful. Different forms of the same word might help eliminate some of this seeming monotony. The word *brute*, for example, might be significant in a paragraph about an abusive parent. In order to provide some variation on the same theme, you might want to rely on different forms of *brute*, such as *brutal, brutally* or *brutality*. Keeping the same idea in the reader's mind by using these different forms provides the needed stress and variety that will make your compostion clear.

Examine this fine piece of prose by F.L. Lucas, who repeats the word *signature* numerous times, to achieve stylistic emphasis rather than to connect thoughts. Notice also the emphatic repetition of *unique* in the concluding phrases of the first sentence:

> Even the most rigid Communist, or Organization-man, is compelled by Nature to have a unique voice, unique fingerprints, unique handwriting. Even the signatures of the letters on your breakfast table may reveal more than their writers guess. There are blustering signatures that swish across the page like cornstalks bowed before a tempest. There are cryptic signatures, like scrabble or lightning across a cloud, suggesting that behind is a lofty divinity whom all must know, or an aloof divinity whom none is worthy to know (though, as this might be highly inconvenient, a docile typist sometimes interprets the mystery in a bracket underneath). There are impetuous squiggles implying that the author is a sort of strenuous Sputnik streaking round the globe every eighty minutes. There are florid signatures, all curlicues and danglements and flamboyance, like the youthful Disraeli (though these seem rather out of fashion). There are humble, humdrum signatures. And there are also, some-

times, signatures that are courteously clear, yet mindful of a certain simple grace and artistic economy—in short, of style.

F.L. Lucas, "Party of One" (frequently anthologized as "What Is Style?")

In the following excerpt, *voice* is repeated for emphasis. The author is alluding to "The Song of Solomon" 2:12 and the rebirth associated with spring:

The voice of the turtle is heard in the land, heard in all the arts—in literature, painting, and music—and in the voices of men and women speaking to one another. It is not the voice of the dove, that sweet and melancholy sound which the translators of the Authorized Version presumably had in mind; it is the croak of isolation and alienation issuing from within a vault of defensive armor—the voice of the reptilian turtle.

John N. Bleibtreu, *The Parable of the Beast*

Synonyms   To avoid monotonous repetition of the same word, use synonyms to emphasize an important concept. Just as pronouns help establish connections among sentences, so synonyms keep the main idea before your reader. For example, *stormy* has many synonyms, such as *wild, blustery, fiery, frenzied, passionate, tempestuous,* or *explosive.* Try combining one of these modifiers with a noun like *fighter* or one of its synonyms: *contender, opponent, brawler, scrapper, boxer, soldier,* or *warrior.* In short, repeating a word or using a variation or a synonym will help you link key ideas.

Repetition of Pronouns   Pronouns will also help provide a different form of repetition within a sentence, among sentences, or within a paragraph. Repetition of the same pronoun creates a *pronoun reference pattern.* Look at the following illustrative paragraph and note how an experienced writer relies on *sleeper, he,* and *him* to tie thoughts together:

Pronoun reference pattern

It is curious to be awake and watch a sleeper. Seldom, when he awakes, can he remember anything of his sleep. It is a dead part of his life. But watching him, we know he was alive, and part of his life was thought. His body moved. His eyelids fluttered, as his eyes saw moving visions in the darkness. His limbs sketched tiny motions, because his sleeping fancy was guiding him through a crowd, or making him imagine a race, a fight, a hunt, a dance.

Gilbert Highet, Man's Unconquerable Mind

The arrows and lines from the pronouns point toward the antecedent. Note how monotonous this series of sentences would sound if the noun *sleeper* appeared each time instead of a pronoun. Observe how this pointing back by pronouns helps establish a "tied-in" relationship among sentences.

Note how the author of the following description enhances the image of her central character by including a series of pronouns (*his, her, your*) that form a pattern. By replacing the name *Michael* several times with *him* and *his,* the author reinforces the coherence of her description. Can you also locate a number of repetitions of significant words that further enhance the coherence of this portrait of a very disturbed young man?

Nearly everybody in the Red Lion Tavern became aware that Michael Levanthal, the hyperactive young professor whose career seemed so promising, was on the verge of a nervous collapse. Only he seemed unaware of what was happening to him. His wife had recently noticed changes in his eating habits; no longer was he as conscious of his carefully matched suits and ties, or the shirts so smartly monogrammed and color coordinated. And his children had started to frown when he yelled at them and found no interest in their model airplanes or their accomplishments at school. And now around him at the tavern the old regulars seemed to take notice of Michael for the first time, wondering, when they took time to think about someone else, what exactly was wrong with him. Only he didn't seem to recognize the strikingly obvious reality that something was wrong, terribly wrong.

A pronoun must have a clear antecedent. An *antecedent* is a word coming before the pronoun that the pronoun refers to. For example, in the sentence. "The woman is looking for her daugher," *woman* is the antecedent for *her*. If you have two or more nouns before the pronoun, your reader may become confused about which antecedent and which noun the pronoun refers to. Observe the confusion in the following example:

> As I watched the rider on the ferris wheel and the operator, I couldn't decide in whose position I would rather be. Who would have more fun? Would he be straining and working harder than he? A careless move by either the rider or the operator might result in their death. I believe I prefer being on the ground observing each in his work or fun.

It is doubtful that you would ever write with such ambiguous pronouns. Who is "he"—the rider or the operator? Where is the plural antecedent for their? But these sentences illustrate one pitfall of using pronouns: they must agree with the number, gender, and person of the noun nearest them. These terms can be confusing to beginning writers or to those new to English grammar terminology.

Gender   Does the pronoun replace a noun that is either masculine, feminine, or neuter? Gender distinctions occur *only* in third-person singular pronouns.

Number   Is the pronoun singular or plural?

Person   Is the pronoun first-, second-, or third-person?

What pronouns work best in these repeated patterns? Use *personal pronouns* in any of the three cases (nominative, objective, or possessive). The following chart will guide you:

he	she	it	we	you	they
his	his	its	our	your	their
him	hers		ours	yours	theirs
					them

First-person pronouns *I, me, my, mine* are not listed because they rarely have a noun antecedent. Try to have at least two pronouns looking back to the same noun; otherwise no *pattern of repetition* has been achieved. Try also to have these pronouns connect several different sentences.

> "Hey, *that* tub has stronger looking plants, even though *these* have variegated leaves and many buds."

> "You know *those* could be Martha Washingtons or *those* scented-leaf varieties; *these* aren't, I don't believe. They're just common reds and pinks."

Repetition of a Sentence Pattern   Another device for achieving coherence is repeating a key sentence pattern within a paragraph. The pattern must be highly styled; it should be compact; it must be forceful, as it will call attention to itself through the repetition. The reader follows the pattern, hearing the repetition and paying attention to the message that the pattern holds together. You need not always repeat the entire sentence, however; occasionally, for variation, you might want to repeat only a phrase or a portion of the key sentence, then repeat the whole sentence at the conclusion of your remarks — before your most important point.

Repeating a key sentence is a rhetorical device that effective speakers frequently use. The repetition appeals to the emotions of the audience. Imagine a rural meeting hall where a charismatic minister stirs the audience with the repeated phrase, "We shall overcome!" Then the repeated exclamation begins to echo throughout the audience, who join in the chant.

In another example, at the end of a speech the former Chancellor of the University of Texas system used "We had better be . . ." at the start of several paragraphs to stress major points. The echo effect achieved by this repetition helped reinforce the ideas he wanted his audience to remember:

> We had better be thinking about how we are going to preserve the individual in a society that is becoming increasingly impersonal. . . .

> We had better be thinking about how we are going to protect our privacy in a society that has developed the electronic equipment to eavesdrop on anyone, anywhere in the world. . . .

We had better be thinking about what kind of ethics our society wants to demand of its citizens in an age when permissiveness has almost become a religion in itself. . . .

We had better be thinking about how we are going to build bridges of common interest and friendship among nations. . . .

E. D. Walker, "The Addendum"

CAUTION

Be careful not to overwork this device. Your writing may become monotonous if you repeat too many key sentences. You must have chosen a pattern deserving emphasis and repetition. It should have eye appeal; it should be something that will stick in your reader's mind; it doesn't have to be as trite as an advertising jingle, but think of how many of them you remember.

Even as fine a stylist as Mark Twain can lapse into monotonous repetition of unimportant, melodramatic phrases in an absurdly long sentence (despite its rich detail). Examine his needless repetitions in the following excerpt from his *Autobiography*:

I know how a prize watermelon looks when it is sunning its fat rotundity among pumpkin vines and "simblins"; I know how to tell when it is ripe without "plugging" it; I know how inviting it looks when it is cooling itself in a tub of water under the bed, waiting; I know how it looks when it lies on the table in the sheltered great floor space between house and kitchen, and the children gathered for the sacrifice and their mouths watering; I know the crackling sound it makes when the carving knife enters its end, and I can see the split fly along in front of the blade as the knife cleaves its way to the other end; I can see its halves fall apart and display the rich red meat and the black seeds, and the heart standing up, a luxury fit for the elect; I know how a boy looks behind a yard-long slice of that melon, and I know how he feels; for I have been there.

Now let's look at an excerpt from James Baldwin's *Go Tell It on the Mountain*. Baldwin skillfully repeats "Dirt was in" (and variations of the same word group) to stress the filth John encounters in his kitchen as a youth and the shame he still bears for having to live in such squalor:

> The room was narrow and dirty; nothing could alter its dimensions, and no labor could ever make it clean. Dirt was in the walls and the floorboards, and triumphed beneath the sink where roaches spawned; was in the fine ridges of the pots and pans, scoured daily, burnt black on the bottom, hanging above the stove; was in the wall against which they hung, and revealed itself where the paint had cracked and leaned outward in stiff squares and fragments, the paper-thin underside webbed with black. Dirt was in every corner, angle, crevice of the monstrous stove, and lived behind it in delirious communion with the corrupted wall. Dirt was in the baseboard that John scrubbed every Saturday, and roughened the cupboard shelves that held the cracked and gleaming dishes. Under this dark weight the walls leaned, under it the ceiling, with a great crack like lightning in its center, sagged. The windows gleamed like beaten gold or silver, but now John saw, in the yellow light, how fine dust veiled their doubtful glory. Dirt crawled in the gray mop hung out the windows to dry. John thought with shame and horror, yet in angry hardness of heart: He who is filthy, let him be filthy still.

> James Baldwin, *Go Tell It on the Mountain*

Demonstrative Pronouns   Demonstrative pronouns will also help you establish a pronoun reference by acting as pointers. There are four of these "pointer words" in the English language: *this*, *that*, *these*, and *those*. After using a noun, you might need to point to it in subsequent sentences by using one of these pronouns. Here is a bit of dialogue illustrating the use of demonstrative pronouns:

"Oh look at *these* lovely geranium plants!"

"Yeah," Sara replied, "*those* have many buds, but look at *these* in *this* tub."

Sexism and Pronouns

You should be careful not to offend your audience by repeatedly using the word *he* as a generic pronoun for *he* and *she*. If the group referred to is all males, use the pronouns *he* and *him*, as in "The waiter found a tip the customer had left for him." If a group is restricted to females, use *she* and *her*. To avoid stereotypical writing, do not use *his* to refer to groups with mixed company. Revise "Everyone should have his own ticket to the Rockets game" to "Everyone should have his or her own ticket to the Rockets game." An alternate form to indicate gender mixture is *s/he* or *he/she*, but neither of these forms is used with great frequency. In conversation, you may say, "Everyone should have their ticket to the Rockets game." But be careful in writing not to make this agreement error. The important point to remember is to be sensitive.

GUIDELINES

1. Change generic-based pronoun to the plural.

Example: A student must turn in his paper on time.
Revision: Students must turn in their papers on time.

2. Alter biased titles.

Chairman becomes *chair* or *chairperson*.

3. Substitute *he or she* for the generic *he*.

Example: A juror must be certain he reaches an unbiased conclusion.
Revision: A juror must be certain he or she reaches an unbiased conclusion.

4. Substitute an infinitive for a generic *he* pronoun.

Example: The director of the play must be careful he blocks the scene according to the playwright's directions.
Revision: The director of the play must be careful to block the scene according to the playwright's directions.

Sequence of Sentences: Basic Patterns

CHAPTER
5

Effective writing is carefully planned. Even the most experienced professional writer seldom writes spontaneously. Behind every article in *Playboy, Omni, Ladies' Home Journal,* or any other magazine lies some sort of plan that the writer designed. What is remarkable about articles in these magazines is that they seem to have been written with little effort. Even though the author may have labored through many drafts, the finished work appears to have been written effortlessly. Fine writing has a sense of spontaneity, seldom betraying the hard work needed to create it.

As you write, you must plan. And knowing some basic patterns for developing paragraphs will help. There are several patterns that your reader will be likely to expect or anticipate. They will provide style for your message and a logical structure for delivering it. Your thoughts will be clearer if you have followed an underlying pattern. If there is no apparent pattern for your thinking, your message will betray disorganization. Your ideas simply will not move logically from point to point.

Audience Analysis

There are many reasons why you might choose one paragraph pattern instead of another—why you might decide that a movement from particular ideas to general ones would be more effective, for instance, than a cause–effect pattern. Consideration of your audience is one of the primary reasons for choosing a specific pattern. You want to reach the audience with your message in the clearest way possible. To do so, you must assess the audience's needs and be conscious of the stance you adopt; you want to have an immediate, forceful impact, which you can achieve only through audience analysis.

Who are your readers? What exactly is your message to them? What are their sympathies, knowledges, prejudices? Are they of one nationality, ethnic group, economic status? Are they of one particular age group, political persuasion, religious sympathy? Do they live in the same part of the country? Will they likely be receptive or hostile to your message? There are at least five general types of audiences.

1. Sympathetic—shares your beliefs/biases always, wholly supportive;
2. Lukewarm—possibly receptive;
3. Indifferent, neutral—ho hum, who cares? so what!
4. Ignorant or vacuous;
5. Unsympathetic, hostile, unaccepting, feeling threatened and frightened.

Let's pretend that you're writing a position paper on banning the highly controversial exploder bullet. Is your audience a group of local policemen? members of the National Rifle Association? a lobbyist for a political action committee? For each audience you need to adopt particular tactics that will make your position persuasive. It is unlikely that some audiences will change their positions, but they may modify their stand if presented with a convincing argument.

Your considerations shift, however, when your audience primarily is seeking information. The special needs and the particular perspective each audience has about your topic will influence the tactics and stance you adopt. Suppose that you are writing an informative proposal about recording a new musical group. A businessman will need to know about the financial potential. A music critic will be interested in aesthetic matters. A recording engineer might want to know about harmony, balance, and sound overlay. Each of these audiences has a perspective that you need to consider.

Can you think of other things you might consider about your audience? As you evaluate, try also to keep in mind the type of pattern that will create the most significant impact. A sophisticated audience will grasp subtle analogies that are part of the comparison–contrast structure. One can assume that an audience interested in facts and statistical evidence might prefer a cause–effect arrangement. As you experiment with particular patterns and learn of their impact on a variety of audiences, you might discover the appropriateness of some patterns for presenting factual information or other types of messages. Aim your writing, therefore, to a specific audience.

Mastering these patterns will save time. Once you are aware of the difference between a cause–effect and a problem–solution pattern (see Chapter 6), you can plan strategies early in the writing stages, keeping in mind that you must choose the pattern appropriate for the thought as well as for the audience. Using these patterns will lead to more efficient communication.

Rhetorical Stance

Early in any piece of writing you want to establish a *rhetorical stance*, the position or role you will take in presenting a point of view. Verbs will mark this stance. The choice of verb, such as *define, analyze, inform* or *persuade*, indicates the rhetorical position, which in turn dictates the paragraph patterns you need.

Definition

A specific marker verb in your topic sentence (or in your thesis statement for a longer paper) will emphasize your rhetorical stance and thereby ease your writing task. Once you have chosen this key verb, you will be able to select the most appropriate materials and arrangements for clear communication.

CAUTION

The marker verb will determine the overall approach you take, rhetorically, in your paper, but it will not dictate the form of every single paragraph. Rather, you will mix approaches—that is, at times you will use analytical paragraphs; at other times you will state a problem and present a solution for it within the paragraph. Rhetorical stance involves the key approach you are taking in the whole paper, not merely in a part of it. If you are writing only a paragraph, then your stance can emerge in the marker verb of the topic sentence.

Order of Importance

"What do I say first?" "What do I say last?"

These questions are probably the first ones beginning writers have in mind after they select a topic and complete their early brainstorming activities.

These questions are important not only for helping you get started, but for deciding *where* particular ideas belong. Also, you must decide *what* ideas are crucial and which ones are less important. Arranging information by order of importance gives you at least two options for structuring. You can move from least important items toward most important ones or reverse the process, moving from most to least important. The former approach, however, is more emphatic. It allows you in the first few sentences to dispense with the less important data and focus on the climax. In explaining a very complicated mechanical process, you might want to skip over some of the less important details and emphasize forcefully, at the end, the key points your reader needs to remember.

Let's imagine walking on campus between classes. Have you ever analyzed how you look at other people? Do you focus first on their faces? their clothes? their manner of walking? Most of us probably first notice the face of a person approaching; we then concentrate on the individual's eyes and the messages they send—sometimes friendly, sometimes hostile, many times neutral. Some eyes appear to ignore us, perhaps because the individual is daydreaming, is concentrating elsewhere, or is simply slow to perceive. A trained observer (such as a detective or a psychologist) might see more than you, in fact, possibly seeing the whole body from head to toe at a single glance. (Reread "The Camera Eye," p. 53.)

In transferring these observations to paper, we make choices about what to include or discard. Our readers expect logical order, not a jumbled, disorganized presentation. In writing we must be orderly. Only in particular forms of writer-based prose, such as diaries or journals, can we be less conscious of order. Arranging details forces us to make choices.

Focal Points

The two key focal points within the paragraph are the beginning and the end. Your reader will be less likely to remember ideas in the middle parts of the paragraph. If you place the key idea toward the end, either in or just before the clincher, it will more likely be recalled.

Order of Importance:

    Most Important———➤ Least Important

What type of system should a world traveler use when packing a suitcase? She probably should arrange items carefully and efficiently in order to get everything to her destination in the best possible shape. The major items — dresses, skirts, blazers — should be folded flat. Most important Blazers and jackets should be folded inside-out to minimize wrinkling. Next, t-shirts, blouses, vests, and Important other tops should be arranged on top of these larger items. Accessories for each outfit (scarves, handkerchiefs, gloves, belts) lie atop the blouses. Lingerie and hosiery are normally rolled up and squeezed into corners and open spaces; whether they arrive wrinkled is Less important unimportant. Shoes, packed heel-to-toe, might be stuffed with casual socks or small items like a travel clock or a face cloth. Finally, pesky items that she really needs, but less often, such as her hair dryer, bottle Least important opener, paring knife, curling iron, or even a convertor — adaptor for electrical appliances — rest on top of all her clothing in this carefully packed suitcase.

Order of Importance:

    Least Important ———➤ Most Important

Arranging a suitcase mentally before packing it is an important strategy. Mapping out where everything will go, laying out all items to be packed, and deciding

Least important

Less important

More important
Most important

what more important items belong on the bottom and what less important items, on top will help the experienced world traveler pack carefully and efficiently. Less important items like accessories — jewelry, gloves, scarves, belts — probably belong on top of larger items. Underneath accessories are the various tops (t-shirts, blouses, and vests) that coordinate with each outfit. Right below these tops such items as lingerie and hosiery can be squeezed into any open spaces around the shoes, packed heel-to-toe, and containing small items like a travel clock or spare face cloth tucked inside. Larger items rest at the base of the suitcase stack. The most important garments such as dresses, skirts, and blazers are at the bottom; jackets and blazers are best folded inside out to minimize wrinkling. Orderly planning ahead and packing by a systematic arrangement will help the traveler arrive with garments that look as though they have just come off the store rack!

Chronology: The Time Order Pattern

Happening 1		Event 1
Happening 2	or	Event 2
Happening 3		Event 3
etc.		etc.

Definition

Chronology derives from the Greek word *chronos*, meaning "time." Arranging ideas chronologically is useful in a number of different writing situations, yet in each case you proceed in an orderly manner from first to last.

In organizing a paragraph by a time sequence, you do not always have to begin with a topic sentence. "Once upon a time" indicates that a story will be developed; it is an appropriate opener to begin a narration. One must be careful to organize narratives logically so that events fall into a natural sequence. Special signal markers for this pattern will provide this logical sequencing of events. Such words as *later, afterward, earlier, next, before, now,* and many others indicate the order of happenings.

Factual Writing

But when is a chronological pattern most appropriate? When you need to write a factual account of an event (such as a traffic acccident), a historical account (such as on a history exam), or the proceedings of a trial, you may wish to arrange facts in a logical time sequence in the order in which they occurred. Order is also important if you are giving recipe directions where time is crucial, such as when to add specific ingredients and in which order. Steps in a process analysis also follow chronological order.

Flashback

Your paragraph may use a variety of different time sequences other than linear time (or forward-moving time), however. One of these is the *flashback*, the recalling of an event that happened earlier. You interrupt the forward progress of your narrative and shift backwards in time to an earlier moment. Flashbacks often appear in films, especially in sequels like *Rocky II* and *III* and *Superman II* and *III*.

Definition

A paragraph with nostalgic moments may rely on flashbacks to evoke the key events in the past that a person remembers and longs for. The paragraph may focus on the person dreaming about the past and recalling it in an orderly or sometimes jumbled fashion. A special type of flashback is *time tripping*, which involves trips ahead to the future or huge steps backwards into the past. H.G. Wells' *The Time Machine* and Kurt Vonnegut's *Slaughterhouse Five* are classic novels that illustrate time tripping, as do some science fiction stories.

Nostalgia and time-tripping

Exercise 5–1

Get into the habit of analyzing paragraphs, not only those you write, but also those of strong professional writers. Use the following eight points to analyze some of the professional and student paragraphs in this book. You might want to write them on a separate sheet of paper for quick reference.

1. Locate the topic sentence — if there is none explicitly stated, phrase one of your own.
2. Determine the author's purpose or aim.

3. Determine the author's pattern of organization.
4. Identify the supporting materials used for development.
5. Identify the devices for coherence and transition.
6. Define the tone and point of view.
7. Look for unique styling devices the author has used.
8. Identify the intended audience.

Examples for Analysis

1. She laid her crucifix on her chair. The chief executioner took it as a perquisite, but was ordered instantly to lay it down. The lawn veil was lifted carefully off, not to disturb the hair, and was hung upon the rail. The black robe was next removed. Below it was a petticoat of crimson velvet. The black jacket followed, and under the jacket was a body of crimson satin. One of her ladies handed her a pair of crimson sleeves, with which she hastily covered her arms; and thus she stood on the black scaffold with the black figures all around her, blood-red from head to foot.

    James Anthony Froude,
    "The Execution of Mary Queen of Scots"

2. It is a summer morning in 1936. Wendell Mac Rae, official photographer of the new Rockefeller Center, is riding on top of an elevator rising, one floor at a time, toward the top of the RCA building. Each time the elevator stops, he shines a 1,000 watt floodlight into the empty adjoining shaft. Thirty seconds pass. Mac Rae kills the light and rises to the next floor, and the next, methodically repeating the process, as he has for nearly an hour and a half. When he reaches the 70th and last floor, he will descend to the ground and close the shutter of a heavy 8 × 10 Deardorff view camera aimed upward in the neighboring shaft. The final photograph will show the 850-foot length of the shaft, a technical tour de force, the product (like the skyscraper itself) of skill, ingenuity, and patience.

    Erla Zwingle, "Elegance at Shutter Speed"

Writing Assignment

Narration

In a paragraph relate a brief personal experience—one memorable happening, one with strong emotional involvement. Narrate a key turning point in your life—the breakup of a relationship, your achievement of a goal such as being chosen for the Olympics or being elected a class officer, the separation from or death of a close relative or friend. Possibly incorporate bits of dialogue into your story to establish a sense of realism.

The Spatial Pattern

The spatial pattern is difficult to illustrate, because the pattern is an attempt to capture space, to describe an area—an exterior or an interior area. Spatial patterning becomes evident when you analyze a painting, a photograph, a landscape, or even a piece of descriptive writing. Actually, as you analyze, you are imposing a pattern on space.

Eye Movement

The analysis traces the movement of eyes from one portion of the observed object to another. That is, your eyes move in multiple ways—from left to right (or vice versa), from the foreground to the background, possibly from top to bottom just as a movie camera pans across objects being photographed on a Hollywood film set. In Western cultures, the movement describing space is from left to right; certain Eastern cultures frequently move from right to left. (Examine a page from the Torah or Koran or the ideograms on an Oriental scroll.)

But when do you select a spatial pattern? More often than not, you select descriptive writing for spatial arrangements of a scene, such as the outside of a barn or the interior of a health spa. You also might use this pattern to describe a person, beginning with facial features (focusing on the eyes), then moving to other portions of the face, and later to other parts of the body.

Normally, you will not need a topic sentence, as your focus is the total image implied throughout the entire description. For example, a seascape is incomplete if, in trying to describe it, you focus on only a single shell. Likewise, your picture of a person is only partial if you give merely the details about hairstyle.

Vantage Point

A second need for the spatial pattern is establishing an observer's stance, the vantage point the observer selects. There should be a clearly perceived spot whence the observer views the scene. As a writer, you must be careful not to shift vantage points abruptly without preparing your audience for the move. Suppose you are observing an art gallery. Position yourself under one arch or on a bench with a full view of the room. Write from this observation point, allowing your eyes, not your body, to move. Observe steadily and consistently from this one position. In recording the observations, adopt a similar stance.

Signal Words

You will need to provide signals for your audience about directions and movement. A spatial pattern relies on such signals as *to the left, up above, below, from north to south, east to west,* and many others. Another type of signal in the spatial pattern is the shift from one side of the object to another, from less important details to more important ones. Such shifts must be logical; you usually don't describe doorways and arches until it's clear to your reader you are describing a building. The reader must be aware of the logic of your particular perspective. Logically, one moves from the foreground to the background, from the near to the far, from the left to the right.

Examples for Analysis

1.   It was like every other house in Jalco, probably larger. The adobe walls were thick, a foot or more, with patches of whitewash where the thatched overhang protected the adobe from the rain. There were no windows. The entrance doorway was at one end of the front wall, and directly opposite the door that led to the corral. The doors were made of planks

axed smooth from tree trunks and joined with two cross pieces and a diagonal brace between them hammered together with large nails bent into the wood on the inside. Next to each door and always handy for instant use, there was the cross bar, the *tranca*. On both sides of the door frame there was a notched stub, mortared into the adobe bricks and about six inches long. The door was secured from the inside by dropping the *tranca* into the two notches.

Ernesto Galaraza, Barrio Boy

2.   After our meal we went for a stroll across the plateau. The day was already drawing to a close as we sat down upon a ledge of rock near the lip of the western precipice. From where we sat, as though perched high upon a cloud, we looked out into a gigantic void. Far below, the stream we had crossed that afternoon was a pencil-thin trickle of silver barely visible in the gloaming. Across it, on the other side, the red hills rose one upon another in gentle folds, fading into the distance where the purple thumb-like mountains of Adua and Yeha stretched against the sky like a twisting serpent. As we sat, the sun sank fast, and the heavens in the western sky began to glow. It was a coppery fire at first, the orange streaked with aquamarine; but rapidly the firmament expanded into an explosion of red and orange that burst across the sky sending tongues of flame through the feathery clouds to the very limits of the heavens. When the flames had reached their zenith, a great quantity of storks came flying from the south. They circled above us once, their slender bodies sleek and black against the orange sky. Then gathering together, they flew off into the setting sun, leaving us alone in peace to contemplate. One of the monks who sat with us, hushed by the intensity of the moment, muttered a prayer. The sun died beyond the hills; and the fire withdrew.

Robert Dick-Read, *Sanamu: Adventures in Search of African Art*

3.   To the right a few steps, you ducked through the entry way to the main "cuevas." Ahead was the

smoke stained ceiling of a large cooking/dining room. Behind that a small puddle that once was a large, fresh filled reservoir. To the right, carved from limestone, were the columns that led to chamber after chamber after chamber; underground bed and living rooms. The only thing on the walls were chip marks. No paintings or inscriptions. Then, I thought, paintings and inscriptions were made by happy people. What happiness was here underground? The Mayans weren't cave dwellers. Except here, by necessity.

Jim Weiser, "In the Steps of Conquerors"

4.   Now the door to the store was open. Inside it was bright and natural-looking. To the left was the counter where slabs of white meat, rock candy, and tobacco were kept. Behind this were shelves of salted white meat and meal. The right side of the store was mostly filled wtih farm implements and such. At the back of the store, to the left, was the door leading up the stairs, and it was open. And at the far right of the store there was another door which led to a little room that Miss Amelia called her office. This door was also open. And at eight o'clock that evening Miss Amelia could be seen there sitting before her rolltop desk, figuring with a fountain pen and some pieces of paper.

Carson McCullers, *The Ballad of the Sad Cafe*

Writing Assignment

Description

1. Write a vivid description of an event, such as one of these: a church wedding, an auto race, an opening-night performance, a crucial basketball game.

2. Write a very factual, basic description of a place you know very well—a room, building, car, park—keeping your description very simple. Then rewrite the same paragraph, this time giving vivid descriptive details that bring the place alive.

The Kite Pattern

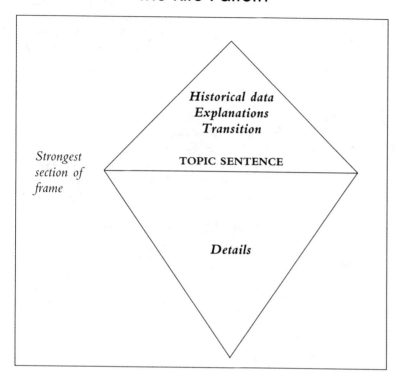

The *kite pattern* derives its name from its similarity to   Definition
the structure of an ordinary kite, as illustrated in the box
above. Its frame has two sections: a shorter, upper half
above the middle wooden support bar, and a more elon-
gated lower section that leads toward the tip at the base of
the frame. String, paper, and a tail made from bits of cloth
are other parts of the kite. In this pattern, the topic sentence is delayed so that background information, transition, explanatory detail, or historical fact may be briefly
introduced. These abbreviated details prepare for the topic
sentence. Just as the horizontal brace in the center of the
kite's frame strengthens the structure, so the topic sentence
gives focus and vigor to the entire paragraph.

The uniqueness of this paradigm lies in its variation
from more traditional structures that provide explanatory
materials *after* the topic sentence. The kite pattern is illustrated in Rachel Carson's paragraph below. Note how she
places explanatory material before the topic sentence, creat-

ing a need later for additional specifics about the snapping shrimp's life within a sponge. Introductory explanations and historical background arouse the curiosity of the audience and prepare for the main idea. Transitional elements supply links. Once the topic sentence is stated, various types of supporting materials create the substance.

Introductory explanation

Topic sentence

Narrative and descriptive detail

Note: absence of clincher sentence

The intricate passageways, the shelter and available food they offer, have attracted many small creatures to live within the sponge. Some come and go; others never leave the sponge once they have taken up residence within it. One such permanent lodger is a small shrimp — one of the group known as snapping shrimp because of the sound made by snapping the large claw. Although the adults are imprisoned, the young shrimp, hatched from eggs adhering to the appendages of their mothers, pass out with the water currents into the sea and live for a time in the currents and tides, drifting, swimming, perhaps carried far afield. By mischance they may occasionally find their way into deep water where no sponges grow. But many of the young shrimp will in time find and approach the dark bulk of some loggerhead sponge and, entering it, will take up the strange life of their parents. Wandering through its dark halls, they scrape food from the walls of the sponge. As they creep along these cylindrical passageways, they carry their antennae and their large claws extended before them, as though to sense the approach of a larger and possibly dangerous creature, for the sponge has many lodgers of many species — other shrimps, amphipods, worms, isopods — and their numbers may reach into the thousands if the sponge is large.

Rachel Carson, "The Habitation of the Shrimp," from *The Edge of the Sea*

Examples for Analysis

Read over the following kite paragraphs, then answer these questions:

1. List the special details that precede the actual topic sentence.

2. Write out the topic sentence, quoted directly. Can you find an "idea word" in the topic sentence? What seems to be the writer's feeling about the topic discussed? What specific words in either the topic sentence, or elsewhere in the paragraph, help identify the author's feeling?

3. Each of these paragraphs has been lifted from a section of a book. Identify special words and phrases within each paragraph you analyze that suggest the paragraph comes from a larger context. (Try to find references to other issues the writer might be talking about elsewhere but referred to here.)

4. Look closely at the second paragraph from *Parkinson's Law*. How serious is the writer? What is amusing about what he says?

1.   May was a round boulder sinking before a tide. Time sloughed off the last implication of urgency, and the days moved imperceptibly one into the other. The few world news items which Dyer read to me from time to time seemed almost as meaningless and blurred as they might to a Martian. My world was insulated against the shocks running through distant economies. Advance Base was geared to different laws. On getting up in the morning, it was enough for me to say to myself: Today is the day to change the barograph sheet, or, Today is the day to fill the stove tank. The night was settling down in earnest. By May 17th, one month after the sun had sunk below the horizon, the noon twilight was dwindling to a mere chink in the darkness, lit by a cold reddish glow. Days when the wind brooded in the north or east, the Barrier became a vast stagnant shadow surmounted by swollen masses of clouds, one layer of darkness piled on top of the other. This was the polar night, the morbid countenance of the Ice Age. Nothing moved; nothing was visible. This was the soul of inertness. One could almost hear a distant creaking as if a great weight were settling.

Richard E. Byrd, "Alone in the Antarctic," from *Alone*

2.   The first sign of danger is represented by the appearance in the organization's hierarchy of an individual who combines in himself a high concentration of incompetence and jealousy. Neither quality is significant in itself and most people have a certain proportion of both. But when these two qualities reach a certain concentration—represented at present by the formula I^3J^5—there is a chemical reaction. The two elements fuse, producing a new substance that we have termed "injelitance." The presence of this substance can be safely inferred from the actions of any individual who, having failed to make anything of his own department, tries constantly to interfere with other departments and gain control of the central administration. The specialist who observes this particular mixture of failure and ambition will at once shake his head and murmur, "Primary or idiopathic injelitance." The symptoms, as we shall see, are quite unmistakable.

C. Northcote Parkinson, *Parkinson's Law*

3.   One can argue over the merits of most books, and in arguing understand the point of view of one's opponent. One may even come to the conclusion that possibly he is right after all. One does not argue about *The Wind in the Willows*. The young man gives it to the girl with whom he is in love, and if she does not like it, asks her to return his letters. The older man tries it on his nephew, and alters his will accordingly. The book is a test of character. We can't criticize it, because it is criticizing us. As I wrote once: It is a Household Book; a book which everybody in the household loves, and quotes continually; a book which is read aloud to every new guest and is regarded as the touchstone of his worth. But I must give you one word of warning. When you sit down to it, don't be so ridiculous as to suppose that you are sitting in judgment on my taste, or on the art of Kenneth Grahame. You I don't know. But it is you who is on trial.

A.A. Milne, Introduction to *The Wind in the Willows*

Writing Assignment

Formulate a topic sentence, one that will need explanation and a specific example or personal illustration before it. Place this explanatory information before the topic sentence, as it is essential to the clarity of your subject. Then follow the topic sentence with thoughts and statements that will support or prove your opinion. Select a subject of your own or use one of the following ideas:

Your favorite videogame or television sitcom

A place where elves and unicorns live

A beloved pet

Packing up to move to a new city (what to leave, what to take)

A Student Example

Gabby gives some background on her subject that leads up to her topic sentence; then she begins to develop it with examples that conclude with the clincher. Can you find Gabby's kite pattern?

Legal Options

The one choice is a position with a high flying law firm in Houston. The other option is a prosecuting attorney's job in a small town in west Texas, Fort Stockton. Deciding between a high paying, high status position, or a lower paying one with more modest status can cause considerable tension for a senior in law school. Admittedly, it's nice having a choice, but is the increased tension worth it? First, having such options distracts the law students from their studies. They begin to spend more time reading circulars from the Houston and Fort Stockton Chambers of Commerce than reading their law books. Real estate flyers from the two cities pour in, beckoning them to consider one house over another. With such distractions, it is difficult to find time to study for their senior exams. Second, the young lawyers find that they have less time for social and other leisure time activities. Given the options of the competing law firms, these seniors have less time to attend plays or sports events on the U.T. campus or even see the latest movies. Dates have to be postponed, as contrasting thoughts about the future in Houston or Fort Stockton are compared. Their future careers, indeed their whole lives, are at stake, whether to become Houston high flyers or possibly opt for less money and more modest status in Fort Stockton.

The Circular Pattern

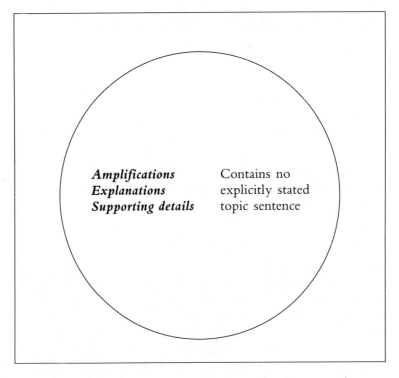

Amplifications
Explanations
Supporting details

Contains no
explicitly stated
topic sentence

You needn't become zealous about having a topic sentence in every single paragraph. Not all paragraphs need one; many clearly structured paragraphs merely hint at or suggest a thought. The smooth flow of sentences and ideas creates the essential unity; this characteristic is especially true of narrative and descriptive paragraphs, which rarely state the main idea. Instead, it is suggested by the supporting details and explanations, and the reader's job is to infer the core meaning, the major thought. Each sentence of the paragraph becomes a part of the implied idea.

The majority of paragraphs written by well-established,

professional essayists will not have stated topic sentences. Richard Braddock has analyzed this writing characteristic in an important study ("The Frequency and Placement of Topic Sentences in Expository Prose"). But in a classroom situation, composition instructors will probably prefer paragraphs to have a well-structured topic sentence, particularly if they are single-paragraph papers or the major or main paragraphs of a composition.

The pattern for the paragraph with an implied topic sentence is somewhat like a circle, but not one that suggests the writer is wandering aimlessly in a welter of details. Nor does the circular shape indicate lack of planning and organizing. It does, however, suggest that the writer feels confident the main idea is clear and that the reader will have no problem understanding. In short, it reaffirms the writer's feeling that the point is obvious, that there need be no topic sentence to make the point more explicit.

Examples for Analysis

Create an appropriate topic sentence for each of the following paragraphs:

1. _____

_____

_____

2. _____

_____

_____

3. Explain how the writer in the second paragraph uses direction words to point your eyes toward the steps the black flies took in their journey.

_____

_____

_____

4. What special effects are achieved in the second paragraph by the writer's asking you questions?

_____

_____

_____

5. What does the writer make you think of in the last sentence by referring to Israel and the wilderness? What is *allusion*? Does this reference in the last sentence seem lost on you, or does it enhance your understanding of the flight of the black flies by using the comparison suggested by the allusion?

_____

_____

_____

1.   If a number of boys were in a lodge where older people were sitting, very likely the young people would be talking and laughing about their own concerns, and making so much noise that the elders could say nothing. If this continued too long, one of the older men would be likely to get up and go out and get a long stick and bring it in with him. When he had seated himself, he would hold it up, so that the children could see it and would repeat a cautionary formula, "I will give you gum!" This was a warning to them to make less noise, and was always heeded—for a time. After a little, however, the boys might forget and begin to chatter again, and presently the man, without further warning, would reach over and rap one of them on the head with the stick, when quiet would again be had for a time.

> George Bird Grinnell, "Education of the Blackfoot Children,"
> from *Pawnee, Blackfoot and Cheyenne*

2.   How can something become a significant event, unless it already is one? One winter or rather spring morning while on my usual way to work along the shores

of Beebe lake I saw a curious sight. A scattering of
wingless flies, I did not know what kind, were crawl-
ing across the surface of the new snow. All were
moving in the same direction, from the slope on the
lake side of the path across it toward the trees. It was
an immense journey through a barren wilderness for
the tiny creatures, over drifts of empty snow, down
into valleys formed by footprints, up the other bank
to the tree trunks which seemed to be their goal.
They struggled on, each alone, one about every two
feet. Some had failed already and lay quiet, black
specks on the white expanse. There must have been
scores, perhaps hundreds altogether; I could not see,
looking along the slope, where the movement ended.
These flies must have been hatched by the force of
the early spring sun on the slope, which faced south.
Their emergence had been premature. Several were
very feeble, and struggled on with an effort painful
to see. But how could one help black flies? It was
some relief to watch one or two reach the rough
junction of snow and bark and tumble into the cre-
vices. I trust these found what they wanted. The
March snow must have interrupted a brood which
should otherwise have been able to feed immediately.
Nature had anticipated herself. Here was Israel in the
wilderness indeed.

Jonathan Bishop, "The Black Flies," from *Something Else*

Writing Assignment

1. Try writing without a topic sentence. Deliberately
    block out your natural tendency to formulate a pur-
    pose for writing. Let your thoughts wander and write
    freely, beginning with a single point and returning to
    it but after presenting numerous concrete examples
    or narrative illustrations. Select your own subject or
    try one of these:

    Life inside an arcade of videogames
    Your personal hangups

Several of your favorite restaurants
Articles in a time capsule
A typical day in your neighborhood
Falling out of love
Dumb things your pet does
A picnic in the park
A skiing vacation.

2. Bring to class an example of a paragraph developed without a clearly stated, obvious topic sentence. Look for one in factual, nonfiction books, texts, journals, or magazines.

The Sandwich Pattern

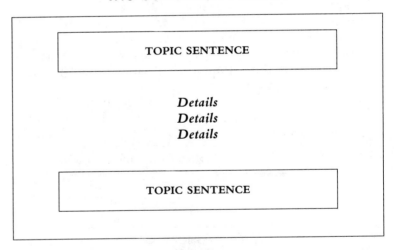

By its very structure, the sandwich pattern will help remind your reader of a key idea. This reminder will occur in the last sentence, which will restate, but in different words, the main point from the topic sentence. This final sentence is a restatement, not a clincher as described in Chapter 2.

What concept underlies this "sandwich pattern"? Think of the topic and final sentences as being analogous to a sandwich—two slices of bread—whereas the supporting materials between them function as filler.

To use this pattern, begin with your topic sentence. Follow it with the necessary supporting details, using those that are particularly appropriate for developing each idea. Then end with a climactic retelling that reiterates the idea in a modification of the topic sentence.

Changing the Final Sentence

This variation in deductive development creates two crucial changes. The first occurs when you construct the final sentence, since it will be more reiterative than usual in order to emphasize your key point. It functions as a mirror reflecting the topic sentence, recalling again the main point. The second change is that the paragraph is less open-ended than other deductive structures. That is, you are inclined to "close off" development by stating it in the topic sentence rather than restating it at the end. Your reader will feel you have finished developing the idea because of the emphatic closing sentence.

Examples for Analysis

Read over the following two paragraphs, then try to answer these questions.

1. How is a sandwich effect achieved by the first and last sentences of the second paragraph?

    _____

    _____

2. (a) What key word is repeated in the final sentence of the first paragraph that helps create an echo of the first sentence? (b) How is an echo of the main idea created in the second paragraph by particular words?

    a. _____

    b. _____

    _____

    _____

1.   The foremost characteristic of deductive arguments is that they may be considered valid or invalid. Validity is a function of the form or the arrangement of the terms in the premises that are stated in support of the conclusion. Validity is not concerned with the contents, or the subject matter, of the premises or the conclusion. If all the items mentioned in the conclusion are mentioned in the premises, and, if the terms are properly arranged, then, whether or not the premises are true in fact, the argument is a valid argument.

Gerald Levin, *Prose Models*

2.   Examine a South African railway timetable, and you'll find that all passenger trains stop at a small town called Wellington. This has been the rule for more than a century. The owner of the land needed for the railway line was a farsighted farmer named P. J. Malan. To make sure that the people of Wellington would always be able to catch trains to the north and south, he gave the land to the railway on condition that all passenger trains stop at Wellington. Over the years, kings, queens and presidents have strolled along the Wellington platform — thanks to Farmer Malan.

Lawrence G. Green, *When the Journey's Over*

Writing Assignment

1.   The sandwich pattern is exceptionally strong since it has two explicitly stated topic sentences, one as introduction, the other as conclusion, — one reinforcing the other but using different wording. Select your own subject or use one of the following ideas for a paragraph of 8 to 10 sentences.

Enforcing a strict dress code at your school

Objecting to a smoking policy in the work place

Toxic waste pollution in a nearby stream or river

Eliminating required physical activities in elementary grades so that academics will receive greater emphasis

Student Example

Heroin in Pain Therapy

There are therapeutic properties in heroin that make the drug potentially beneficial to terminal cancer or AIDS patients and burn victims. Patients receive almost total relief from their pain. They gain a euphoria and feeling of relaxation from the drug that lasts as long as six hours. For patients with such terminal illnesses or those in severe pain perhaps they do deserve such euphoria. The drug is at least twenty times stronger than morphine yet is only twice as addictive as morphine. A 1922 law prevents the use of heroin for pain therapy. Many unenlightened people associate heroin only with hard core drug users and ignore the deadly but nevertheless therapeutic properties of the drug. Even so, they outweigh the dangerous consequences of taking it, particularly for those who are in agony from terminal cancer, enduring the final stages of AIDS, or experiencing the excruciating pain associated with burned flesh.

Particular-to-General Pattern

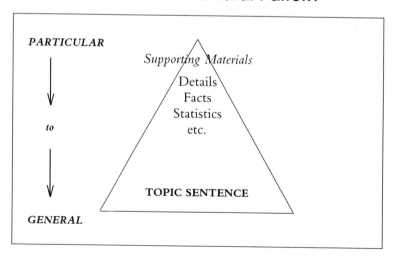

What might motivate you to keep information from your reader? Possibly because you want to create suspense, you may conceal your topic or merely hint at it. Norton

Mockridge surprises us in this brief introduction to a long essay about his . . . Well, let's wait and see:

> Every morning when we're in our city apartment, Cleo walks out of the kitchen at 7:30, marches down the hall, across the living room, through my dressing room, into the bathroom—and calls me for breakfast. There's nothing too much unusual about this, I guess, except for the fact that Cleo happens to be a cat.
>
> Norton Mockridge, "Cleo Calls"

Eventually we learn who Cleo is, yet we were probably misled at first, thinking she may have been a maid or a relative. Details reveal Cleo's identity.

Inductive process: definition   This method of withholding information follows the *inductive process*, one in which you collect data and from them draw inferences. In a single paragraph you will probably draw only one inference, which then becomes your topic sentence at the end of the paragraph. The preceding diagram illustrates how the paragraph triangle leads from the various types of supporting materials toward the topic sentence which, because it is the last sentence, "clinches" the thought. You must be careful, however, to organize details so that they logically "induce" the generality at the end. Each detail must be purposeful, significant, and clearly essential to formulating the generalization.

Method of implication   Another name for this paragraph pattern is *method of implication* because it relies heavily on hints and suggestions about the general idea although never stating it explicitly. Such implications are useful, particularly when you want to manipulate an audience quite deliberately. As suspense builds, so grows a desire to know what your elusive topic is. You are really toying with the audience's emotions. Note how effective this method is, though, even in the following letter to an editor, the topic of which you probably will know before you finish.

Dear Editor:

> Looking around for something to take the place of a daily, dreary vitamin pill I discovered a liquid product that has all the known indispensables for good health, plus a few extras.

After making sure it had the regular A, B, C, D, and E vitamins I checked out the other fairly well-known ones: riboflavin, niacin, pyridoxine, pantothenic acid and folic acid (all in the so-called vitamin B complex). It had them all.

Then, I turned to the minerals. I found this drink had every single mineral known to be necessary to the human body! These include phosphorus, potassium, magnesium chloride, calcium, sodium, and iron.

I found that we need 19 minerals. This drink had them all and 10 more besides.

Then it struck me! The pill peddlers have been pushing a protein pill lately. Could it be . . . ? I found 10 different proteins (amino acids) we need for good health. This drink had them all plus another eight.

Just to be sure, I called a doctor and asked him his opinion of the product. He told me "It favors growth and development in youth, confers health and vigor throughout life and postpones old age."

I tried a dietician and he praised it. I got similar answers from a dentist, nurse, beauty expert, and a food editor.

They all agreed. It was the most convenient, pleasant and effective way to fill the nutritional gaps of ordinary diets and to promote growth, health and energy.

This stuff must cost plenty I thought. Would you believe it? The price in my area is about 80 cents a gallon.

They call it milk.

A Farmer

Laurence M. Hursh, "'Liquid Product' Has Essential Diet Items"

One final characteristic of this pattern is that there are no variations. A paragraph is either inductive or it is not. Note how skillfully the author of this *TV Guide* profile creates suspense about his subject, an American scientific martyr:

He was thin and stooped, almost ascetic in appearance. Wisps of smoke curled from an ever-present pipe or cigarette. At times he spoke so softly that students and colleagues complained he could not be heard in the lecture hall. Yet he was also a superb conversationalist, a man of both charm and acerbic wit. Though his specialty was theoretical physics, he could discourse on obscure Hindu poetry as readily as on quantum mechanics. This formidable presence was J. Robert Oppenheimer, physicist extraordinary, father of the atomic bomb and perhaps America's only scientific martyr.

Frederic Golden, "Oppenheimer: Scientist and Martyr"

Examples for Analysis

1.   Thousands of miles from Corbett, a luth turtle was dragging its damp shell up a dune where she would dig a hole for her eggs. Some unknown force within her had enabled her to find, along the endless coast of South America, the exact spot in Guiana where, seven years earlier, she had been saved by chance from the voracious beak of a frigate bird. Deep in the jungle, in the fork of a great tree, a sloth was sleeping. In other jungles in other places, herds of elephants would also sleep. Like thousands of other animals born on a planet teeming with billions of human beings, they are, for the moment, left in peace. But for how long?

Christian Zubar, *Animals in Danger*, trans. J. F. Bernard

a.   What is the subject implied in the question at the end of the first paragraph?

_____

_____

b.   What instances of specific animals stand out in the paragraph?

_____

_____

_____

c. Rewrite the following information in one paragraph. Add transitional words and phrases, if necessary, to link the sentences together.

_____

_____

_____

_____

_____

_____

2. Here is a multiple-paragraph example using journalistic style:

It is a joy to learn that another child has discovered a wonderful device.

It is simple to operate. Anyone with even an elementary school education can use it without instruction. And when a child uses it, it opens up a whole new world of wonder.

If handled carefully it will last for generations and function perfectly every time. It has no wire or electric motors. If left idle and unused for 50 years it will still be ready to serve at a minute's notice.

The device is so small it can be held in one hand and operated with the other or it may be used on a table or a desk.

This gadget does many things to and for children. It can amuse them, instruct them, excite them and at times scare the britches off them. It has been known to bring tears of sorrow trickling down their chubby little cheeks.

Now, you and I have known about this device for years and most of us use it daily but when a child discovers it, it brings a brand new thrill.

This device of which I write is called a "book."

Bish Thompson, "A Very Wonderful Device"

Writing Assignment

Induction

Select a current issue and conduct an informal survey among your friends to determine whether they favor the issue. Then write a paragraph summarizing your findings, citing pertinent data. Create an inductive structure by ending the paragraph with the conclusion you have drawn from an analysis of your data.

A Student Example

He ran through the patio door just as fast as his little feet would carry him. He ran right to the big hamburger shaped tunnel and climbing stand. How did he know how to climb up the slippery sides? He managed without much effort. He slipped off quickly and ran in circles. Which ride should he try? He passed up the yellow lion and settled on a blue bug. Jump, jump, jump. Another little boy in a red sweater riding the merry-go-round eyed him suspiciously. Some one had invaded his private world. They eyed each other. But soon both boys were slipping and sliding down the big hamburger. It's fun to eat at McDonald's and play on the rides.

Paragraph Patterns: General to Particular

CHAPTER 6

The Deductive Pattern

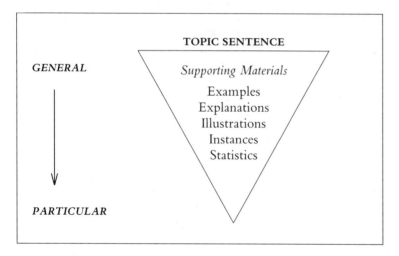

GENERAL

TOPIC SENTENCE

Supporting Materials

Examples
Explanations
Illustrations
Instances
Statistics

PARTICULAR

The most common structure in English prose is the general-to-particular pattern. As the preceding diagram illustrates, this pattern begins with a topic sentence, which states a general idea. From this idea the paragraph moves toward particularities — examples, explanations, illustrations, instances, statistics — that explore various parts of the general statement.

Frequently called the *deductive method* or the *deductive order*, this pattern will help you present specific points that make

Deductive method

up a general truth. You will deduce from this general point (that is, draw from it) particulars, issues, and specifics. The following illustration shows how this paragraph pattern moves out from the general idea (represented within the circle) toward a specific point (represented by the dot).

The triangular shape in the box on page 129 is a mnemonic device (a memory jogger) for recalling this pattern. The pyramid is turned upside down, moving from the base (the topic sentence) toward the apex (the final clincher sentence). You may want to reach definite conclusions by the end of the paragraph, or you may decide to leave your paragraph *open ended* — that is, reach no definite conclusions. You may leave your audience questioning and thinking, depending upon the topic — such as subjects involving ethical decisions, whether to terminate a pregnancy, whether to commit involuntary euthanasia, whether to accept or reject a particular religious dogma (transubstantiation or the immaculate conception).

Numerous examples of the general-to-particular pattern appear in textbooks and magazines or newspapers. A few examples of this structure follow, and questions after each paragraph will help you remember the pattern and become more analytical about the paragraphs you read as well as those you are planning to write.

E.B. White's portrait of New York is a fine example of the general-to-particular paragraph structure. As you read, try to pick out the particular details that illustrate the topic sentence; then answer the questions that follow the paragraph.

It is a miracle that New York works at all. The whole thing is implausible. Every time the residents brush their teeth, millions of gallons of water must be drawn from the Catskills and the hills of Westchester. When a young man in Manhattan writes a letter to his girl in Brooklyn, the love message gets blown to her through a pneumatic tube — pfft — just like that. The subterranean system of telephone cables, power lines, steam pipes, gas mains and sewer pipes is enough reason to abandon the island to the gods and weevils. Every time an incision is made in the pavement, the noisy surgeons expose ganglia that are tangled beyond belief. By rights, New York should have destroyed itself long ago, from panic or fire or rioting or failure of some vital supply line in its circulatory system or from some deep labyrinthine short circuit.

E.B. White, "Here Is New York"

Exercise 6–1

1. The topic sentence is: _____

    _____

2. Make a list of supporting details or "particularities" that illustrate the topic sentence.

    a. _____   c. _____

    b. _____   d. _____

3. What is White's purpose in writing this description?

    _____

    _____

4. a. What type of audience do you believe he is addressing?

    _____

    _____

    b. What type of audience would be unsuitable for this information and his method of presenting it?

    _____

    _____

5. Find at least two transitional elements that help tie the thoughts together.

    a. _____

    b. _____

6. Find at least two memorable "word pictures" that you remember after reading White's remarks:

    a. _____

    b. _____

The following description of the western artist C. M. Russell is a lively paragraph in the general-to-particular pattern. The key words are *grubbiest cowboy*; *cowboy* is the idea word and *grubbiest* suggests an attitude. This general desription is then particularized as the writer develops the portrait:

> By most reports Russell was one of the grubbiest cowboys who ever rode the range. He would wear a shirt until it became so dirty and greasy that it almost stood up by itself. Then instead of taking it off, he'd pull a new one on over it—until at the end of the winter he'd be wearing half a dozen shirts. He and another friend once had a competition to see who could find the largest, fiercest louse on his body. His ripeness finally prompted a group of cowboys with whom he was batching to strip him and scrub him in boiling water, nearly destroying the bunkhouse in the process.
>
> Barnaby Conrad III, "C.M. Russell and the Buckskin Paradise of the West."

Exercise 6–2

1. The topic sentence is: _____

2. What special details help illustrate *grubbiest cowboy*?

    a. _____   c. _____

    b. _____   d. _____

3. Can you identify Conrad's audience? Is he writing for
    a group of cowboys, a general audience, western fic-
    tion writers, scholars, or some other group? Explain
    why you selected the particular audience.

    _____

    _____

    _____

These paragraphs from professional writers present a
challenge to beginning writers who can imitate them.
Writing about her friend, Denise, Gloria follows the general-to-particular pattern:

One of the most important considerations that a pregnant teenager contemplating an abortion must have is
money. Denise debated with herself, "Do I have the money
to support a baby—alone?" The question did come to Denise's mind even though she had a family, a boyfriend
who wanted her to have the child, and many supportive
friends. Even so, thought Denise, "What if my family or my
boyfriend won't help me—financially? How will I pay my
way out of this mess, even if that is possible?" Denise
knew about the various programs in St. Louis that helped
pregnant teenagers. She visited the Planned Parenthood
office to learn about abortion and alternatives she possibly
could afford. She began to consider the financial demands
a new baby might represent; clothing, food, and shelter
were just a few of them. She decided she needed to ask
her boyfriend if he could help her financially. Was he, for
example, ready to give her monthly child support pay-
ments? Moreover, she knew that she had to face her parents and ask them whether they could, and in fact would,
be able to help her out financially with the new baby. After
all, it would be their grandchild. Clearly, financial matters
were something that Denise had to face, but she had other
things on her mind, too, as she debated with herself
whether to have the baby or abort it.

Examples for Analysis

1.   Many of the Founding Fathers were passionate lovers or practitioners of music. Jefferson used to rise at five in the morning to practice the violin; his expense books record many a purchase of "the latest minuets" and of fiddle strings for string-quartet sessions; and he was well acquainted with the technique and construction of various instruments. Samuel Adams organized the people of Boston into secret singing clubs to stir up enthusiasm for independence. And Thomas Paine wrote at least two fine songs, "The Liberty Tree" and "Bunker Hill." In addition to having made a famous ride, Paul Revere might go down in history as having been the engraver of the first volume of original hymns and anthems ever published in this country. And Benjamin Franklin — most versatile of all — not only was a writer of ballad verses and a music publisher, but even invented a new musical instrument — the glass Armonica, for which Gluck, Mozart, and Beethoven composed a number of pieces.

Elie Siegmeister, "Music in Early America"

Exercise 6–3

1.   Write out the topic sentence for this paragraph.

_____

_____

2.   (a) Refer to the earlier discussion of "cases" and "instances" (see Chapter 3); which technique has the writer used to support his point in this paragraph? (b) List two specific examples.

a. _____

_____

_____

b. _____

_____

_____

2.   The latest blight to afflict the spoken word in the United States is the rapidly spreading reiteration of the phrase "you know." I don't know just when it began moving like a rainstorm through the language, but I tremble at its increasing garbling of meaning, ruining of rhythm, and drumming upon my hapless ears. One man, in a phone conversation with me last summer, used the phrase thirty-four times in about five minutes, by my own count; a young matron in Chicago got seven "you knows" into one wavy sentence, and I have also heard it as far west as Denver, where an otherwise charming woman at a garden party in August said it almost as often as a whippoorwill says, "Whippoorwill." Once, speaking of whippoorwills, I was waked after midnight by one of those feathered hellions and lay there counting his chants. He got up to one hundred and fifty-eight and then suddenly said, "Whip—" and stopped dead. I like to believe that his mate, at the end of her patience, finally let him have it.

James Thurber, "The Spreading 'You Know,'"
in *Lanterns and Lances*

Exercise 6–4

1.   What is Thurber's implied comment about the English language, particularly with phrases such as "you know"?

_____

_____

2. What phrase have you heard people using when they seem to be at a loss for words? Give several specific examples.

    _____

    _____

    _____

3. (a) What is the tone of this paragraph? After identifying the tone, indicate what in the paragraph leads you to make this conclusion. (b) Is Thurber trying to make a serious point?

    _____

    _____

    _____

4. What does the whippoorwill example add, if anything, to the paragraph to stress Thurber's point?

    _____

    _____

    _____

3. Here is a one-paragraph book review of Laurence Olivier's *Confessions of an Actor*. It is similar to what you might write for a history, sociology, or political science project. You might find this pattern useful for an essay exam in any discipline. Note the writer's careful analysis, his critical evaluation, and numerous specific examples that give texture to the review.

Topic sentence establishing unfavorable point of view

    Few people will dispute the fact that for more than three decades Sir Laurence has been King of the legitimate theatre. But his autobiography lacks the literary fireworks which would have made this another triumph; it is a weak telling of his life with people rushing hither and yon as mere characters on a theatrical program. While he goes into better detail about his performances, and those of others, on the London stage, the frame of reference for most readers will be nil. His Hollywood efforts seem to be only interruptions in his life. When he came to Hollywood in the early 1930s, they billed him as another Ronald Colman [*sic*], but Olivier left Hollywood to do a movie in England with Gloria Swanson (seen here as *What a Widow!*) an effort that is blithely dismissed. Even when he returned to star in *Wuthering Heights*, there's little here to hang your hat on. And when he starred in *Rebecca*, Alfred Hitchcock's first American film, the director is only a footnote in Olivier's life. Even David O. Sleznick who produced the film, the producer of Vivien Leigh's *Gone with the Wind*, and that film certainly changed their fortunes as husband and wife, fellow stars, etc. doesn't get much attention here. We do get a detailed story about working with Marilyn Monroe in *The Prince and the Showgirl* and feel the harrowing experience it was to a perfectionist as Olivier, but it is all surface emotion. When Vivien Leigh suffers a mental breakdown, while Olivier's telling of this is compassionate, it is never affectionate. Obviously, Olivier's life and love really is The Theatre. But that's not enough for most readers. Added to all this disappointment is the lack of an Index. Perhaps what was most needed was a hardlined editor or co-author who would have asked the tough questions and gotten some tough answers.

Chronological presentation of examples

Example 1
Example 2

Example 3

Example 4

Example 5

Example 6

Conclusion and final evaluation

David Winston York, *West Coast Review of Books: The 1983 Year Book*

The Question-to-Answer Pattern

The question-to-answer pattern moves from a generality, stated in an initial question, toward an answer. The question, either the first sentence or one near the beginning of the paragraph, makes your audience want to know *who, what, when, where,* or *how.* It makes clear that the purpose of the paragraph is to provide answers. And these answers relate to the topic and attitude words posed in the question. As the paragraph develops, your subsequent sentences

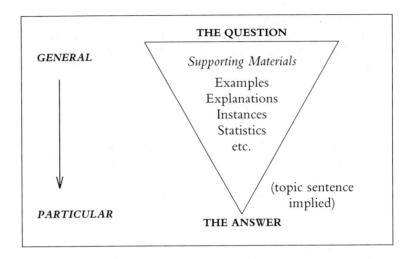

reveal the answer or the several answers to the question. Each subdivision presents part of a single answer, if the answer is unusually complex and invites such division. Other questions, however, suggest multiple answers, all of which can be elaborated upon in explanatory sentences.

As you formulate the question, ask yourself if you have clearly stated a main topic. Have you included an attitude word that suggests your position? Or is where you stand clearly implied? In "The American Scholar," Emerson asks, "Who reads an American book?" He is writing about nineteenth-century American intellectuals, yet by implication suggests that few bother to read "things" American. That he should pose such a question implies that he probably believes American books deserve to be read, even by his contemporaries in Cambridge and Concord, Massachusetts.

The question-to-answer pattern is dramatic. It promotes a sense of urgency: the question needs to be answered. The reader wants answers quickly; if the answers aren't there, the urgency increases. Emerson feels it important enough to stir up his audience's interest in American literature. The answer he provides shamed his "caved" and "trustless" audience that so regularly ignored American books and devoted most of their time to those printed in England.

The diagram of this pattern illustrates its similarity to the didactic method. Both use the inverted pyramidal structure. The question serves as an introduction to the paragraph; the explanatory sentences that develop the answer become the body sentences.

CAUTION

Remember to end your implied topic sentence with a question mark.

Student Examples

Smoker's Rights

How do smokers feel when non-smokers object to their habit? Smokers need to realize that if they are health hazards to others, there is a serious problem that cannot be ignored. It is no matter to others (besides their close friends and family) if smokers are harming themselves, but when their behavior begins to affect non-smokers, then someone must establish reasonable rules of behavior. Those rules must consider the rights of smokers and non-smokers as well. Smokers cannot be dismissed as second class citizens, banished from the office place or the public arena. Not only do smokers often sense their diminished social status, but sometimes they also believe non-smokers lump them with groups of heroin and cocaine addicts who cannot break their habit. And finally, smokers feel as if they aren't decent; they are made to feel they are dirty people by many non-smokers who regard them and their habit with contempt. But do smokers really deserve to feel the way many of them do?

National Service: An Obligation

Is national service a good idea that deserves consideration? National service provides a grant to young people to help defray college tuition expenses. To be eligible for the grant, the college student must have completed two years of either military or community service. The program has definite advantages for economically disadvantaged youths. Young Latinos and Afro Americans would find the program attractive, particularly if they did not have adequate funding for college. But the program is for all students. It would foster in all participants a sense of public responsibility, derived from service in local shelters, immigration centers, and possibly even near-by Indian reservations. Those who participate might even discover they have talents they were unaware of; possibly even a career goal might emerge from such participation. The concept of a national service policy—and the National Service Act of 1989—deserve our attention and support.

Weirdo Calls

Do you ever get weird phone calls? Funny ones that use bad words. No one likes or wants them. What can you do to stop them? Well, the phone people say just ignore and hang up. And don't talk back. Don't say anything as that's what the caller wants you to do. He wants to scare you, but don't let him. Just hang up. However, if he keeps phoning and annoying you, tell the phone people. They'll tell you what to do. But if you still get calls, you may have to get a different phone number. And if that doesn't work, then you may have to get the police to help trace down the caller. Just remember, you have to do something yourself to put an end to these weirdo calls.

Examples for Analysis

1.

The Myth

What is the myth of the Texas lady? Texas ladies resemble the True Woman of the nineteenth century. Additionally, stereotypes of two generations come to mind: the polite, carefully done, and ultimately vapid matron with the immovable coiffure and her daughter, the pretty undergraduate who is becoming a lady via membership in a sorority. Her frothy young sisters wear appropriately faded blue jeans, gold-filled earrings, lipstick and eyeshadow. Mother and daughter talk softly and smile a great deal. They speak when spoken to, and when they speak, they say nothing unpleasant, nothing immodest, and nothing substantive, especially in the presence of men.

Celia Genishi, "Texas Ladies' Talk: A View from the Tower"

Although traditionally a paragraph has a topic sentence in the form of a declarative statement (see p. 17), this pattern begins with a question. Presumably, the question is the topic sentence. Actually, though, the question merely implies the topic idea: "the myth of the Texas lady." Here, the topic sentence is implied, not stated. The description of a mythical Texas lady answers the question. How she acts, how she dresses, and how she speaks foster this myth. As the details in this paragraph unfold, they reveal the myth.

2.   Has anyone ever resisted the charm of the Swiss Family? Indeed, can anyone think of it as just another book? Someone once likened Chaucer's stories to an English river, slow, quietly beautiful, and winding all the way. In the same terms, *The Swiss Family Robinson* is like a mountain lake. It is contained and motionless. It does not go anywhere. It has no story. Details, and detached incidents, are looked at separately without regard to what is coming next. This is how children live when they are happy, and this is why children will read *The Swiss Family Robinson* backwards and forwards and not bother about the end. To the adult eye, very little seems intended for out-and-out realism. When father Robinson puts together his boat of tubs with the ease and speed of a Popeye who has just eaten spinach, we, and children too, accept a literary convention. Nor are the vague people at all convincing. For Johann Wyss began, not by writing for a wide public but for his children who knew him and his wife and themselves too well to bother about characterization, even if he had been capable of it. Having isolated his characters, Wyss used the book from then onwards as a sort of holdall for conveying moral instruction and scientific information. He did not foresee the outcome of the book. One feels that the lively and capable Miss Montrose was brought in at the end because Wyss's eldest son had got engaged and Wyss wanted to bring his fiancée into the family. The charm of the book, then, lies precisely in the absence of story. The days are endless and time has no meaning. We sink completely into the milieu of these people who are not going anywhere and do not mind. Time is bright and uncomplicated as holidays spent by the sea in childhood.

William Golding, *The Hot Gates and Other Occasional Pieces*

3.   Who were the pioneers? Who were the men who left their homes and went into the wilderness? A man rarely leaves a soft spot and goes deliberately in search of hardship and privation. People become attached to the places they live in; they drive roots. A change of habitat is a painful act of uprooting. A man who has made good and has a standing in his community stays put. The successful businessmen, farmers, and workers usually stayed where they were. Who then left for the wilderness and the unknown? Obviously those who had not made good; men who went broke and never amounted to much; men who though possessed of abilities were too impulsive to stand the daily grind; men who were slaves of their appetites—drunkards, gamblers, and woman-chasers; outcasts—fugitives from justice and ex-jailbirds. There were no doubt some who went in search of health—men suffering with TB, asthma, heart trouble. Finally there was a sprinkling of young and middle-aged in search of adventure.

Eric Hoffer, "The Role of the Undesirables"

4.   Why do I awake each weekday at 5:45 a.m. and go to the Providence, Rhode Island airport, bad weather or good, to fly airborne traffic reports in a fixed-wing airplane? The answer is simple: I'm a pilot and I'm a ham.

Anthony L. Dibiasio, "Ham in the Sky"

5.   Why should we live with such hurry and waste of life? We are determined to be starved before we are hungry. Men say that a stitch in time saves nine, and so they take a thousand stitches to-day to save nine tomorrow. As for *work,* we haven't any of any consequence. We have the Saint Vitus' dance, and cannot possibly keep our heads still. If I should only give a few pulls at the parish bell-rope, as for a fire, that is, without setting the bell, there is hardly a man on his farm in the outskirts of Concord, notwithstanding that press of engagements which was his excuse so many times this morning, nor a boy, nor a woman, I might almost say, but would forsake all and follow that sound, not mainly to save

property from the flames, but, if we will confess the truth, much more to see it burn, since burn it must, and we, be it known, did not set it on fire, — or to see it put out, and have a hand in it, if that is done as handsomely; yes, even if it were the parish church itself. Hardly a man takes a half-hour's nap after dinner, but when he wakes he holds up his head and asks, "What's the news?" as if the rest of mankind had stood his sentinels. Some give directions to be waked every half-hour, doubtless for no other purpose; and then, to pay for it, they tell what they have dreamed. After a night's sleep the news is as indispensable as the breakfast. "Pray tell me anything new that has happened to a man anywhere on this globe," — and he reads it over his coffee and rolls, that a man has had his eyes gouged out this morning on the Wachito River; never dreaming the while that he lives in the dark unfathomed mammoth cave of this world, and has but the rudiment of an eye himself.

Henry David Thoreau, "Why I Went to the Woods"

Writing Assignment

1. Select a subject of your own choosing or one of the suggestions given below. Restrict the topic, phrasing it as a question. Then write a paragraph of 8 to 10 sentences in which you answer the question you have posed.

   Dangers posed by computer hackers

   Stock mergers

   Assault weapons

   Wild horse roundups

   Star gazing

   Bird watching

   Satanism cults

   Dirty tricks

2. Look for an example of question-to-answer paragraphs in your reading and bring it to class to share with other writers.

The Cause-to-Effect or Effect-to-Cause Pattern

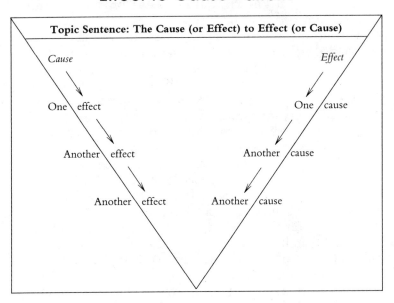

Topic Sentence: The Cause (or Effect) to Effect (or Cause)

Cause

One effect

Another effect

Another effect

Effect

One cause

Another cause

Another cause

Definition

Definition

Process questions

Another variation on the general-to-particular pattern is causal analysis, the cause-to-effect structure, or its reverse, effects to cause. What is a *cause*? What is an *effect*? A *cause* is a phenomenon that makes something happen; the sun shines and *causes* us to be warm, *causes* photosynthesis in plants, *causes* our solar heating system to operate. Each of the things the sun *causes* to happen is an *effect*.

This pattern is useful in writing about *why* something happened. Why did Rome fall? Why were there riots in the London streets? Why is peace so elusive? If you reverse the pattern and work from effects to cause, you begin with a result. The result may be that young people were rioting in the seventies in Picadilly Circus. What caused them to riot? unemployment? nihilism? racial hatred? apprehensiveness about nuclear war?

When determining causes, say of the London riots, you must be careful to distinguish *sufficient* causes from *contributory* causes. The *contributory* cause to the riot in Picadilly Circus may have been the heat, the excitement of other rioters, the presence of a rival gang. But these causes—independent of any others—may not alone have been *sufficient* causes for the riot. That is, a sufficient cause by itself generates an effect, in this case, the riot. Frustration about being unable to get a job, or even a job interview, may be sufficient cause.

One must be cautious when using this pattern, as it may lead you into a common reasoning fallacy—*post hoc ergo propter hoc* (after this, therefore because of this). For example, you might recall the childhood adage, "Step on a crack, break your mother's back." If you step on a crack in the sidewalk and a day later your mother's back begins to hurt, you cannot logically conclude that the first action—the cause—resulted in the pain in your mother's back—the effect. You are oversimplifying and not thinking logically when you suggest there is a relationship between your stepping on the crack and the pain in your mother's back. List several other adages, like "Feed a cold, starve a fever" and analyze them, focusing on cause–effect relationships. Do they evidence sound reasoning? or something else?

It is really simpler if your paragraph concentrates on a single cause–effect relationship. Remember that although there may be an infinite number of possible causes for every event, the effects may also be infinite. It is important that you try to sharpen the focus of your paragraph on only a single cause, making it clear to your reader the relationship between a cause and its effect. Or if you are reversing the pattern, make absolutely clear how the effect derived from one or two clearly developed causes.

A useful formula to remember when writing a cause–effect paragraph is:

1. Where there is a **cause,** there will be an **effect.**
2. Without a **cause,** there can be no **effect.**

Here are some possibilities for structuring. Imagine your sentences moving in one of the following directions:

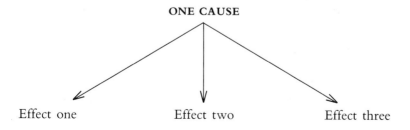

ONE CAUSE

Effect one   Effect two   Effect three

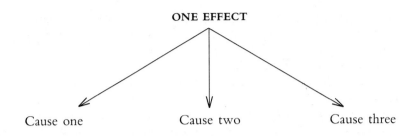

ONE EFFECT

Cause one   Cause two   Cause three

Examples for Analysis

Transition that echos
the causal cycle
(topic sentence)

cause → effect → cause
Example

Analogy to clarify

Result

Transition that
pre-outlines

1.   Now it is clear that the decline of a language must ultimately have political and economic causes: it is not due simply to the bad influence of this or that individual writer. But an effect can become a cause, reinforcing the original cause and producing the same effect in an intensified form, and so on indefinitely. A man may take to drink because he feels himself to be a failure, and then fail all the more completely because he drinks. It is rather the same thing that is happening to the English language. It becomes ugly and inaccurate because our thoughts are foolish, but the slovenliness of our language makes it easier for us to have foolish thoughts. The point is that the process is reversible. Modern English, especially written English, is full of bad habits which spread by imitation and which can be avoided if one is willing to take the necessary trouble. If one gets rid of these habits one can think more clearly, and to think clearly is a necessary first step toward political regeneration: so that the fight against bad English is not frivolous and is not the exclusive concern of professional writers. I will come back to this presently, and I hope that by that time the meaning of what I have said here will have become clearer. Meanwhile, here are five specimens of the English language as it is now habitually written.

From George Orwell, "Politics and the English Language"

2.   In short, the investigators looked into every possible cause except the real one. Benny Paret was killed because the human fist delivers enough impact, when directed against the head, to produce a massive

hemorrhage in the brain. The human brain is the most delicate and complex mechanism in all creation. It has a lacework of millions of highly fragile nerve connections. Nature attempts to protect this exquisitely intricate machinery by encasing it in a hard shell. Fortunately, the shell is thick enough to withstand a great deal of pounding. Nature, however, can protect man against everything except man himself. Not every blow to the head will kill a man—but there is always the risk of concussion and damage to the brain. A prize fighter may be able to survive even repeated brain concussions and go on fighting, but the damage to his brain may be permanent.

Norman Cousins, "Who Killed Benny Paret?"

3.   A child need not be raised by his biological parents. Freud made so much of the Oedipus complex or Oedipal situation that many people believe a male child *must* have a jealous desire for his mother and an envious hatred for his father in order to grow up normally. But there has been much argument among anthropologists about whether or not this Oedipal relationship really exists in all societies. As I see it, the chief thing is to understand the basic principle underlying the Oedipus phenomenon, which is applicable to any family structure. The human infant for many years is entirely dependent upon and in the power of some individual or individuals. If you're in someone's power, for better or worse you have to come to terms with that person. If the person doesn't abuse his power, you come to love him. But in whose power the child is, and with whom he has to come to terms, can vary greatly.

Bruno Bettelheim, "The Roots of Radicalism"

Exercise 6–5

1.   What is meant by the term *biological parents*?

    _____

    _____

2. Look up the definition of "Oedipus Complex" and write it in the space provided:

_____

_____

3. What is an Electra Complex? Write the definition of that term here.

_____

_____

4. What does this paragraph suggest about the impact of power in raising children?

_____

_____

4.   In the experimental sense, sensory deprivation means cutting off all the senses from outside stimulation and leaving the brain to its own devices. Lilly's method of doing this was to float for a number of hours in a large tank filled with an extremely dense solution so that the body would float very high. He would float on the surface with the room darkened or with dark goggles over his eyes. He discovered that if the water was kept at 93°F, he wouldn't be able to differentiate hot from cold, and his tactile sense wouldn't function. His hearing would disappear; his ears would be just under the surface and no sound waves were being produced in the tank. Lilly and hundreds of others (myself included) floated in his tanks for varying lengths of time, and each individual experienced the same phenomenon: When deprived of sensory stimulation, the brain is vitally active. Everyone who came out of the tanks said that he'd had very vivid daydreams and seemingly wild fantasies and everyone said that he felt rested.

Diana Nyad, *Other Shores*

Student Examples

1. Seldom does a member of the secular population consider that one of the major effects of celibacy among
priests is personal contentment. A priest gives up everything in order to serve God, and does so willingly. He
studies theology for four years then spends two more
years doing his novitiate work in order to prepare himself
to become faithful to both God and himself. His engagement with his studies prevents him from having a personal life with women. Such commitment to rigorous
study gives the young priest personal satisfaction and
spiritual comfort. He realizes that he has been given a
special gift, his vocation. Part of his responsibility is to
accept the fact that he is a median between God and the
parishoners he serves; he must remain celibate in order
that he not be distracted in serving a wife as well. Jesus
becomes his model. Since Jesus never married, the priest
knows he cannot. Even the Apostles, who were married
prior to joining Jesus' ministry, entered the life of celibacy
in order to serve their master and free themselves from the
demands of the flesh. Such a decision results in personal
satisfaction for the contemporary priest as it no doubt did
for Jesus and his Apostles.

2. There are many disturbing effects that could be related
to a single cause, the banning of handguns in America.
Such a law would be the beginning of dangerous gov-
ernmental infringement that clearly needs to be resisted.
One effect of disarming the public would be the sacrificing
of our rights to protect our families in our homes. Handguns help us protect ourselves against the criminals who
invade our property. Even though many domestic crimes
are a direct result of misused firearms, the local newspapers in our community have detailed four recent cases
of people who shot robbers they caught inside their
homes. One eighty-year-old woman used her small pistol
to protect herself against a six-foot masked bandit whom
she caught emptying her chest of drawers. Another effect
of disarming the public would be to give the advantage of
self-protection to the criminals. They would not register or
turn in their handguns. They would remain armed while
the ordinary citizen who might have turned in his gun to
obey the law would then be unprotected. A final effect of

such a ban would be the compromise and eventual deterioration of rights of hunters who have a constitutional right to bear arms. They could not use small arms in target shooting, small game hunts, or skeet shoots. Antique gun collectors would have to turn in their weapons, too, as their hobby would become illegal. Banning handguns sounds like a good idea, but it has too many negative effects for it to be considered a serious proposal.

Brainstorming Exercise: Cause to Effect, Effect to Cause

Try listing possible causes of and effects of the problem created by drinking alcoholic beverages in a public park.

Causes: No city ordinance preventing drinking
Inadequate provision for security
Inadequate self-discipline
Insufficient control of groups
Parental control of children
Police supervision

(Other Causes?) _____

_____

Effects: Litter

Broken beer bottles _____

_____

_____

Fears

Too many strangers _____

_____

Congestion

    Too many cars _____

_____

_____

Violence

    Knifings _____

_____

_____

Accidents

_____

_____

_____

Writing Assignment

1.   Break up into groups of three within the classroom and select one of the following topics to talk over. Appoint one of the members of the group to record the key observations members of the group make. Take notes as people talk; then compare your notes with the recorder's. Use your notes to write a rough draft of a paragraph out of class on the topic:

    a. Weekend travel
    b. Favorite snack food
    c. Traffic jam
    d. Lighting on campus
    e. Motorcycle accident
    f. Family rituals at Christmas

        g. Lemons

        h. Controlled substances

        i. The pill

2. Get together out of class with a friend and brainstorm on one of the preceding topics. Take notes as you talk. Then develop a paragraph using one of the methods you have learned so far. Bring the rough draft of the paragraph to class.

Cause and Effect

1. Select an issue, plan, or policy with which you are familiar and write a paragraph predicting what the *effects* will be. For example, what effects might logically follow if the NFL players strike?

2. Select a strong personal belief, bias, hobby, or special interest you hold and write a paragraph in which you search for causes.

3. In a well-developed paragraph analyze the causes and effects of clinging to a certain superstition. For example, why does opening an umbrella inside a building bring bad luck?

Problem-to-Solution Pattern

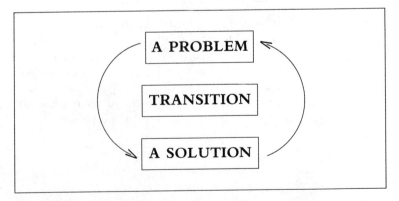

When writing about problems and solutions for history, political science, or sociology courses, you may want to rely on a special structure that offers many options for presenting information. Half of your paper may present a discussion of a single problem or several related ones; the remainder will then discuss the solution to the problem — a reasonable solution, that is — or numerous possible solutions, some of which are reasonable, some perhaps fanciful. This structure is particularly useful for argumentation or persuasion, from the mildly controversial to the really momentous.

Before you really start writing, think about what motivates you to select a particular problem to analyze. Is the problem worthy of discussion? or is it just a waste of time? A *problem* worthy of concern is one that causes either injury or pain to other people, that possibly could degrade a whole race or cause danger to a few or multitudes, that promotes tremendous inefficiency, or that possibly allows neither individuals nor groups to grow, or that inhibits or limits their growth and development. A significant problem is one fundamental to either the individual or society; hunger is certainly a fundamental problem that is a concern for a whole country or the world. If you have a choice of a problem to write about, try to select one that is timely or timeless, one that deals with growth and survival, either of the individual or a large group. But above all else, choose a problem worthy of consideration.

Processs questions

Definition

Problem–Solution Structure

On a scale less grand, a paragraph may also have this problem-to-solution structure. That is, its topic sentence presents a problem to analyze. Explanatory sentences may present historical background, if this information is essential. They may also describe various parts of the problem or troublesome ramifications, if you feel they are relevant and need to be addressed.

Causes of the problem and effects the problem generates are concerns for an alternative approach. What caused the increase in traffic deaths in your city last year? Was it poor traffic lighting or inadequate street maintenance? the new right-turn-on-red law? drunk drivers? unrestrained interference with cars by joggers, pedestrians, loose animals? What have been some of the effects of this increase in traffic deaths? Have chapters of Mothers Against Drunk Drivers been formed? Have more police been hired? traffic tickets issued? A complete analysis of cause–effect relationships related to the problem thus becomes the material for a long essay.

Think of paragraphs using this structure as having two parts. The second half describes a solution to the problem posed earlier, or possibly more than one solution. It is important to avoid oversimplified solutions your audience will dismiss hastily. Each must be fully developed, showing how it eliminates the problem in practical ways. Clear advantages of some solutions are that they are painless, that they cost less, and that they are quick and long lasting.

Note Faulkner's brevity in presenting the problem, a "universal physical fear" of being blown up, and a solution that young writers have at their disposal:

> Our tragedy today is a general and universal physical fear so long sustained by now that we can even bear it. There are no longer problems of the spirit. There is only the question: When will I be blown up? Because of this, the young man or woman writing today has forgotten the problems of the human heart in conflict with itself which alone can make good writing because only that is worth writing about, worth the agony and the sweat.
>
> William Faulkner, "On Accepting the Nobel Prize for Literature"

The Pro-and-Con Structure

A variation of the problem-to-solution pattern is a complex structure that presents the pro and con of an issue. *Definition* *Pro* and *con* are latinate in origin; *pro* means "for" and *con* (*contra*) means "against"; you can think up a long list of words in your vocabulary that begin with either prefix. Useful for balanced analysis, such a pattern presents the pro of an issue (or its advantages) in the first half and the con of the issue (or its disadvantages) in the second half. That is, pose the affirmative of an issue—why we should be in favor of gun control or neutering of stray animals—in the first half. Then follow with the negative in the second half, that is, why we should not favor gun control, why we should not neuter stray animals.

Reversal Words

A number of signal words that provide transition between the two halves of your paragraph will help you divide the pro and con sections. Words and phrases like *but, yet, however, on the contrary, on the other hand, in contrast, while this may be true, in spite of,* or *conversely* alert your reader to the shift or reversal from an affirmative to a negative position. In most instances your topic sentence with its attitude word will make clear where you stand on the issue, even though you are presenting both sides. It should be clear where you stand so that you do not appear wishy-washy or evasive. Occasionally, this pattern used in an introductory paragraph suggests how the whole paper will explore two halves of an issue. The following paragraph is fairly typical of the pro-and-con structure:

The NCAA transfer rule stipulates that athletes must sit out an entire academic year and earn a full year's credits before being eligible to participate in intercollegiate sports. There are several reasons why this rule is advantageous both to these players and the university. It discourages players from jumping from one university to another simply because the new one has a better chance of winning an NCAA title, thereby giving the players greater visibility to pro scouts. Also, players will be less likely to change schools when personal problems develop, such as an argument with a coach. And the application of the rules gives players an opportunity to become an integral part of the campus rather than only Saturday "participants" in university life. Even so, the transfer rule has inherent disadvantages, such as discounting legitimate reasons why students must need to transfer to another school. Also, it discriminates between the activities of scholarship and non-scholarship students. The college chorus and band scholarship students, for instance, do not have to abide by the same NCAA rules as the athletes. Nor do the athletes and musicians who are not on scholarship. The rule seems more clearly designed to benefit institutions and coaches rather than students.

Topic Sentence

The "pro" (the advantages)

Pivot Term

The "con" (the disadvantages)

Occasionally, however, you may wish to leave your reader in the dark on where you stand, wishing to reveal your position as the paper develops. If you are stating two sides in one paragraph, however, early on you should make your position clear. Vigorous, positive statements such as these will affirm your stand: "Those who want a community free of rabies threats should continue to support the spaying of stray animals." Or "This example alone shows why handgun control is a reasonable position."

Examples for Analysis

1. When the passage of the 26th Amendment gave eighteen-year-olds the right to vote, it created a major difficulty for states that decided to lower the drinking age from 21. The prevailing thinking in the early seventies was that if a young man could be drafted, was eligible to pay federal income tax, or be held responsible for debts incurred, he should also—it seemed logical to assume—be allowed to buy liquor. Yet reports from the National Highway Traffic Safety Administration indicated that alcohol is involved in more than half of the fatalities of people under 35. Road accidents in Maine, Michigan, and Texas increased appreciably once the drinking age was lowered. To solve the problems created by what was then considered enlightened thinking in the seventies, a number of states, like Montana, Iowa, Michigan, Texas, and Minnesota, raised the drinking age. In New Hampshire, one must be 20 to buy liquor; in Massachusetts, one must be 20 and also provide a Massachusetts driver's license and a state-issued identification card in order to purchase liquor. The solution does not help bar owners, however. They want to allow people under 20 or 21 to buy or serve drinks but also to deny them the right to buy liquor by the bottle. The solution may seem simple to legislators, but students at colleges and universities throughout the country find little logic in a law that legislates prohibition for someone who has been drinking legally for a year or so.

Exercise 6–6

1. What is the topic sentence for the previous paragraph?

    _____

    _____

2. What specific problem is identified in the paragraph?

    _____

    _____

3. List several solutions that various states introduced.

    _____

    _____

    _____

4. What is the drinking age in your state?

    _____

2.   What do you do when the wings of your sumptuous, all-weather Duke Blueline plane begin to collect ice? You may have obtained a forecast of icing danger, but you felt confident that your new plane, the Mercedes Benz of small aircraft, could stand the test. Soon a problem develops! There's ice outside! What do you do? One of the first things is seek a higher altitude. Climb to 20,000 feet! There, you will be free of clouds and can escape icing. Consulting various approach charts to airports in the area is another important step in case you need to make an emergency landing. These charts must be available as well as a full set of terrain charts, with the lowest terrain indicated. Ground-based radar controls also help if you experience icing problems. Respect all weather, especially ice. Being prepared for ice — even in a new Duke Blueline — is a step intelligent pilots, conscious of air safety, always take.

Exercise 6–7

1. What is the problem the small aircraft has?

    _____

2. What does the author mean by calling the Duke Blueline "the Mercedes Benz of small aircraft"?

    _____

    _____

    _____

3. What are three proposed solutions to the problems the pilot has?

    _____

    _____

    _____

4. Look at this subtopic sentence, then try to develop one or two explanatory sentences that develop it in more detail:
    Ground based radar controls will also help if you are experiencing icing problems.

    _____

    _____

    _____

A Student Example

As you read Albert's description of his goals in running, identify the *problem* section of his paragraph, then find the *solution* section. Could you offer suggestions for improving Albert's paragraph? Does it have too much detail? Has he confused you with the many references to times and miles? Does he have an effective beginning and finish for his paper? Does he have an *idea* and an *attitude* word in his topic sentence? Has he kept the same topic before his readers throughout the paragraph?

Why I Run

My reason for running is that I like to see the improvement in distance and speed in myself week after week. My problem is that for the past 3 weeks I haven't seen any improvement in either the distance or the speed at which I run. Before, I would first get to where I could do the first 3 miles at about 7 minutes a mile, and until then would I add another mile to the distance and another minute for each mile. Now my goal is to run the 9 miles at a time of 9 minutes per mile, which would equal eighty to ninety minutes of running. What I need to do is learn to run at an even pace so I don't become exhausted after ninety minutes. A solution I believe will work is to run each mile on a time interval. That is, to increase the time for each mile. I could start with the first 3 miles at 11 minutes a mile; the second 3 miles at 12 minutes per mile, and finally the last 3 miles at 13 minutes a mile. This would equal aproximately 108 minutes, which is about 18 minutes more than my goal of 90 minutes for 9 miles, but by doing this I would be increasing my distance. As for the speed I'm sure it would increase also after a few weeks. By the time I run these nine miles at a controlled pace a few times, the endurance components of my muscles will be stronger and able to handle more speed.

Writing Assignment

1. Write a paragraph in which you analyze with some depth a personal problem, one that is important to you. Analyze your audience and select concrete details, and have several examples that will make the problem clear to your reader. What should your reader know in order to understand your problem? Avoid selecting a problem that is too big or too complex for one paragraph. Suggestions for possible topics are:

    Oversleeping in the morning
    Sticking to a diet

Stopping smoking
Conversing with others
Sleeping through lectures
Being tongue-tied at parties
Running up credit card charges
Interviewing for a job

2. Write a second paragraph in which you provide your reader with a solution to your problem. Have a full description of the solution with many samples that will be meaningful to your readers.

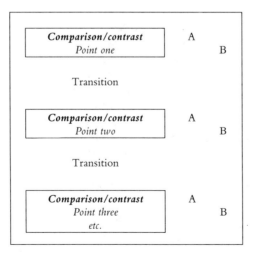

	CHAPTER
The Analytical Patterns	7

The following five patterns are deductive, but essentially different because each is in some manner analytical. Analytical patterns break down the main idea into its related parts. This chapter presents these patterns from the simplest to the most complex form.

The Comparison–Contrast Pattern

THE BLOCK A/B PATTERN

Comparison   A

Pivot term

Contast   B

THE ALTERNATING A/B PATTERN

Comparison/contrast
Point one   A   B

Transition

Comparison/contrast
Point two   A   B

Transition

Comparison/contrast
Point three
etc.   A   B

The preceding diagrams illustrate two basic approaches to writing comparison and contrast, a variation of the general-to-particular pattern. Although in Chapter 4 we talked about comparison and contrast as one type of supporting material (see page 71), now we adapt the pattern to entire paragraphs. The most elementary form separates a paragraph into two equal halves. The first introduces A and its characteristics. The second half presents those of B, normally beginning with similarities and then pointing out appropriate differences. The writer assumes that an alert reader will discern any implied contrasts as similarities are enumerated.

Note how John Fischer invites the discerning reader to make the mental leap necessary for recognizing the similarities in origin, behavior, and dress between Texans and Ukrainians. He relies on metaphor to compare Texans and Ukrainians by using such words as *saddle, borderland,* and *outlaw*. A *metaphor* suggests that one thing, a person for example, is something else, as in "He is a blockheaded Texan," suggesting a comparison between the man and a block and identifying the man's stubbornness. The contrasts are inherent in the parallels Fischer details.

Note metaphor:
Ukrainians = Texans

The Ukrainians are the Texans of Russia. They believe they can fight, drink, ride, sing, and make love better than anybody else in the world, and if pressed will admit it. Their country, too, was a borderland—that's what "Ukraine" means—and like Texas it was originally settled by outlaws, horse thieves, land-hungry farmers, and people who hadn't made a go of it somewhere else. Some of these hard cases banded together, long ago, to raise hell and livestock. They called themselves Cossacks, and they would have felt right at home in any Western movie. Even today the Ukrainians cherish a wistful tradition of horsemanship, although most of them would feel as uncomfortable in a saddle as any Dallas banker. They still like to wear knee-high boots and big, furry hats, made of gray or black Persian lamb, which are the local equivalent of the Stetson.

John Fischer, *Why They Behave Like Russians*

Questions for Analysis

1. Does this paragraph follow the block A/B or alter-
    nating A/B pattern? _____ What structural
    details led you to this conclusion?

    _____

    _____

2. What is the topic sentence of the paragraph?

    _____

    _____

3. What image of a Texan is created? What image of a
    Ukrainian is created?

    _____

    _____

4. What descriptive details stimulate these pictures?

    _____

    _____

5. A *stereotype* ignores individual differences and includes
    generalizations about a particular group, such as that
    all Texans are cowboys and braggarts. What stereo-
    types about Texans and Ukrainians do you find in
    Fischer's paragraph?

    _____

    _____

Comparison and contrast is a common pattern of thinking. Quite naturally, as we encounter a new or an unknown
phenomenon, our mind triggers connections between it

and previously experienced phenomena. Every fall, for example, when new-model automobiles are displayed, we naturally compare them with last year's. Automatically, we contrast this year's Super Bowl teams with those we've known in the past.

Pivot Term

A striking feature of the first comparison and contrast pattern is a pivot term that separates the A and B halves. The term appears in the last sentence of the comparison or near the beginning of the first sentence of the contrast. If none appears, then the reader must make the necessary mental connections between the comparison and the contrast. A few typical pivot terms are *but, however,* and *on the other hand*; a more comprehensive list appears in Chapter 4.

Example for Analysis

Nostalgia is a recurrent theme in Chinese poetry. An American reader of translated Chinese poems may well be taken aback — even put off — by the frequency, as well as the sentimentality, of the lament for home. To understand the strength of this sentiment, we need to know that the Chinese desire for stability and rootedness in place is prompted by the constant threat of war, exile, and the natural disasters of flood and drought. Forcible removal makes the Chinese keenly aware of their loss. By contrast, Americans move, for the most part, voluntarily. Their nostalgia for home town is really longing for a childhood to which they cannot return: in the meantime the future beckons and the future is "out there," in open space. When we criticize American rootlessness, we tend to forget that it is a result of ideals we admire, namely, social mobility and optimism about the future. When we admire Chinese rootedness, we forget that the word "place" means both a location in space and position in society: to be tied to place is also to be bound to one's station in life, with little hope of betterment. Space symbolizes hope; place, achievement and stability.

Pivot term

Yi-Fu Tuan, "American Space, Chinese Place"

Exercise 7–1

1. This paragraph has no topic sentence, but its central idea is implied. What is the implied idea?

    _____

    _____

2. Compose a topic sentence for this paragraph.

    _____

    _____

3. Where would you place it in the paragraph?

    _____

    Why there? _____

4. To understand this paragraph, you must distinguish *rootedness* from *rootlessness*. What is the difference?

    _____

    _____

5. What is different about the American and Chinese attitudes about home?

    _____

    _____

A Variation

A variation of the A/B pattern requires two separate paragraphs: one with similarities (the A part); the other with differences (the B part). This variant, as illustrated below in McGinley's two paragraphs, will help even when you have so much supporting detail that possibly it would overpower your reader if it were in one cumbersome paragraph.

Indeed, the reading habits alone of the younger generation mark them off from their betters. What does an adult do when he feels like having a go at a detective story or the evening paper? Why, he picks out a convenient chair or props himself up on his pillows, arranges the light correctly for good vision, turns down the radio, and reaches for a cigarette or a piece of chocolate fudge.

Children, however, when the literary urge seizes them, take their comic books to the darkest corner of the room or else put their heads under the bedcovers. Nor do they sit *down* to read. They wander. They lie on the floor with their legs draped over the coffee table, or, alternatively, they sit on the coffee table and put the book on the floor. Or else they lean against the refrigerator, usually with the refrigerator door wide open. Sometimes I have seen them retire to closets.

Phyllis McGinley, "Are Children People?"

The following A/B structure separates the bodily movements characteristic of a walker from those typical of a cyclist.

In walking the leg muscles must not only support the rest of the body in an erect posture but also raise and lower the entire body as well as accelerate and decelerate the lower limbs. All these actions consume energy without doing any useful external work. Walking uphill requires that additional work be done against gravity. Apart from these ways of consuming energy, every time the foot strikes the ground some energy is lost, as evidenced by the wear of footpaths, shoes and socks. The swing of the arms and legs also causes wear and loss of energy by chafing.

Contrast this with the cyclist, who first of all saves energy by sitting, thus relieving his leg muscles of their supporting function and accompanying energy consumption. The only reciprocating parts of his body are his knees and thighs; his feet rotate smoothly at a constant speed and the rest of his body is still. Even the acceleration and deceleration of his legs are achieved efficiently, since the strongest muscles are used almost exclusively; the rising leg does not have to be lifted but is raised by the downward thrust of the other leg. The back muscles must be used to support the trunk, but the arms can also help to do this, resulting (in the normal cycling attitude) in a little residual strain on the hands and arms.

S. S. Wilson, "Bicycle Technology"

Exercise 7–2

1. Can you find three similarities between the walker and the cyclist?

   _____

   _____

2. Are there three differences between them?

   _____

   _____

The Alternating Pattern

The second pattern presents an alternating point-by-point analysis. You begin by viewing the similarities and differences of A and B in terms of a single feature, such as the physical appearance of two dancers. Then with this singular focus you begin listing similarities and differences. Next, you analyze another feature, such as their stage presence. Continue enumerating as many features as are essential to make your comparison–contrast complete, alternately listing details about both dancers, being careful to have adequate support to clarify each artist's distinguishing features.

Observe the way Miller makes his point-by-point analysis of Paul Gauguin (the French impressionist painter of the latter part of the nineteenth century) and Somerset Maugham's central character, Strickland, in *The Moon and Sixpence*. Note how the sentence structure makes the comparison and contrast between Gauguin and the character in Maugham's novel so forceful. One-half of a sentence is devoted to Gauguin; the other, to Strickland. Miller uses compound sentences to draw attention to both men. But in the fifth sentence and in the last two sentences, he extends the alternating pattern beyond a single sentence.

There is no doubt that Maugham drew the concept of his story from Gauguin's life. But as for similarity of character between his hero and Gauguin, there was none. Maugham often referred to Strickland as "dull"; Gauguin, a fierce, intense man, was never dull. Strickland, at 40, left his wife unexpectedly and went to Paris to learn to paint. But Gauguin, who had been a Sunday painter for many years, quit his job at 35 (a less romantic age for taking chances, as Maugham obviously realized), but remained with his wife and family until it was agonizingly clear that he had to make a choice between marital responsibility and art. Strickland was secretive; Gauguin compulsively self-revealing. Strickland was callous, uncaring about leaving his wife and family; Gauguin was torn, anguished, guilt-ridden. Strickland did not care what others thought of him; Gauguin did—passionately. Strickland had a "poor gift of expression"; Gauguin was eloquent, an accomplished writer. Strickland cared nothing for fame; Gauguin hungered for it openly, desperately. Strickland's Tahitian wife promised, at his insistence, to burn his hut and all his paintings when he died, and she did so. Gauguin would never have done such a thing. He loved and protected his works, could hardly wait to get the world's reaction to them.

J.P. Miller, "Gauguin the Savage"

Examples for Analysis

1. In *Sixpence in Her Shoe*, Phyllis McGinley makes a number of charming comparisons and contrasts between children and adults. Can you recognize the particular pattern and some of the strategies she uses in the following examples?

Children admittedly are human beings, equipped with such human paraphernalia as appetites, whims, intelligence, and even hearts, but any resemblance between them and people is purely coincidental. The two nations, child and grown-up, don't behave alike or think alike or even see with the same eyes.

Take that matter of seeing, for example. An adult looks in the mirror and notices what? A familiar face, a figure currently over-weight, maybe, but well-known and resignedly accepted; two arms, two legs, an entity. A child can stare into the looking glass for minutes at a time and see only the bone buttons on a snowsuit or a pair of red shoes.

Phyllis McGinley, "Are Children People?"

2. Here in his contrast between two great Russian dancers of two different generations — Vaslav Nijinsky of the Ballet Russe and Rudolf Nureyev of the Kirov Ballet — Rosenwald presents the differences (B) before pointing out the similarities (A):

Physically, Nureyev and Nijinsky are very different. Nureyev has a cat-like presence. His legs are long, his waist narrow, and his shoulders broad and well-proportioned. Photographs of Nijinsky show him to be larger in the waist and with arms of unusually massive proportions and a large neck protruding from slightly sloping shoulders and supporting his relatively small head. Despite the physical differences, both dancers are known for their plasticity, that unique ability to assume a desired form whether in motion or at rest. Both have great elevation, and Nureyev is as renowned for his jumps as Nijinsky was for his.

Peter J. Rosenwald, "Homage to Diaghilev"

Exercise 7–3

1. This paragraph has a number of very difficult words. Look up each of the following and write appropriate definitions in the space provided.

a. Well-proportioned: _____

b. Massive: _____

c. Protruding: _____

d. Plasticity: _____

e. Renowned: _____

2. An image is a picture created with words. What are two outstanding images of dancers in this paragraph?

a. _____

b. _____

3. Here is another example of the B/A pattern, this one focusing on two former presidential candidates:

> In the 1960 presidential campaign the Republicans ran Vice-President Richard M. Nixon and the Democrats, Senator John F. Kennedy. The backgrounds of the two men presented striking contrasts: Kennedy, a Roman Catholic from Massachusetts, was the son of a wealthy man who had served as chairman of the Securities Exchange Commission and as United States ambassador to Britain; Nixon, born a Quaker in California, had to work his way up from relative poverty. But both were young; Nixon was forty-seven years old, and Kennedy was forty-three. Both were experienced and astute politicians, who showed at the national conventions that nominated them that they intended to dominate their parties and run their own campaigns. Both insisted on relatively liberal platforms.
>
> Henry W. Bragdon and Samuel P. McCutcheon,
> *History of a Free People*

4. This clever point-by-point structure from *The New Yorker* details a number of comparisons and contrasts between two food processors. Pay particular attention to the vivid imagery used by the author, Suzannah Lessard:

> . . .The two machines stood side by side, taking up two-thirds of her counter space. Alone, either would have been neutral and fairly uninteresting, but in

conjunction they summoned up a silent, uncompromising war between two entirely different worlds. The KitchenAid reminded one of a nineteen-forties Oldsmobile. It was heavy and rounded, at once motherly and powerful-looking, its shape serenely functional and suggesting a long term of service. It had a quality of modesty and dutifulness, of readiness to go to work but only when asked. In comparison, the Cuisinart looked vain, high-strung, and predatory, and much too eager to prove how smart it was. Those few parts of it whose shape followed their function, such as the plastic cylinder on top, were dinky, giving it an air of here today and gone tomorrow. The heavy base exuded power, but, perhaps because of the lightness of the parts on top, it was a willful, unbalanced kind of power. It gave no sign of loyalty. Clearly, it would as soon chop up you as your mushrooms. The KitchenAid made you think of roomy country houses, of the smell of something baking in the afternoon, of coming in out of the snow, of children. It made you think of cooking as generosity, as an integral part of a texture. It made you think of families. The Cuisinart did not make you think of families. It reminded you of clever, unencumbered adults whose conversation is as swift and sharp as its light blades. It suggested not comfort but competition. Especially after you had seen it work, it made you feel as though you had better watch out and hurry. And it made you think of cooking not as part of a texture but as a hedonistic obsession. The KitchenAid projected a sense of proportion in life, the Cusinart a kind of disproportion in which the importance of some things becomes crazily magnified while others completely disappear.

Suzannah Lessard, "The Talk of the Town"

Exercise 7-4

This paragraph has a number of complicated words that may be unfamiliar to you. Look up each of them in your dictionary and write an appropriate definition:

1. Uncompromising: _____

2. Dutifulness: _____

3. Predatory: _____

4. Exuded: _____

5. Integral: _____

6. Texture: _____

7. Unencumbered: _____

8. Hedonistic: _____ _

9. Obsession: _____

10. Disproportion: _____

Writing Assignment

Compare and Contrast

Write a paragraph of comparison and contrast using two comparable objects. Select objects in the same class, such as these: two luxury foreign cars (Mercedes and BMW); two subcompacts; two kinds of pets; two novels, movies, or dramas; city life and country life; a seashore resort and a mountain village.

The Process Analysis Pattern

The whole-to-parts structure is particularly useful if you are giving a set of directions or describing steps in an operation. These two writing techniques are referred to as *analysis of a process*, which is telling how something is done or how something works.

Directional writing   Have you ever tried to give someone directions to your house? It may be easy to *tell* directions in person or over the phone, but have you ever written out a set of directions? It is often a lengthy process, and it's easy to become confused by such things as the number of stop lights, turns, specific places where you turn, landmarks, or distance. One form process writing takes is *directional writing,* as in maps, recipes, or technical instructions for manuals. Another form of process analysis is *operational writing,* which informs or describes how something works, such as in a set of instructions for a fraternal installation, the registration process at your college, or the steps legislators follow in maneuvering a bill through Congress. Robert's *Rules of Order* is an example of operational writing, a systematic scheme for conducting meetings; it outlines the process a PTA president or DAR regent is likely to follow. Instructions for games, from those included in Monopoly to more formal ones like those established for boxing under the Marquess of Queensbury rules, outline processes.

Operational writing

Audience Analysis

When using either of the two forms, begin by identifying your audience and assessing its needs. How much does the audience know—or need to know—about the process? Questions about age, education, technical knowledge, or other basic areas may of course need to be addressed. But the key audience consideration is *communication.* To communicate you must be clear and logical. Unclear directions will confuse and delay; illogical directions will mislead; incomplete data will lead to an uninformed audience. Occasionally, graphics (drawings, charts, diagrams) will enhance the clarity of your presentation and save time.

Communication

Both directional and operational writing require a logical sequencing of steps or parts. A chronological arrangement may be helpful and may aid clarity. Or you can enumerate the steps or parts of the process by using words like *first, second,* and *third.* Questions a historian might ask—such as who? what? where? why? and when?—may provide structure for special process analyses. Chemistry and math textbooks list steps for experiments and problem-solving strategies using this format. Check your political science or history text for analytical patterns. For an even more graphic example, however, check the instructions on a self-service gas pump:

1. Lift nozzle and insert
2. Turn switch to right
3. Rotate handle to on position

4. Fill tank
5. Return handle to off
6. Replace nozzle in pump

CAUTION

1. Maintain a consistent point of view throughout. For example, if you begin with *you* and imperative mood verbs (those that give orders), use these same pronouns and verbs throughout.
2. Adopt a single stance: be personal and casual or strictly formal in tone.
3. Be totally familiar with the material before trying to describe the process. Plan how you will write before starting.
4. Try to use sensory verbs and create vivid images.
5. Include, if appropriate, negative reminders, such as "don't overheat."

Examples for Analysis

1. Using "I" point of view:

To make up a dance, I will need . . . a pot of tea, walking space, privacy and an idea. . . .

When I first visualize the dance, I see the characters moving in color and costume. Before I go into rehearsal, I know what costumes the people wear and generally what color and texture. I also, to a large extent, hear the orchestral effects. Since I can have ideas only under the stress of emotion, I must create artificially an atmosphere which will induce this excitement. I shut myself in a studio and play gramophone music, Bach, Mozart, Smetana, or almost any folk music in interesting arrangements. At this point I avoid using the score because it could easily become threadbare.

Agnes De Mille, *Dance to the Piper*

2. Using "he" (historical point of view):

First he irrigated the wound with normal salt solution of 100 degrees Fahrenheit, which by that time
was about room temperature. Then he grasped the
edges of the pulsating wound with long smooth for-
ceps. With not a little difficulty, he held the flutter-
ing edges together and, using a continuous suture of
fine catgut, he managed to close the wound. Next he
closed the intercostal and sub-cartilaginous wounds,
again using catgut. For the cartilages and the skin,
he changed to silkworm gut and left a few long
sutures in the external stitches. They would permit
easy removal in case infection or hemorrhage should
develop, though he prayed it would not. Then he
applied a dry dressing, straightened his aching back,
and mopped his brow. The silent, intent circle
around him stirred; someone spoke. The historic
operation was over.

> Note: The past tense is frequently used for reporting scientific information

Helen Buckler, *Dr. Dan: Pioneer in American Surgery*

3. Using "we" point of view:

So we lurched out across the pampa to the first
owl-hole. . . . The hole we had found turned out to
be some eight feet in length, curving slightly like
the letter "C," and about two feet at the greatest
depths below the surface. We discovered all this by
probing gently with a long and slender bamboo.
Having marked out with sticks a rough plan of how
the burrow lay, we proceeded to dig down, sinking
a shaft into the tunnel at intervals of about two feet.
Then each section of tunnel between the shafts was
carefully searched to make sure nothing was hiding
in it, and blocked off with clods of earth. At length
we came to the final shaft, which, if our primitive
reckoning was correct, should lead us down into the
nesting chamber. We worked in excited silence,
gently chipping away the hard-baked soil. At intervals during our excavations we had pressed our ears
to the turf, but there had been no sound from inside, and I was half convinced that the burrow
would prove empty. Then the last crust of earth

gave way, and cascaded into the nesting chamber, and glaring up out of the gloomy hole were two little ash-grey faces, with great dandelion-golden eyes. We all gave a whoop of triumph, and the owls blinked very rapidly and clicked their beaks like castanets. They looked so fluffy and adorable that I completely forgot all about owls' habits, and reached into the ruins of the nest-chamber and tried to pick one up. Immediately they transformed themselves from bewildered bundles consisting of soft plumage and great eyes, to swollen belligerent furies. Puffing out the feathers on their backs, so that they looked twice their real size, they opened their wings on each side of their bodies like feathered shields, and, with clutching talons and snapping beaks, swooped at my hand. I sat back and sucked my bloodstained fingers.

Gerald M. Durrell, *The Drunken Forest.*

4.   Using "you" (understood) point of view:

Prepare a steel rod about five or six feet long, about half an inch thick at its largest end, and tapering to a sharp point. This point should be gilded to prevent its rusting. Secure to the big end of the rod a strong eye or a ring half an inch in diameter. Fix the rod upright to the chimney or the highest part of a house. It should be fixed with some sort of staples or special nails to keep it steady. The pointed end should extend upward, and should rise three or four feet above the chimney or building to which the rod is fixed. Drive into the ground an iron rod about one inch in diameter, and ten or twelve feet long. This rod should also have an eye or ring fixed to its upper end. It is best to place the iron rod some distance from the foundation of the house. Ten feet away is a good distance, if the size of the property permits. Then take as much length of iron rod of a smaller diameter as will be necessary to reach from the eye on the rod above to the eye on the rod below. Fasten this securely to the fixed rods by passing it through the eyes and bending the ends to form rings too. Then close all the joints with lead.

This is easily done by making a small bag of strong paper around the joints, tying it tight below, and then pouring in the molten lead. It is useful to have these joints treated in this way so that there will be a considerable area of contact between each piece. To prevent the wind from shaking this long rod, it may be fastened to the building by several staples. If the building is especially large or long, extending more than one hundred feet for example, it is wise to erect a rod at each end. If there is a well sufficiently near to the building to permit placing the iron rod in the water, this is even better than the use of the iron rod in the ground. It may also be wise to paint the iron to prevent it from rusting. A building so protected will not be damaged by lightning.

Ben Franklin, Letter to David Hume

5. Using "you" point of view:

A very trivial circumstance will serve to exemplify this. Suppose you go into a fruiterer's shop, wanting an apple — you take up one, and, on biting it, you find it sour; you look at it, and see that it is hard and green. You take up another one, and that too is hard, green, and sour. The shopman offers you a third; but, before biting it, you examine it, and find that it is hard and green, and you immediately say that you will not have it, as it must be sour, like those that you have already tried.

Thomas Huxley, *Scientific Investigation*

6. Using third-person (objective) point of view:

Large-scale preparations began on the day before the wedding. The cooks, married couples numbering thirty persons in all, began to arrive at the bride's home at seven o'clock in the morning. Custom requires that the bridegroom cut off the heads of the fowl. Men picked the chickens, ducks, and turkeys. The women washed and dressed them. The women prepared the dressing, stuffed the fowl, washed dishes, baked quantities of pies, peeled two bushels of potatoes, and cracked nuts. The men cleaned celery, supplied plenty of hot water from large kettles, emptied garbage, and constructed temporary tables for the main rooms in the house. These tables, made of wide pine boards and trestles, were placed around three sides of the living room. Two tables were in the kitchen and one in the bedroom, making the equivalent of about six tables with a total seating capacity of one hundred. The dressed, stuffed fowl were placed in the large outside bake oven on the evening before the wedding.

John Hostetler, Amish Society

Writing Assignment

Process

1. Write a paragraph in which you give detailed steps involved in frying an egg.

2. Write a paragraph in which you give step-by-step instructions on how to perform a specific activity, such as how to perform a card trick, water ski, scuba dive, change a tire, administer CPR, or something similar. Prepare a list of numbered steps and use as an outline to write from.

3. Write a *directional* process paragraph on a subject of your choosing or select one of the following:
    a. Give directions for going from your home to your school or job or the nearest bus stop.
    b. Give directions for going from the center of your city to a specific park, lake, stadium, or a key attraction for tourists.

4. Write an *operational* process paragraph on a subject of your choosing or select one of the following:
    a. A fraternal initiation
    b. A marriage ceremony
    c. A holiday custom in your family
    d. Instructions for playing a game

The Enumerative Pattern

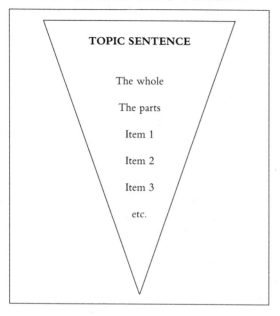

Let's imagine that someone asked you to describe a Mexican pastry, an *empanada*. How would you begin? Would you give a picture of the whole: its color, its size, its shape? Would you be more likely to focus on the various fillings — cherry, mince, and apple — or its crust, color, and texture? The way you look at an empanada — as a whole with separate parts — is analogous to the thinking process used in writing the enumerative-patterned paragraph.

Process questions

This pattern begins by announcing the whole of the subject in the topic sentence. Then it moves quickly away from this whole to enumerate (number) its parts. This type of paragraph needs special markers for coherence as you move from one part to another. The most useful of these is numbering. Many writers use the numerals 1, 2, and 3, enclosing them, occasionally, in parentheses. But to create a more graceful style you might try an alternative approach using enumerative words, such as *first, second, third,* or a word with a similar function: *next, another, initially, still another, last, final, finally, one, two, three,* or phrases such as *first of all, last of all,* or *in addition.* Each of these signals the start of a subtopic sentence that clarifies one part of the whole.

Here is a short paragraph that illustrates this enumerative pattern. Note how the author specifies two problems in the topic sentence and then develops brief comments on each:

The whole

Part one

Part two

    Basically, there are two problems that get in the way of management research. The first is that managers are a diversely educated lot, and their research tools consequently reflect their past education rather than their current needs. The second great hurdle is that managers don't understand the tasks their reference books are supposed to perform. Every journalist knows the difference between fresh-from-the-horse's-mouth primary information and secondary sources, but most managers rely on their reference books for data, which because of the lapse between publication time and use, is almost always old. Having a shelfful of old, out-of-date references just doesn't compare with having a handy telephone and a few books that tell you exactly where to get what you need now and in its most up-to-date form.

Stephen Kindel, "Knowing Where to Look"

Exercise 7–5

1. Is the first "part" of management search problems adequately developed?

2. Does the writer provide sufficient, convincing detail? What additional detail might he have added?

3. What is the second problem management researchers have?

4. What do you think is the difference between a "primary" and a "secondary" source?

_____

_____

_____

The enumerative pattern is useful in summarizing. It provides reminders for the reader about the whole topic and the parts. Since it presents a convenient list, it will help your reader remember the argument advanced, the topic discussed, and the particular items.

This analytical process leads naturally from whole to parts. You have to be careful, however, to present your ideas logically. The enumerative pattern provides you with this organizing structure.

CAUTION

Develop each "part" of the "whole" with a sufficient number of supporting materials. Don't merely list divisions.

Examples for Analysis

1. I suspect that we have a good deal to learn from the 18th-century travelers. First, they saw that their books were printed with dignity, with fine type and wide margins on paper that had some texture to it. Second, they took with them an attitude of mind that delighted in the extravagance and eccentricities of the people they met on their journeys; they were far from being moralists. Third, they had a fine feeling for monuments, by which they meant palaces and castles, towers, churches and gateways, and all carved stonework and woodwork wherever it met the eye. Finally, they were in no hurry.

Robert Payne, "Florence Was Exciting, Venice Overrated"

2. Occasionally, in very casual writing the author might choose to separate ideas into several brief paragraphs. The needs and the educational background of the audience, and the type of publication (in this case, a pop psychology journal) determine the writer's stylistic choices. Carefully note the slight supporting evidence, the brief sentence structure, and the level of vocabulary.

Of course, as I said, I was usually doing these jobs because in one way or another I had chosen to. Also, I knew I was not going to have to do them forever, and I had enough control of my work so that if I did find a better way to do a task, I could then do it that way. Many people, perhaps most people, are not so lucky.

In the second place, students working for money are to some degree being useful, if not to the world at large, at least to someone. Young people are rarely able to feel useful and needed, and for most of them it is both necessary and helpful.

In the third place, work gives young people a chance to get some money without having to beg from their parents. Though begging is bad, having no money is even worse. In a money-based and money-worshipping society, to be without money is to have no dignity, no rights, no place in the world. Young people today feel badly enough about themselves as it is. With no money and no way to get it, they feel even worse. The fact that they spend their money quickly and often foolishly is beside the point. In any case, it is adults who, with expensive advertising and promotion, persuade them to do that.

John Holt, "Growing Up Engaged"

3. A common enumerative pattern in advertising and business communication relies on a list of numbers enclosed in parentheses. These numbered items the writer considers important enough to emphasize separately, possibly even in boldface:

Wayward Tours offers travelers four types of elegant menus, all offering considerable variety. (1) **A**

la carte, a selection of everything—appetizers, entrées, beverages, desserts, all priced separately. (2) **Table d'hôte,** a menu offering complete dinners at a fixed price. (3) **American plan,** a menu that includes meals with the price of the room. (4) **Special menu,** a set meal designed particularly for a special occasion. Each of these permits clients of Wayward Tours to enjoy freedom of choice at a reasonable cost.

4. Look for five words in this student's example that have an enumerative function:

One of the major problems a parent has is getting a young child packed and ready for camp. What do I put in? What do I leave out? These are typical questions the parent might ask. Experienced trunk packers provide a number of useful warnings. Initially, it's best to disregard the clothing suggested in the camp brochure. A child who wears two pairs of tattered blue jeans and one pair of sneakers all summer long does not need either five or six pairs of trousers or several pairs of shoes. Another bit of advice is to include many types of hats for a variety of occasions. They make packing a comb and brush almost unnecessary! Other experienced trunk packers say it's important to label everything, from sheets and underwear to orthodontal appliances. Still others suggest pasting a complete clothing and supplies list inside a child's trunk, as it will help the child locate possessions and provide the parent with an inventory of what's been lost. A final suggestion is to leave some vacant space in the trunk for items the child collects over the summer, from craft projects to other kinds of litter!

Exercise 7–6

Write an enumerative paragraph on vacations or trips. What items, for example, should you take on a wilderness hike? a ride down the Colorado River rapids? a ski vacation in Vermont or northern California?

Classification

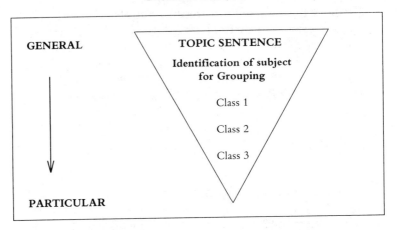

I am a man of medium height. I keep my records in a Weiss Folder Re-order Number 8003. The unpaid balance of my estimated tax for the year 1945 is item 3 less the sum of items 4 and 5. My eyes are gray. My Selective Service order number is 10789. The serial number is T1654. I am in Class IV-A, and have been variously in Class 3-A, Class I-A(H), and Class 4-H. My social security number is 067-01-9841. I am married to U.S. Woman Number 067-01-9807. Her eyes are gray. This is not a joint declaration, nor is it made by an agent; therefore it need be signed only by me—and, as I said, I am a man of medium height.

E. B. White, "About Myself"

E. B. White here takes a close look at himself. He is relying on a very common, man-made categorizing technique to help us see him: classification. He uses sizes, numbers, and colors to classify himself in an amusing way.

Definition   Paragraphs that *classify,* depending on the writer's particular purpose, help identify specific, significant differences within a group. For example, ribbons classify six categories of winners in horse shows: *blue* (first place), *red* (second place), *yellow* (third place), *white* (fourth place), *pink* (fifth place), *green* (sixth place). Soldiers are classified and thereby differentiated by rank, such as privates, captains, majors, generals, commissioned or noncommissioned officers.

But categories may also be divided. *Division* is the act   **Definition**
of refining within a category. The category of "general" may
be further divided into the five categories: brigadier general,
major general, lieutenant general, general, and general of the
armies. The following chart about dogs illustrates divisions
with classification.

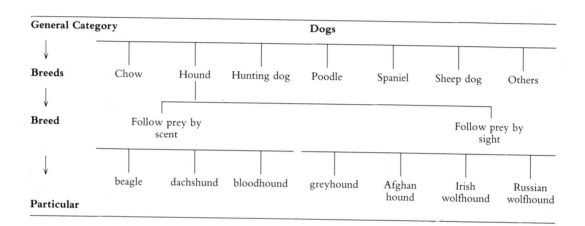

In the chart we are extending what we did earlier with
the list of five divisions of generals. We have refined the
category "dogs" by general breeds, then focused on one
breed, the hound, further dividing this single breed into
dogs characterized by how they follow their prey. Such
refinement of categories is a natural part of our thinking
about or writing about a subject. The second chart shows
how a paragraph might be organized using the categorizing
and dividing methods.

In writing classification paragraphs, keep these writing
principles in mind:

1. Use clear and sharp distinctions.   **Process points**
2. In refining categories, remember to divide into two
   or more categories; it is impossible to *divide* (a
   mathematical principle, remember) into one part.
3. Use the same criteria when establishing your groups.
4. Make clear whether you have an exhaustive list of
   distinctions or one that is fairly general or incomplete.

TOPIC SENTENCE NAMES A NUMBER OF CATEGORIES

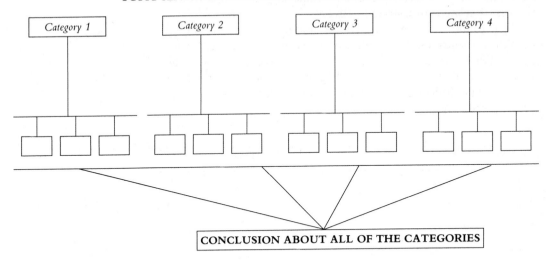

Examples for Analysis

1. This is a portion of the opening paragraph of a well-known essay using classification organization.

We have divided men into Red-Bloods and Mollycoddles. "A Red-blood man" is a phrase which explains itself; "mollycoddle" is its opposite. We have adopted it from a famous speech by Mr. Roosevelt, and redeemed it—perverted it, if you will—to other uses. A few examples will make the notion clear. Shakespeare's Henry V is a typical Red-blood; so was Bismarck; so was Palmerston; so is almost any business man. On the other hand, typical Mollycoddles were Socrates, Voltaire, and Shelley. The terms, you will observe, are comprehensive and the types very broad. Generally speaking, men of action are Red-bloods. Not but what the Mollycoddle may act, and act efficiently. But, if so, he acts from principle, not from the instinct for action. . . .

G. Lowes Dickinson, "Red-Bloods and
Mollycoddles," *A Reader for Writers*

Class one   2.   There are three kinds of book owners. The first has all the standard sets and best-sellers—unread, untouched. (This deluded individual owns wood-pulp and ink, not books.) The second has a great many books — a few of them read through, most of them dipped into, but all of them as clean and shiny as the day they were bought. (This person would probably like to make books his own, but is restrained by a false respect for their physical appearance.) The third has a few books or many — every one of them dog-eared and dilapidated, shaken and loosened by continued use, marked and scribbled in from front to back. (This man owns books.)

Class two

Class three

Mortimer J. Adler, "How to Mark a Book"

3.   Watchers of sandpiles know that not all sandpiles are alike. They know that there are sandpiles in public playgrounds, they know that the beach is a haven of other public sandpiles, and they know that at last there are SANDPILES, though proficiency in sandpile-watching may demonstrate the existence of other classes. The expert knows that the sandpile in the public playground has the same composition as any in private yards, save for the greater incidence of rocks, toy soldiers, spoons, and shovels, but he also knows that it doesn't permit that sovereign sense the child has in his own domain. The expert also understands that the beach sandpile, composed much like that in the public playground but for a new ingredient, shells, and a new sense, the sound of ocean, which makes forts all the more desirable in sand, likewise forbids the exercise of monarchy except temporarily. But he who *knows* sandpiles, knows that the private sandpile in the backyard is an empire untroubled except by brothers and sisters and occasional friends, and they can be managed when the vision is strong.

Topic sentence

Class one: Public sandpiles

Class two: Beach sandpiles

Class three: Private sandpiles

Jim W. Corder and Lyle H. Kendall, Jr., *A College Rhetoric*

4.   There are different kinds of feminine blushes. There is the coarse brick-red blush which romantic writers always use so freely when they let their heroines blush all over. There is the delicate blush; it is the blush of the spirit's dawn. In a young girl it is priceless. The passing blush produced by a

happy idea is beautiful in a man, more beautiful in a young man, charming in a woman. It is a gleam of lightning, the heat lightning of the spirit. It is most beautiful in the young, charming in a girl because it appears in her girlishness, and therefore it has also the modesty of surprise. The older one becomes, the more rarely one blushes.

Sören Kierkegaard, *Either/Or*

5.   With respect to my own observations, I've noticed many sociolinguistic elements that fit the stereotype. First, Texas ladies often — but certainly not always — sound "Southern." They have evident drawls although they are not identical to the sounds of the Deep South. Second, certain lexical items and syntactic structures not in my dialect caught my ear, e.g., "I'm fixin' to grab me a bite" or "Is this y'all's iced tea?" Third, the *gestalt* of the Texas lady is incomplete without the nonverbal elements of her communication. Clearly, the way a lady socializes is crucial, and her success at socializing depends largely on how appropriately she uses paralinguistic as well as linguistic features.

Celia Genishi, "Texas Ladies' Talk: A View from the Tower"

6. Classification may also use enumerative techinques to provide a list of distinguishing characteristics, as in the following paragraph:

These features may not be unique to Texas ladies, but they are highly exaggerated forms of ladies'/women's talk in general. Robin Lakoff enumerates features of what she terms women's talk that set it apart from men's:

1.   The frequency of words related to interests associated with women, e.g., cooking and sewing: *braise, dart,* etc.

2.   Adjectives like *charming, cute, darling*

3.   Frequent question intonation

4.   Hedges like "sort of," "kind of," etc.

5.   Use of the intensive *so,* as in "I like him so much."

6. Hypercorrect grammar
7. Superpolite forms (no swearing or off-color remarks)
8. Absence of jokes
9. Oral italics to emphasize certain parts of utterances.

> Celia Genishi, "Texas Ladies' Talk:
> A View from the Tower"

7. There are many ways people in the Southwest fight windstorms that usually blow into town in mid-March. Note how Craig Phelon gives us a few personality types that emerge from the way people battle the wind:

> Despite all these handicaps, the man managed to come up with a pretty logical theory on wind positions. Here is a sample of the personality types he recognized in downtown El Paso. THE BULL-DOZER. This is the type who trudges straight into the wind, with head lowered and eyes closed. He is self-reliant and aggressive but also pretty dumb. Walking around like that, he is likely to bump into telephone poles, knock over little old ladies or get run over in traffic. That's why we don't see very many bulldozer types in El Paso. THE SIDEWIND-ER. A majority appear to be in this category. It includes those who use a shoulder like the prow of a ship to offer less resistance to the oncoming wind. This type knows how to deal with the give-and-take situations of life. He is more likely to compromise his position than the bulldozer type, but less likely to run into telephone poles. . . . THE CLINGER. Often one will see a person who flits from one solid object to another. He'll grab a lamp post for security, then make a mad dash for the side of a building, a parking meter or telephone pole. Between stops, the wind blows the clinger around in circles as if he were a rag doll. The clinger is a basically insecure individual, not ready to deal with reality — which is a perfectly normal response to El Paso's windy season.

> Craig Phelon, *El Paso Times*

Writing Assignment

1. Write a paragraph in which you classify three or four personality types; select types you know well and give them appropriate name tags as Craig Phelon does — Sidewinder and Clinger. You might choose to classify blind dates, clerks in stores, fast-food servers, instructors, classmates, and the like.

2. Write a paragraph in which you classify items in comparable levels, such as classifying makes of sports cars, subcompact cars, types of music, musical instruments, students, teachers, dates, customers, news commentators, and the like.

The Argument Pattern

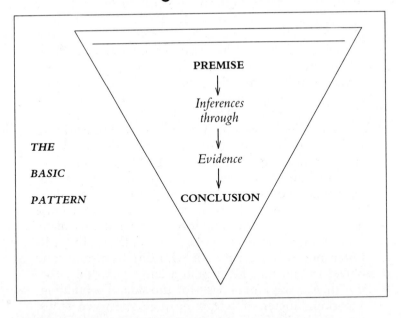

THE

BASIC

PATTERN

PREMISE
↓
*Inferences
through*
↓
Evidence
↓
CONCLUSION

Definition   Simply stated, an *argument* means the drawing of conclusions from a premise. It makes a claim supported by evidence (whatever legitimizes the claim) or by implication (whatever conclusions may be drawn from the claim). An argument becomes persuasive when your evidence convinces an audience that your conclusions are valid. There are three basic parts to an argument outlined in the diagram above: (1) the premise that states the claim; (2) the inferences drawn from evidence about the premise; and (3) the conclusion drawn from the evidence that proves the claim. For this argument there must be a known audience whose needs, biases, and beliefs have been previously considered and examined.

Three parts

A second feature of an argumentative paragraph is that the topic sentence becomes a premise that you want to prove and have the audience accept, or at least understand if they can't accept. This *premise* must be an arguable statement, not merely a personal opinion or assumption. (See Chapter 3.) It should be a precisely worded, absolute statement, subject to only one interpretation, either negative or affirmative. Even though you may have strong personal feelings about a particular side of the argument, the premise itself is objective, free from personal bias. Were personal bias a part of the premise, then you would be expressing only an opinion, not an arguable point. To phrase a premise, the beginning writer might find the following pattern helpful:

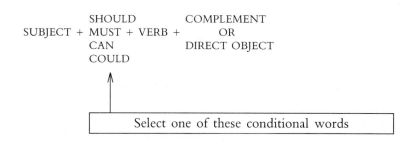

```
                SHOULD        COMPLEMENT
SUBJECT +  MUST  +  VERB  +        OR
                CAN           DIRECT OBJECT
                COULD
                  ↑
                  |
      ┌───────────────────────────────────────┐
      │  Select one of these conditional words │
      └───────────────────────────────────────┘
```

Examples: Professional soccer players should have the right to strike.

All automobiles should be equipped with automatic seat restraints.

Dieters must participate in a regular exercise program.

Shared responsibilities for home chores can strengthen family ties.

Exercise 7–7

Using the preceding examples as models, write a premise on each of the following topics:

1. Apartheid in South Africa

    _____

2. Trade with Japan

    _____

3. Travel in Mexico

    _____

4. Car seats for children

    _____

5. Single-parent family

    _____

6. Bicycle messengers

    _____

If your argument requires a special language that may be unfamiliar, you will need to define key terms. Ambiguity in terminology is a genuine problem in argumentation. Abstract words, technical terms, foreign terminology—all of these will need defining in the context of your argument to ensure that unambiguous communication can take place.

Support for premises

Aristotelian appeals

For support of the premises you can rely on a number of appeals. The three most common are the Aristotelian appeals—ethical, logical, and emotional. Select one or two consistent with your audience. With some, an emotional appeal would be preferable (for example, a Save the Children solicitation), whereas others might reject an emotional appeal but might be persuaded by a logical one (for example, a college admissions board or a promotion review committee).

Ethical appeal

To advance an ethical argument, you need to create a

self-image of trustworthiness and unselfishness. You need to project a high moral character and common sense; above all, you must have the good will of the public in your rhetoric. For instance, both the television evangelist and the politician project an image of high moral character and common sense. If the public learns that their personal lives are not above reproach, the ethical appeals of both become suspect. Above all, to be effective an ethical appeal must have credibility.

To project a logical appeal for the argument, your concern shifts from self to reasoned appeals and universal truths. For this approach, use either inductive or deductive patterns as suggested by the accompanying charts.

Logical appeal

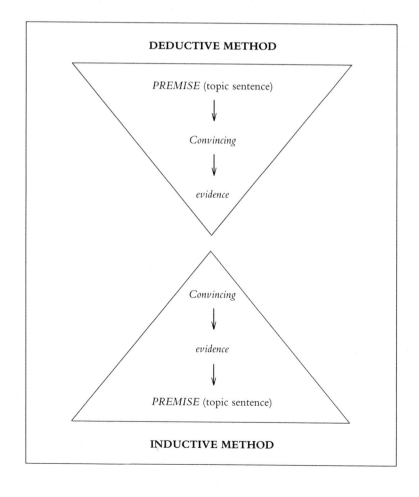

Evidence must include some of the following: facts, statistics, expert testimony that convinces, reliable documentation, and possibly even appropriate literary allusions for purposes of clarification. (See Chapter 4 for an explanation of supporting materials.)

Psychological Strategies

Maslow's Hierarchy of Needs   To create an emotional appeal, your argument must include psychological strategies and consider fundamental human needs, such as those Abraham Maslow categories as forces human beings to respond to and act on. Briefly summarized, they are:

1. *Physiological needs* — basic biological survival needs: food, air, water, shelter
2. *Safety needs* — security, desire for order, law, freedom from fear and harm
3. *Belongingness needs* — love, need for approval of and acceptance by family, children, peer groups
4. *Esteem needs* — self-esteem, desire for recognition, prestige, status
5. *Self-actualization needs* — desire to fulfill a sense of self-worth, achieving what we believe we are capable of achieving.

Abraham Maslow, "A Theory of Human Motivation"

TWO TOPICS USING MASLOW'S HIERARCHY AND EMOTIONAL APPEALS

Topic	*Need*
1. Disposal of nuclear waste	Physiological need (threat to air, environment, food) Safety need (threat to personal security; freedom from fear of nuclear contamination and disease, such as radiation poisoning)
2. Immigrants and their children	Belongingness needs (acceptance by peers in school, achieving naturalization, desire of child to achieve parental approval)

Esteem needs (achieving high scholastic recognition or honors at school, attending an Ivy League or other prestigious school, acquiring a title, having recognition on the job)

The Motivated Sequence   Another paradigm for argument that you might like to follow in a long paper is a five-step "motivated sequence" developed by Douglas Ehninger and Alan Monroe (*Principles and Types of Speech Communication*, 8th ed.).

1. *Attention step.* Design a strategy that will attract and hold the attention of your audience. Your first words should startle or shock.

2. *Need step.* Begin with an analysis of the problem, illustrating by typical examples and other concrete evidence. Illustrate the gravity of the need by citing expert testimony, statistics, or other supporting materials. (See Chapter 3.) It is vital here to point out how this need relates to your audience.

3. *Satisfaction step.* Present a convincing solution to the problem. Show how it satisfies the audience's needs. Use positive proof with facts and evidence to support your claim.

4. *Visualization step.* Help your audience imagine the results of accepting your solution. Propel them into the future. Picture the results of the solution or the devastating consequences of not adopting it.

5. *Action step.* Sum up with a forceful clincher. Ask your audience to act, to do one specific thing. Possibly use emotion to incite your audience to respond to your solution.

The motivated sequence is a simple, effective structure for presenting an argument. Look for examples of it in solicitations from charitable organizations, in letters from political action groups, or in public addresses by those advocating a cause. This opening attention step in a solicitation letter from the National Headquarters of the Disabled American Veterans illustrates how effective only one part of the motivated sequence is:

We're all for belt tightening . . .
BUT WHAT ABOUT THE VETERAN
WITH NO HANDS
TO WORK HIS BUCKLE?

The dramatic question and the capital letters create a dynamic impression.

Refuting the Opposition

When there is strong opposition to your argument, you will need to develop a systematic response to the objections. For a rebuttal to be effective you need to avoid personal attacks (the *ad hominem* argument) that would threaten your opponent and might possibly backfire. Instead of attacking your opponent personally, you need to adopt a reasonable, logical response that persuades rather than annoys. Organize your refutation into clearly defined parts that point out fallacies in the opposing argument, which may be illogical, false, or absurd. And make concessions whenever they are appropriate.

Let's imagine that you are before a local school board advocating the implementation of a bilingual-education program in an elementary school curriculum. After considerable research and consultation with professionals, you have concluded that such a program is valid. Each member of the school board has a copy of your proposal. Your task now is to defend it before the whole board. How do you proceed?

First, restate clearly your opponents' objections, clarifying any misunderstandings you have about their position. Acknowledge or concede worthwhile points your opponent has.

Second, question evidence. Is it logical, relevant, accurate, or absurd? Confront your opponent with your objections in a tactful, objective manner.

Third, maintain a courteous, sensitive stance, being particularly careful not to offend the opponents.

Fourth, present counterevidence that persuades the validity of your position. Refutation is more appropriate in long papers than in short ones.

Fifth, be willing to concede if the opponent's arguments have some merit. Be moderate and reasonable. The opposition is not totally wrong, yet you need not be conciliatory if the opponent's position is basically unacceptable. If you want to concede points, you might rely on such switch words as *but, however, nevertheless,* and *on the other hand.*

Sixth, express conviction about your position, yet do so with moderation, not stubbornness.

Effective argument — whether your appeal is ethical, logical, or emotional — depends upon the evidence and the selection of effective supporting material rather than on your personality or your ability to use emotionally scented words, name-calling, or other manipulative tactics. An irresponsible arguer may rely on personality and shoddy tactics to sway the audience. Politicians often rely on these shoddy devices and unreliable advertising gimmickry to win votes or persuade uncommitted voters, but even they can't fool all of the people all of the time, to paraphrase Abraham Lincoln. The three most effective types of supporting material are typical examples, reliable expert testimony, and defensible statistics. There are, of course, other types of support, such as comparisons or contrasts, definitions, instances, case studies, or those discussed fully in Chapter 3. They are also useful, but not always needed.

CHECKLIST

1. Is the premise stated so that the arguable issue is clear?
2. Are ambiguous terms defined?
3. Is the tone consistent and appropriate?
4. Is the language suitable for the treatment of the subject, occasion, and audience?
5. Is the audience clearly defined by its needs? Are these needs addressed?
6. Is there a logical progression from premise to evidence to conclusion?
7. Is there adequate supporting material — reliable facts, typical examples, appropriate comparisons or contrasts, accurate statistics?
8. Is the expert testimony from expert sources?

9.   Are logical conclusions reached?

10.   Is the opponent's point of view successfully refuted?

Examples for Analysis

1.   From work we move to culture. There is much that we could say about the shabbiness and tawdriness of American mass culture, about neon signs and hot-dog stands, but it has been well said elsewhere, and is of no special concern here. Our concern is with culture and consciousness. Culture in America provides one more manifestation of the concept of impoverishment by substitution. Because of the substitution phenomenon, one of the prime characteristics of American culture is that the genuine is replaced by the simulated. When the radio gives us five minutes of news, there is staccato noise or music in the background, sounds of explosions, fighting, or catastrophes to simulate excitement; we are not allowed to find excitement in the news itself. It is possible to buy pre-mixed peanut butter and jelly, and frozen "Japanese style" vegetables. Restaurants in shopping centers offer "Chinese" or "French" food that is an ersatz version of the real thing. Deodorants obliterate the smells of the human body, and then perfumes and sprays coat the body with a manufactured smell. The problem with this ersatz culture is that all that is meaningful in the experience is lost in the substitution. Homemade ice cream is an experience that makes an impact on consciousness. When something is put in its place, the ability to experience the genuine is reduced. In this sense, fake Chinese food is worse than none, for it deadens our curiosity and makes our ignorance more stubborn.

Premise

Evidence

General example

Specific example

Specific example

Specific example

Conclusion

Charles A. Reich, *The Greening of America*

2.   It is possible to stop most drug addiction in the United States within a very short time. Simply make all drugs available and sell them at cost. Label each drug with a precise description of what effect—good or bad—the drug will have on whoever takes it. This

will require heroic honesty. Don't say that marijuana is addictive or dangerous when it is neither, as millions of people know—unlike "speed," which kills most unpleasantly, or heroin, which is addictive and difficult to kick.

Gore Vidal

| Exercise 7–8 |

1. What is the basic argument of Vidal's paragraph?

    _____

    _____

2. Does he sound serious or humorous about his position? What words or phrases lead you to this conclusion?

    _____

    _____

3. Should other drugs be included in his list, such as alcohol? If so, list them.

    _____

    _____

3.   One of the hardest things for a woman with aspirations to do in our society is to admit, first to herself and then to others, that she has ambitions that go beyond the routine—a good marriage, clever children. Early on, we learn that men don't take kindly to the notion of a woman entering the competitive lists. It is in the nature of power and position that those who have it do not relinquish it graciously, as all colonial peoples and all minority groups discover at a certain stage in their development. Well, O.K. so be it. But infinitely more damaging to our psyche is the realization that our ambitions are met with equal hostility—pooh-poohed, sniffed at, scoffed at, ignored, or worse, not taken seriously—by mothers, sisters,

cousins, aunts, and friends, who won't believe that we
have set our sights on a different sort of goal than *they*
have envisioned, preferring instead to believe that our
ambition is merely a "passing phase" — which, unfortunately, it often is because of lack of encouragement.

Susan Brownmiller, "The Enemy Within"

Exercise 7–9

1. Briefly summarize the main idea of Susan Brownmiller's
    paragraph.

    _____

    _____

2. What is Ms. Brownmiller's position about competitive-
    ness between men and women?

    _____

    _____

3. When she refers to "colonial peoples," what exactly
    does she mean? What groups do you know that once
    were "colonial peoples"?

    _____

    _____

4. How does Ms. Brownmiller concede a point in the
    second sentence of the preceding paragraph?

    _____

5. Examine carefully the verbs in sentence four. How
    do they convey Ms. Brownmiller's feeling about her
    subject?

    _____

    _____

6. What does Ms. Brownmiller mean by a "passing phase"?

_____

_____

7. This paragraph originally appeared in *Mademoiselle*. How do you think Ms. Brownmiller expresses sensitivity to a particular audience in this paragraph? Or do you believe she is writing for a general audience? How can you tell?

_____

_____

_____

_____

8. Formulate a premise that is similar to the one you worked out earlier in this chapter. (See pp. 191.) You may use some of the ideas from Ms. Brownmiller's paragraph to help develop an argumentative edge to your thinking. Develop a brief argumentative paragraph that includes a topic sentence, at least three subtopic sentences, and supporting sentences for each subtopic. Be sure to clinch your argument in the last sentence with a forceful summary sentence.

9. Go to the library and look up Susan Brownmiller in your card catalogue or computer. List two of her books.

_____

_____

_____

Writing Assignment

Deduction

1. Examine one strongly held opinion, yours or another's (example: I hate peanut butter), and carefully analyze the assumption, or assumptions, it is based upon.

2. Examine advertisements in a popular magazine seeking examples of deductive reasoning. Then write a paragraph in which you analyze the underlying assumptions and determine the truth or validity of the deduction you have made.

# Special Paragraphs for the Whole Theme	# CHAPTER 8

Some paragraphs are mainly functional. That is, they do not develop ideas or argue positions. Instead, they play an organizational role by performing a special task within a larger context. They can provide bridges among sections of a long paper; they can introduce or conclude. These special paragraphs follow no set pattern, but within each there are strategies you will want to learn.

Minor Paragraphs

A *minor paragraph* can be a one- or two-sentence unit of a longer piece of writing. Possibly a fragment. It neither has a topic sentence nor develops an idea. Usually, we can identify it by length, yet its length has no real bearing on its function. (Sometimes length may merely indicate inadequate development of a major idea.) It is important for beginning writers to distinguish a developmental paragraph from a minor one. Take time now to review the definition of a *developmental paragraph* (see pp. 4–5). Definition

A minor paragraph is functional, serving many different purposes: Functions

1.   to introduce a piece of writing
2.   to conclude a piece of writing

3. to bridge thought units (transitional)

4. to provide additional supporting material for a lengthy developmental paragraph

CAUTION

Be careful, though, as the label *minor* might be a bit misleading. The paragraph itself is important in the development of an entire essay. Only because it is functional does it have the name *minor*. For example, both the introductory and concluding paragraphs of a long theme are extremely crucial because they either introduce your main idea or help draw inferences from your whole argument that will stay in your reader's mind. Thus, it's very important for you to draw clear distinctions in your mind between those paragraphs that develop an idea fully and those that serve a functional purpose.

Introductory Paragraphs

Prince Charles wears one, but then so does Frank Sinatra. Baron Stackelberg's son has one that was designed by Fabergé. Actor George Hamilton wears one. And the Countess Carimati has two—a gold one and one with her husband's coat of arms emblazoned on a large emerald. Count Carimati's is made of steel, lined in gold to keep his finger from turning green.

Ellen Bilgore, "The Return of the Signet Ring"

What is Ellen Bilgore doing in this brief description? Is she playing with us? Tantalizing us? Or does she have a serious purpose? In actuality, what she has done is capture our interest by concealing her aim; she has piqued our curiosity.

Bilgore's second paragraph reveals the real subject matter of her article—signet rings:

Since the middle of the twelfth century signet rings have routinely adorned the pinkies of European landed classes. And in the eight centuries since then, the custom that was once purely utilitarian has acquired as many flourishes as the intricate engraving on the planed surfaces of the rings themselves.

What makes an introductory paragraph unique, however, is that it is functional rather than developmental. That is, it lacks a topic sentence, it provides no supporting material in subtopic sentences, it does not develop single points. Rather, as in the Bilgore example, it introduces. It gets things started and shows where you are going in your paper.

Arouse Reader Interest

The major function of any type of introduction in any form of communication—a single paragraph, multiparagraphs, entire chapters, employment interviews, banquet speeches, persuasive letters—is to arouse reader interest. To entice, to grab or snare the reader's attention, to overcome the "ho-hum, why-should-I-read-this" attitude, we rely on a number of different rhetorical strategies. Readers can be fickle. If you don't grab them with your opening words, they will abandon you.

Strategies

There is no single formula or pattern for writing introductions, but the following strategies—used alone or at times in combinations—might be helpful:

1. Use an anecdote (a brief story—real or fictional) that establishes mood and possibly presents a character profile.
2. Use multiple anecdotes (several examples of problems at local savings and loan associations, parking chaos at a number of malls in the community).
3. Begin with a shocker sentence ("They laid Jesse James in his grave and Dante Gabriel Rossetti died immediately."—Thomas Beer, *The Mauve Decade*).
4. Use a bold jest, witty saying, quotation, or fable (a story using animal characters) that relates to the subject matter. ("A man with clenched fists can't shake hands.")
5. Try stating a paradox or apparent contradiction. (Tell what something is; then undercut your comments by stating exceptions.)
6. Provide some historical background.

Hernando de Soto passed through here in 1540. Elvis Presley was born here in 1935. That was about it in Tupelo, Mississippi history, until . . .

7. Echo a key word or idea from your title.
8. Begin with a question.

("Does maintaining a reasonable weight seem like an uphill struggle — on a skateboard?")

— or a series of questions.

"Is inflation about to surge? And where is it coming from? What will the Federal Reserve do about interest rates?" Be sure you plan to answer them in your paper.

9. Tell the other side of the story or discuss various divisions of the subject, which you do not plan to treat. Try using an unconventional story.
10. Define key terms.
11. Develop a literary allusion or an analogy that imaginatively connects to your subject.
12. Give instructions in memo form to a real or imaginary person.
13. Leave out a key detail that the reader will not expect you to omit, delaying it until the end of the introductory paragraph.
14. Establish a catchy comparison or contrast (two eccentric chefs, two unconventional dancers).
15. Begin with a stream of consciousness, allowing a character to reminisce, to open up his or her thoughts — particularly useful in narratives or character sketches.
16. Begin with a problem you hope to solve.

The Purpose Statement

A second major function is to state the *purpose* and *thesis* of the communication, especially in long essays or formal addresses. A *purpose statement* establishes the rhetorical control a writer uses to approach the subject, the occasion, and the audience. That is, it identifies in its verb the writer's

Definition

rhetorial stance, whether the paper will analyze, argue, define, explain, narrate, and so forth. Many instructors prefer the purpose statement to have infinitive phrasing, as in the following examples:

> The purpose of this library research paper is to argue that the federal laws for the possession of marijuana are unjust.

> The controlling purpose of this investigation is to analyze two reasons why the orangutang is on the brink of extinction.

> My purpose is to analyze apparently contradictory interpretations of Ernest Hemingway's ending in "The Short Happy Life of Francis Macomber" and to determine the validity of each point of view.

> The purpose of this analysis is to account for the sudden rise to popularity of the Beatles during the 1960s.

The Thesis Statement

A *thesis statement** sets forth the main conclusion of the entire composition that will be verified. Some instructors prefer that it be a single sentence, declarative in form, subject to only one interpretation, and narrowed to a single idea. It is a proposition the writer hopes to prove.

Definition

> The orangutang faces extinction because of the demands of zoos and because its natural habitat is being destroyed.

> The phenomenal success of the Beatles throughout the 1960s is the result of their early musical experimentation in Germany, their conscientious management by Brian Epstein, and their willingness to alter their musical style.

Some instructors prefer that both the purpose statement and the thesis appear in a particular order or place in the introduction. Other instructors may have a different format for constructing both statements. Regardless of placement, the purpose and thesis statements will help you limit your focus and subject.

*Students should not confuse a thesis statement with a master's thesis, which is a substantial, formal paper completed as part of the requirements for a master's degree.

Audience Connections

Another function of the introduction is to establish rapport between you and the audience. The introduction helps create an image of you that the audience can accept, particularly if you wish to establish yourself as someone who is informed and reliable. Introductions should put the audience in a receptive frame of mind. Introductions confirm that the subject matter is worthy of the audience's time and attention and relevant to their lives. Here, you connect yourself to the topic by explaining, however briefly, how you became involved in it. You can also connect yourself to the audience by pointing out things you have in common. Harmony between you and the audience will make your ideas or arguments acceptable.

Length

How long should an introduction be? For a book, an entire chapter might serve as introduction, whereas in a freshman-level research paper perhaps one or two paragraphs will suffice. In an extremely short piece of writing a single sentence might serve as an introduction. Only you can know whether you have fully and completely introduced your topic. Note this effective but brief introduction:

Beginning now, count to 60, slowly.
   During those 60 seconds, about seven cars were stolen or broken into somewhere in the United States. Chances are that none of the thieves will be caught.

Carin Rubenstein, *Psychology Today*.

Introductions: False Starts

But when do you write an introduction? Do you write it first? Or do you delay? There is no set time, primarily because in the writing process there are so many false starts: you write, stop, discard, write again, toss out, start over. This is true because writing, as you recall, is not a linear process; it's recursive; it loops back and forward and back again. Normally you write the finished introduction *after* you have developed the middle (the body or discussion portion) of your paper or possibly after you have composed a first draft. That is, you write the introduction when you have something to introduce. As you write, constantly think about tightening the thesis, omitting material, rearranging, or even discarding ideas. You seldom fully understand or control a subject until you have written about it. Thus, you may have to delay writing the introduction until you have a full grasp of the subject and have decided what precisely you want to do with it.

CAUTION

1. Be careful of tone and attitude. Don't be cute when the subject is grave.
2. Don't be apologetic.
3. Don't be long winded; keep introductions short and precise. Don't announce what you're going to do. Simply begin.
4. Avoid triteness and phoniness.
5. Avoid being repetitious and misleading, vague and ambiguous.
6. Define unfamiliar terms.

Exercise 8–1

1. Raul's teacher has made the following comment on his introductory paragraph: "Combine short paragraphs into a forceful introduction. What's your thesis? What position do you take?" Revise Raul's paragraph, introducing a possible thesis and combining the three short paragraphs into one:

The Dilemma of Steroid Legalization

The use of steroids has reached epidemic proportions. Predictions are that we will see a continued increase in the use of this drug throughout the world during the rest of this century. It is therefore becoming increasingly important to address the question of whether or not steroids should be legalized.

Currently, it is against the law to have anabolic steroids without a medical prescription. It is also illegal to

have them with the intent to sell. It is not illegal to pos-
sess steroids.

Among those who argue for the legalization of steroids
are some users, trainers and coaches, and pharmaceutical
companies.

2. Deborah's teacher asks, "Where is your thesis? What
    will you argue about wage discrimination? Several
    vague, sketchy sentences." Rethink the paragraph.
    What might Deborah's thesis be? (She has paragraphs
    about equal pay for equal work, sex differential in
    ranks within corporations, classification of employees,
    and wage discrimination.) Do you find some vague,
    sketchy sentences in Deborah's introduction that
    might be deleted, expanded, or made more specific?

Wage Discrimination: Is It a Reality of Life?

Many people believe that our society has changed for
the better. Yes, in some cases it has changed for the better.
Yet, rights for people or, as I should say, for women have
changed since the 1950's. They have been given rights
that are supposed to help and not hinder themselves. Yet,
the courts have decided in favor of what is right, which in
most cases means the men. Women have fought the courts
to receive equal pay for equal work. Granted in some cases,
women are treated with the respect they deserve for doing
the same job as a man. Yet in a lot of other cases they are
treated as a lower class species.

3. At the end of Hector's full-page introduction for a
    research paper, the teacher asks, "Where's your
    thesis?" Hector's title is circled, with the teacher's
    comment "Vague — can you make this title more spe-
    cific?" Provide a better one. Where might you echo
    it within the paragraph?

Amnesty

Throughout the years, the population of illegal aliens
has been increasing in the United States. No one really has
a correct figure on how many illegals are in the United

States. An estimate of hundreds of thousands migrate to the United States each year. To help curve the problem, the United States under the pressure of political powerful growers of California and Florida, who need to meet a labor necessity introduced the Immigration Reform and Control Act of 1986. This act states illegal aliens are allowed to apply for residency if living in the United States before January 1, 1982. Under the Immigration Reform and Control Act of 1986, the Seasonal Agricultural Worker Program (SAW), was established for farm workers. This program which is more lenient to the farm workers need to meet two requirements: To have worked in seasonal U.S. agricultural jobs for at least 90 days in each of three consecutive years, and worked at least 90 days during the year ending May 1, 1986. Farm workers were given an extra year and a half to meet these requirements.

4.   Eddie's teacher writes in the margin next to his introduction, "Good intro." Do you agree? List three effective characteristics of Eddie's paragraph. Where might the paragraph still be improved?

Clean Air in Demand

As I entered the corridor at the Special Events Center for the basketball game, I had arrived at a polluted arena filled with smoke. As I walked half way around the arena to my seating section my eyes began to burn and my allergies began to react to the smoke. This was the first time in my entire life that smoke had ever affected me in that way. I suddenly began to realize how devastating the effects of smoke could be, especially for those people with health problems such as emphysema. Because this issue is so very serious, it must be treated seriously. So, I argue that smoking must be banned in public places.

Examples for Analysis

1. Let's first look at a fairly successful introductory paragraph that Rosalind wrote to classify types of husbands. It's light, it's laden with irony, it's full of humor. Even the

categories themselves establish the humorous tone she uses throughout:

> For generations the human female has been conditioned to regard the matrimonial state as her ultimate goal in life. Although she is aware that such a state involves a husband, no one has ever definitely categorized husbands—at the laywoman's level. There is a great body of scientific research on this subject and it is the objective of this report to present a condensed version of the findings in the above research and to present them in everyday language. As regards husbandly types, there are innumerable variations and combinations but we shall concern ourselves with only the three major categories. Among trained observers the primary types of husbands are known as: Husbands Absentia, Husbands Presentia, and Are-You-Sure-He's-Still-Breathing? For the benefit of the laywoman we shall dispense with such highly scientific terminology and refer to the categories as "Here husbands," "There husbands," and "Where? husbands."

2. Note the surprise of the first sentence of this paragraph:

> Morgan can talk about mud for hours, earnestly, enthusiastically. It's a science in itself. Out at the drill sites, it flows in closed loops, recirculating after being filtered and cleaned by a series of massive, oily machines. Good mud is characterized by its ability to grip the rubble and carry it upward, Morgan explains. For optimum performance, the mud must be altered slightly to fit the specifics of the earth through which the drill is chewing. So Morgan flies to the rigs each day with a testing kit, packaged neatly in a metal box. He bakes the mud, shakes it and mixes small samples with chemicals. Like a master chef with a bubbling broth, he contemplates the mud, and if it doesn't satisfy him, he recommends one additive or another. He flies 500 hours every year on such errands. His logbook now shows about 1,500 hours, of which more than half are off the water.
>
> William Lagewiesche, "Down on the Bayou"

3. A staff writer for the *Wall Street Journal* began an article on chewing tobacco and its popularity among college men with a series of short one- and two-sentence paragraphs (combined below into one) that rely on an anecdote to begin a serious article:

> It's 9 a.m., and 20-year-old Burly Hauck is setting in for a lecture in Cultures and Traditions, a required course at Wabash College here. The lanky sophomore lays his notebook and pen on the armrest of his chair, and he pulls a yellow plastic cup and a silver-wrapped packet from his coat pocket. Peeling back the wrapper on the packet, he tears off a wad of brown, fibrous material. Then he jams the wad between his upper gum and right cheek. "This is a lecture," the professor begins, "on cross-cultural perspectives. I'm going to talk today about American core values." Without shifting his eyes from the professor, Burly Hauck lifts the plastic cup to his mouth, purses his lips and quietly spits. Mr. Hauck isn't making a subtle comment about the professor's lecture. He's just showing he knows the value of not swallowing his chewing tobacco.
>
> Julie Salamon, "Many College Men Now
> Get Something Worth Chewing On"

4. Here is the third paragraph of a scholarly article where the purpose and thesis statements have been deliberately delayed.

> My purpose here is to discuss a major ironic strain in MOBY DICK, the one relating to the "grand programme of Providence," and to examine its changing stances and emphases. While being indebted to numerous critics in both schools of thought, I feel nevertheless that insufficient attention has been paid to the matter of irony in *Moby Dick* as a whole, to the figure of Ishmael in particular as the very center of this ironic design, and to broader stylistic and cultural implications that this irony suggests. This study, then, tries to establish some new premises. It is generally recognized that the universe of *Moby Dick* is fatalistic, and that this condition never changes. In effect Ishmael moves from the in-

Purpose statement

Thesis statement

itial position of gentle irony in the eighteenth-century comic and sentimental tradition at the expense of the grand programme, to a somber form of Romantic irony, only to progress later beyond irony to a new seriousness as an observer of and participant in the action of the novel.

> Christopher Durer, "Mocking the 'Grand Programme': Irony and After in *Moby Dick*"

5. Note the effective use of fragments in this very brief introduction:

> When winter winds blow and snow piles up on the windowpane, it's time to gather the family together and try your hand at real estate. Or playing detective. Or choosing a new career. In other words, it's time to dust off the board games and settle down for an evening of fun indoors.

> Judi Culbertson, "Tabletop Games"

6. Note the thesis statement at the end:

> When man first strapped shaped animal bones to his feet with skin thongs as a means of traveling the frozen lakes of northern Europe, little did he imagine the impact his innovation would have on future generations. From these humble beginnings developed and grew a versatile and captivating form of recreation, entertainment and sport.

> Ian Anderson, "Skating on Ice"

7. Here is an allusive, single-sentence introduction, which creates humorous echoes to the title, "When Swinemen Convene, the Talk Turns to Mating and Barnyard Odor," for an article concerning a pig trade show in Atlanta, Georgia:

> The pigmen cometh.

> Thomas E. Ricks

The author alludes to Eugene O'Neill's drama *The Iceman Cometh* and takes a little liberty with subject–verb agreement rules.

8. This introduction begins with dialogue:

> "The style of *The Pirates of Penzance*," says Wilford Leach, director and screenwriter of the upcoming multi-million dollar musical, "derived from our knowing that we had to create a world in which all that happens in the story would *logically* happen. The result is that *Penzance* offers a view of what really is *another* planet: one that is smaller, more old-fashioned, optimistic and generous than our own, but no less human."
>
> James H. Burns, "The Pirates of Penzance"

9. This introduction contains the definition of an unfamiliar term.

> Here is a scenario that gives many economists the willies: The population explosion continues, and famine strikes the Southern Hemisphere. The shock waves spread northward, dangerously straining industrial economies. Heads of state are in a helpless dither.
>
> But a bean may prevent such a scenario from coming to pass. And what a bean! Its name is *Psophocarpus tetragonolobus*, known to its fast-multiplying fans as the "winged bean." But those who understand this amazing plant's potential are calling it superbean.
>
> Richard Wolkomir, "It's Coffee! It's Milk! It's Superbean"

10. Here is an introduction with a more formal definition.

> Actors, in particular actors who work on the stage, are among the most superstitious people in the world. *Superstition* as defined by Webster's is "any belief or attitude that is inconsistent with the known laws of science or with what is generally considered in the particular society as true and rational." In the following article I will list perhaps the most popular and widely held theatrical superstitions today and shall attempt to deduce from whence they sprang. But as I and most writers of fiction believe — truth is

a theme on which to practice variations—the superstitions are real. The explanations of their origins are open to debate.

Frank Giordano, "Never Store Your Shoes over Your Head!"

11. This introduction begins with an imaginative analogy:

A major construction project is like a heavy storm at sea. Where all was serene, mountains suddenly arise—of mud, rather than water. Passage through the area is blocked by jetsam, flotsam, and lagan, and the traveler must either change course or simply lay to until the gale blows itself out and peace returns. There the similarity ceases, for at sea the end of the storm leaves the same old waters, now calm and friendly, but unchanged in character. And at a construction site—like the Quadrangle here at the Smithsonian—the turmoil ends with splendid creation; in our case, two new museums whose pavilions will rise where devastation now reigns.

Edwards Park, "Around the Mall and Beyond"

Writing Assignment

In your city have you noticed a large number of motorcyclists and bike riders crowding the streets? Some ride purely for pleasure; others have work tasks to perform, such as delivering mail that is guaranteed to arrive in an hour or so. Using some of the strategies for writing introductions that you have learned so far, write a 10- or 11-sentence paragraph that might lead to a theme about this phenomenon in your town. Use a separate sheet of paper for this activity.

Concluding Paragraphs

The function of the conclusion is to draw your remarks to a meaningful close, to bring together loose ends. The conclusion draws inferences and impressions from all the supporting material, looked at one more time. You stand back from particular sections of your work and view the proof structure and evidence. You make the closing meaningful by formulating inferences, by reaching conclusions based on your data. Readers should feel that you have completed the task established in the introduction and fulfilled the contract advanced in the purpose and thesis statements. Now, at the end, your readers should never be left feeling, "Hey, what's next?"

Strategies

There are no set patterns for paragraphs of conclusion. But usually their shape is from particular to general, with the thesis restated in modified form in the last few sentences. Nor is there a single length. A book might require a full chapter, whereas a research paper in history or political science may need only two or three paragraphs, and a short essay, only one or two sentences. But within these various types of conclusions, you may select some of the following strategies:

1. Echo a key word from the title, making sure of its relationship to the entire theme.

2. Summarize the main points you have made; highlight and emphasize briefly. Remind readers of the importance of your subject.

3. Repeat your thesis in a modified form, using synonyms if necessary.

4. Cite the recommendations of experts in the field.

5. List some of your personal conclusions drawn from data in the paper.

6. Repeat an allusion, an analogy, or a paradox if you have used one earlier.

7. Provide an ironic twist to your thesis.

8. Introduce a question that makes your readers think, or answer questions posed earlier.

9. Predict future actions and results, perhaps suggesting a universal application of your points beyond the limited context of the paper itself.

10. Issue a persuasive challenge, moving readers to act.

Tone in Conclusions

Just as there is no ideal length for conclusions, neither is there a single, appropriate tone. Humor is sometimes right when the essay has a light touch. John Simon, the keeper of the language for *Esquire*, ends on a light note, leaving his reader amused, entertained, but also informed, in the following final paragraph of an essay that lists numerous examples of abused language readers have sent him:

> Finally, for all those among you for whom language is a constantly growing organism for accretions from everywhere, here is a happy note. Gene Shalit, of NBC, forwards a letter from the letters column of the May issue of *Ms.* It begins: "I protest the use of the word 'testimony' when referring to a woman's statements, because its root is 'testes' which has nothing to do with being a female. Why not use 'ovarimony'?" Shalit wonders whether the writer is serious and concludes that she is — as is her condition. And as, I add regretfully, is the condition of the English language.
>
> John Simon, "Bad News from All Over"

Clearly a somber tone, although inappropriate for Simon's essay, suits more serious subjects. Often such an ending might make us think, question, or reevaluate a course of action. Tennyson permits Ulysses to end his reflections about life, old age, and the future affirmatively. Notice the balanced series of infinitives, and the dramatic emphasis on the word *not* in the last line. Ulysses is unyielding. His words convey his passion:

> Tho' much is taken, much abides; and tho'
> We are not now that strength which in old days
> Moved earth and heaven, that which we are, we are,—
> One equal temper of heroic hearts,
> Made weak by time and fate, but strong in will
> To strive, to seek, to find, and not to yield.
>
> (ll. 65–70)

Transitional Elements in Conclusions

In the preceding examples, the conclusions are effective for any number of reasons, chief of which is the emphatic language appropriate for either prose or poetry. Even though these paragraphs are drawn from larger contexts — in one case, from a poem — you must imagine their forcefulness within context. How apparent is it to you? Not all paragraphs have obvious concluding transitional elements, such as *thus, therefore, consequently, in summation, in short, accordingly,* or similar summary statements or concluding terms, which you learned about in Chapter 4. Whether such transitional markers are essential, each writer must decide. Emphatic language rather than obvious markers — particularly one like *in conclusion* — is far more useful in making your point memorable for the audience.

CAUTION

1. Avoid introducing new ideas, angles, or facts.
2. Be succinct. Avoid long-winded, tedious endings.
3. Avoid far-fetched moralizing, pious statements, or absolutes (sweeping generalities) that permit no exceptions.
4. Don't leave the reader hanging, suspended in mid-air.
5. Don't apologize for your lack of knowledge, shortcomings, or omissions.
6. Avoid contradictions or irrelevancies.
7. End gracefully, not all at once; don't just stop because it is 3:00 A.M. and you are out of words. Avoid a Bugs Bunny ending: "So long folks!"

Examples for Analysis

1. Numerous political speeches end on memorable and persuasive challenges, such as Lincoln's conclusion to his *Second Inaugural Address*:

    With malice toward none; with charity for all; with firmness in the right, as God gives us to see the right, let us strive on to finish the work we are in; to bind up the nation's wounds; to care for him who shall have borne the battle, and for his widow, and his orphan—to do all which may achieve and cherish a just, and a lasting peace, among ourselves, and with all nations.

2. The prediction in the following concluding remarks evokes a sense of gloom:

> Thus we face the uncertainty of not knowing what the interaction of natural cycles and pollutants will do to affect Earth's weather. The future is cloudy, but the likelihood is that we are beginning to leave the warmest days of planetary summer and may see greater extremes of weather in seasons to come.
>
> Lowell Ponte, "Why Our Weather Is Going Wild"

3. Herman Wouk ends his article on war with this foreboding thought:

> "*Nation will not lift up sword against nation,*" wrote the prophet Isaiah more than six centuries before the Christian era, "*neither will they learn war any more.*"
> If I do not utterly give up that hope, it is because I cannot and will not. Meantime, men of goodwill have to hang in there. As Victor Henry, the hero of *The Winds of War*, sums up the lessons of the Battle of Leyte Gulf, we are nearing the moment in human history when "*Either war is finished, or we are.*"
>
> Herman Wouk, "Must Wars Occur?"

4. Two vigorously worded sentences conclude an entire book evoking the image of an unending journey:

> For us, the voyage was over. But the adventure goes on.
>
> Christian Zuber, *Animals in Danger,* trans. J. F. Bernard

5. Yet these examples of conclusions do not fully suggest their impact on an audience, since they are excerpted from larger contexts. Imagine Arthur Eddington, after tracing man's evolutionary development, ending the essay "The

Evolution of the Physical World" with this dramatic one-sentence paragraph:

> And so we come to Man.

6. The following brief paragraphs work together to introduce and conclude a short article about Avery Island, Louisiana. Look how the word *heck* echoes a thought in both, creating a bridge:

> It's a heck of a place for one of America's great gardens—on a hill in a land that has no hills. And because it is surrounded by coastal marshlands, a cypress swamp and Bayou Petit Anse, it is called an island. It's made of salt, and it's famous for peppers.
>
> Introduction
>
> While alligators sun in the lagoons, flowers bloom and vinegar and Tabasco peppers age in oak casks, the egrets forage in the swamps and marshes. In the evening their shadows blacken the sky as they turn again toward Bird City in Jungle Gardens. Their home is in a heck of a place for a garden. But then, it's one heck of a garden.
>
> Conclusion
>
> Paul Stahls, Jr., "Island of Salt and Pepper"

7. Who can forget the "promises" calling Robert Frost's speaker in "Stopping by Woods on a Snowy Evening":

> The woods are lovely, dark and deep!
> But I have promises to keep,
> And miles to go before I sleep,
> And miles to go before I sleep.

Writing Assignment

Have you ever thought about the "promises to keep" that you have made to yourself or to others? Develop a concluding paragraph for a theme that you might have written about these promises, using some of the strategies you have learned in this section.

Transitional Paragraph

Definition   A *transitional paragraph* is another type of minor paragraph that forms a bridge, a linking unit among sections of a long paper. In Chapter 4 we learned how to use transitional elements to link ideas *within* a paragraph. Now, a step further, we are going to learn how to link the fully developed ideas of individual paragraphs in reports, essays, articles, lengthy compositions for college courses, or even larger elements of books.

Length

You will spot these transitional paragraphs by recognizing a shift in form from a multisentence to a brief one- or two-sentence structure, or possibly even to a single word. The eye not only will catch this brevity but may also spot dramatically unusual punctuation: exclamation points, question marks, or dashes. Brevity is the most obvious feature of this structure.

Two Functions

This sort of paragraph either *pre-outlines* or *summarizes*. By suggesting what comes next, writers not only prove that they are in control of their material; they also alert readers to the direction of the message. Transitional paragraphs orient the reader. Through a process that might be Pre-outline   called "pre-outlining" (forecasting what comes next), writers create a sense of place, of *where* they are, *where* the idea is going, and *what* the next block of material will be. The following transition in topic sentence form pre-outlines a three-part unit:

In oral communication the speaker delivers the message conscious of its content, structure, and style.

Summarize internally   The second function is to provide a summary in the middle of the paper of what has just been covered to remind the readers of where they have been. The summary is a brief restatement of major points. Careful word choice should recall without being repetitious. Occasionally, both functions appear within the same paragraph to establish relationships between one unit of a composition and another.

The following is an example of an internal summary paragraph that appears in the middle of a long article on home-equity conversion plans:

> In sum, American Homestead's plan provides monthly loan advances based on the borrower's life expectancy and the home's value. Interest accrues at a fixed, below-market rate. At the end of term—that is, when the borrower dies or sells—repayment is due on all principal and interest as well as the agreed-upon share of appreciation during the loan period.
>
> Linda Hubbard, "The Key to Security"

Placement of the Transitional Paragraph

These paragraphs go at the *end* of one thought unit and *before* another begins. The writer must decide when and where they are appropriate. Effective speakers more than writers will also use these linking devices. Sometimes speakers use blunter transitions for clarity. Yet neither all speeches nor all lengthy compositions require transitional paragraphs.

Let's look at some transitional paragraphs, examining how they function. Let's note their form, their punctuation, their length, and any other significant features:

> Why the tizzy over this new bean? After all, is not the reigning champ of the vegetable world that old favorite, the soybean?
>
> Richard Wolkomir, "It's Coffee! It's Milk! It's Superbean!"

These questions refer to a previous discussion of what Wolkomir calls a "tizzy." The second question alerts the reader to contrasts that will come next in the essay on the Asian winged beans.

A later paragraph in the same article uses other strategies to provide transition:

> A perfect plant? Almost. But the winged bean does have one serious drawback: its size.

Note the fragmentary questions, the single-word response, one dramatic sentence that conveys the new subject, the enormous height (12 feet) of the plant.

The following transition pre-outlines a lengthy but unnumbered list. The unusual bullet punctuation format, however, is particularly appropriate for newspapers, magazines, brochures, or advertising copy:

> But these particulars are not listed as taxable income: —

Bullet
> • money one spouse receives when working for the other . . .
> • money one receives from municipal bonds . . .

This example is a common form for pre-outlining a list:

> Naturally, her shopping includes a good many items that are mundane (and hardly worth noting). But, by and large, it reflects the sorts of treats that most people reserve for special occasions — remember the following sampling is from Mrs. Herron's regular weekly shopping list.
>
> Lisa Bergson and Fatima Shaik, "Luxury Plus"

Later sentences describe the "sorts of treats" that Phyllis Herron, a San Francisco attorney, bought: Atlantic smoked salmon at $32 a pound and Reggiano parmesan cheese at $11.75 a pound.

Another writer's transition hints at both what's been said and what will be:

> Obviously, *Pirate's* casting decisions had already been made, but who made Leach choose his initial selections?
>
> James H. Burns, "The Pirates of Penzance"

In "Must Wars Occur?" Herman Wouk uses several transitional paragraphs to keep his narrative flowing, suggesting subjects he has covered or ultimately will cover:

> Developmental section
> of essay

Well, what did I see?

> Developmental section
> of essay

How did we ever get into this paralyzing lock with Russia? And what are our chances of getting out of it alive?

Developmental section
of essay

But let us even say that we free ourselves from that doomsday lock. Will that mean world peace?

Developmental section
of essay

But just because war does go back to the first records of man, gloomy skeptics argue that there will always be war; that it is part of the unchanging human nature.

Journalists often provide a bridge to introduce quotations:

Judge Fremont says that the new revisions in corporate law will have a far-reaching impact:

The colon after Fremont's remarks signals the beginning of the quoted material, the revisions he advocates.

Sometimes the transition will state in topic-sentence form the total idea of the unit to follow:

Recent studies by psychologists on the fear of flying have increased understanding of the problem and have suggested a number of therapeutic measures.

The transition here looks ahead to the various therapies.

Some transitions are invitations. Note how the words *let us* indicate that further development of the subject will follow.

Because looking at the unusual image of film and listening to the sound track represent two different tasks performed simultaneously, let us consider in more detail guidelines for each.

Placing Major Transitions: The Pattern

Although you will not always want to use transitions between two developmental units, the following sketch should help you visualize possible placement of major transitions. Remember, these may be single sentences "hooked" onto a developmental paragraph or a separate minor paragraph.

SKETCH OF A LONG ESSAY OR REPORT

> **INTRODUCTORY UNIT**
> *(one or several paragraphs)*

Transition

> **FIRST DEVELOPMENTAL UNIT**
> *(one or several paragraphs)*

Transition

> **SECOND DEVELOPMENTAL UNIT**
> *(one or several paragraphs)*

Transition

> **THIRD AND ALL SUBSEQUENT UNITS**
> *(multiple paragraphs)*

Transition

> **CONCLUDING UNIT**
> *(one or several paragraphs)*

Minor Paragraphs to Present Examples

Occasionally, a writer will have so many rich, vivid examples to illustrate a point in a developmental paragraph that he or she may want to set them off in short paragraphs. Or the example may be so lengthy and detailed that separating it from the major part will help the reader visualize the whole topic.

Anne Dingus in *Texas Monthly* singles out a special horned toad that achieved a certain notoriety among Texas folklorists. Her focus is on Old Rip, whose personality comes to life through Dingus' intricate details. Her description typifies one function of a minor paragraph: to provide an elaborating example within a larger context:

> The most famous Texas horny toad was Old Rip, who was placed inside the cornerstone of the old Eastland County Courthouse when it was built in 1897. Thirty-one years later the courthouse was torn down and, legend has it, there in the cornerstone was Old Rip, none too perky but still alive. Named after Rip Van Winkle, he went on tour and was exhibited to thousands of people, including then-president Calvin Coolidge (it was reputedly one of the few times that solemn gent smiled). When Old Rip died, his body was embalmed, and it is still on display in Eastland. Biologists scoff at the idea that Old Rip lived 31 years; most horny toads live a mere 6 or so.
>
> Anne Dingus, "The Horny Toad"

Occasionally one or two short sentences will adequately describe a specific example:

> Cassily Adams painted *Custer's Last Fight*, many prints of which still hang in bars and taverns. But the famous original 9½-foot by 16½-foot oil painting of the massacre at Little Bighorn was destroyed in a fire at Fort Bliss, Texas in 1946.
>
> Erwin and Peggy Bauer, "Painting the American West"

A minor paragraph may also give multiple brief instances rather than one lengthy example, as in the earlier paragraph about Old Rip. Within a whole book on various pioneer women, Joanna Stratton presents instances of various settlers on the Kansas prairies:

> First to arrive, in the late 1860s, were a sizable number of Swedish settlers. Populating the Smoky Hill Valley, they established thriving communities at Lindsborg, Freemont and Salemsborg. In 1869 two hundred Scottish families made their homes at Scotch Plains, near the northern border. The Mennonites came in 1867, followed by German-Russian Catholics who founded the towns of Catherine, Herzog and Munjor. Three large British communities were established, at Wakefield and Runnymede as well as at Victoria, and there were scattered enclaves of French, Bohemian, Norwegian, Dutch and Danish families too.

> Joanna L. Stratton, *Pioneer Women: Voices from the Kansas Frontier*

From this rather general list we suspect that Stratton will eventually name, from each of these groups, specific women who played an important role in expanding the frontier.

Sometimes a one-sentence paragraph will provide detail:

> Garlands and wreaths adorn the mansion, and poinsettias, cedar, and evergreen boughs surround the 15-foot fir in the reception hall.

> "Victorian Christmas" from "American Observer"

Another function of the minor paragraph is to define a key term, a foreign phrase, or something likely to be unfamiliar to the reader. The brevity alerts the reader to the importance of the term, as in this one-sentence paragraph:

Key term

> There is a name for such stuff in the trade, a word apparently of Russian origin, Kitsch; it means vulgar showoff, and it is applied to anything that took a lot of trouble to make and is quite hideous.

> Gilbert Highet, *A Clerk of Oxenford*

The following two-sentence paragraph defines a key term:

> Our concern here is with the condition called "senile cataracts," an unsatisfactory term which applies only to the lens and not to the person behind it. Senile cataracts may affect people of any age, but it is more likely to happen to those in their late 40s and 50s.

Wendy Haskell Meyer, "Cataracts: Intraocular Lens Implants Have Created a Quiet Revolution in the World of Cataract Surgery"

Also statistics become emphatic in minor paragraphs — set apart from the remainder of the paper:

> For example, the noise level of rustling leaves in the quiet solitude of a country lane (10 decibels) is louder than a whisper six feet away. The noise in empty theaters averages 25 decibels, but with a "quiet" audience it rises to 42. In the average factory, a constant noise of about 80 decibels is characteristic. This is just about the same level as very loud speaking at a close range.

Douglas Ehninger et al., *Principles of Speech Communication*

And amounts of money gain similar emphasis:

> For example, a 75-year-old widow sells her $105,000 home at 23¾ per cent discount. She receives monthly payments of $873, including interest at 11 per cent, which leaves her $548 for rent. After the mortgage period, the annuity purchased by the investors would maintain the $873 monthly payment to her for life and she would continue to live in the home.

Linda Hubbard, "The Key to Security"

A short paragraph can make memorable a quotation or a bit of dialogue —

> In 1766, for example, William Pitt announced boldly in the House of Commons, "I rejoice that

America has resisted." Eleven years later he cried in the House of Lords, "If I were an American, as I am an Englishman, while a foreign troop was landed in my country, I would never lay down my arms — never — never — never!" He was the greatest and most respected English statesman of his day.

Neil Millar, "The British American Revolution"

—or create dramatic emphasis:

This is impossible, of course. California cannot fall into the sea.

Isaac Asimov, "Hey Alaska, Here We Come"

Conventions for Paragraphing

Indentation

As medieval texts illustrate, early writers did not rely on the most common modern indicator for beginning a paragraph — indentation. Instead, the ornate initial letter indicated the start of a new idea. Other scribes used this symbol to indicate indentation: | Today, indentation is the visual clue to the reader to mark a beginning; it is an eye-catching signal of a shift in thought.

Handwritten materials must have indentation, a space free of any writing. But how wide should it be? A rule of thumb is the width of one's index finger. Typed paragraphs, however, should being with a five-space indentation for all double-spaced work; single-spaced material frequently has blocked format (no indentation) with double spacing between paragraphs. Business correspondence may or may not indent for single-spaced format, depending upon the writer's stylistic choice.

Special Conventions

Blocked-in Quotations   When citing an authority, you may want to use a long verbatim quotation, the equivalent of four or more typed lines. Convention dictates that you inset this quotation at least five spaces from the left-hand margin. But since different disciplines use different formats, such as those for the Modern Language Association (MLA) or for the American Psychological Association (APA), consult an appropriate current style manual. Indent further (generally three additional spaces) if the quoted passage begins a new paragraph, as the following example illustrates:

> In *Hamlet and Oedipus* Ernest Jones argues:
>   The intensity of Hamlet's repulsion
>   against women in general, and Ophelia in particular, is . . .

Poetic Quotations With four or more lines of poetry, use a blocked-in format. If a poem has a unique structure—such as one by e. e. cummings or George Herbert—retain the poet's original format. Ordinarily, however, center the longest line of poetry. For example, if you quote from Robert Herrick's "An Ode for Him" (a tribute to Ben Jonson), you would use the following format, centering the longest line:

> AH, *Ben*!
> Say how or when
> Shall we, thy Guests,
> Meet at those Lyrick Feasts
> Made at the *Sun*,
> The *Dog*, the *Triple Tunne*?
> Where we such clusters had,
> As made us nobly wild, not mad;
> And yet each Verse of thine
> Out-did the meate, out-did the frolick wine.

> J. Max Patrick, ed., *The Complete Poetry of Robert Herrick*

Eccentric Formats For reasons not always immediately apparent to readers, a few distinguished professional writers choose to paragraph in bizarre ways. Look at a few lines from Oscar Wilde's "Preface" to *The Picture of Dorian Gray*. Even though they are in prose form, do they remind you of poetry?

The artist is the creator of beautiful things.

To reveal art and conceal the artist is art's aim. The critic is he who can translate into another manner or a new material his impression of beautiful things.

The highest, as the lowest form of criticism is a mode of autobiography. . . .

Richard Aldington and Stanley Weintraub, eds.,
The Portable Oscar Wilde

John Dos Passos in *U.S.A.* uses unconventional but very dramatic paragraphing and a number of images to stress the character of Thorstein Veblen (economist and sociologist):

Veblen

a greyfaced shambling man lolling resentful at his desk with his cheek on his hand, in a low sarcastic mumble of intricate phrases subtly paying out the logical inescapable rope of materoffact for a society to hang itself by,

dissecting out the century with a scalpel so keen, so comical, so exact that the professors and students ninetenths of the time didn't know it was there, and the magnates and the respected windbags and the applauded loudspeakers never knew it was there. . . .

John Dos Passos, *U.S.A.*

Hanging Indentations   Ocasionally, for an eye-catching effect you might reverse the indentation and let the first line of the paragraph hang into the left margin with subsequent lines indented inwardly, the exact opposite of normal paragraph indentation. This overhanging device, appearing often in brochures or magazines, is primarily for marketing and advertising:

Capture the romantic moment in the dazzling colors
of our newest fully fashioned cotton sweaters with crew neck in vibrant royal blue, cardinal red, deep emerald green, and a very peachy pink.

Paragraphing Conversation and Dialogue

The conventions of dialogue dictate that an extended exchange between speakers is indicated by indentation, regardless of how brief the remarks are. When the speaker shifts, you must begin a new paragraph. Observe how a short-story writer handles these conventions:

> Then as a broad hat was swept off and a muffler was removed from his throat, Lige stood revealed. "Did I skeer you?" he asked, with his comfortable smile.
>
> "You? You?" she choked, her fingers twisting. Then she began to sob in an ecstasy of relief.   Speaker shift
>
> "Thought you might be skeered o' the wind, and so I come to look after you after persuading Bev and Cora to spend the night at my place, after they stopped by to get out of the storm."   Speaker shift
>
> "What's all these here tears about?" he wanted to know.
>
> "Oh, Lige, I've been so miserable! Cora hates me, an' don't want me to stay here! An' it makes everything so hard for Bev and me to stay! and I've been scared half crazy of the wind!"
>
> Dorothy Scarborough, *The Wind*

Interview Format

Interview format requires not only indentation, but also the names of the persons speaking. The following exchange between *Harper's Bazaar* and three successful and prominent women illustrates the format:

> BAZAAR: What about relaxation? What do you do when you have time just for yourself, to unwind?
> *Janet:* I watch television and knit sweaters.
> *Wendy:* I like to talk on the telephone to a friend for an hour, about nonsense.
> *Diane:* I read something irrelevant, knowing I'm *never* going to have to interview the subject or the author. Or I go to two or three movies in a day. Or I sleep—I'm truly a marathon sleeper.

Question–answer exchanges follow a similar format, sometimes even using a *Q* and an *A* to separate paragraphs:

Q: Why do you consider Orson Welles' film *Citizen Kane* so innovative?

A: Well, the camera angles, the scene structures, the use of shadows to support moods — well, there're so many things to talk about —

Q: Could you give us some other illustrations, say of specific scenes?

Special Gimmicks

A number of different type-setting gimmicks can indicate paragraph divisions, particularly in listing similar items. The purpose is to call attention to the item. Here are just a few examples:

1. **Boldface type** for first words of a paragraph:

Carol Kelley (Civil Engineering) organized an interdisciplinary colloquium.

2. Heavy black squares, heavy black dots (bullets), lines, or asterisks:

■ I always notice the dust on the top of the refrigerator.
■ I don't mind if one of those women with the beehive hairdos sits in front of me at the theater.

• SET REALISTIC, REACHABLE GOALS. The important word is *realistic*.
• PLAN AND REHEARSE STRATEGIES FOR REACHING GOALS.

* No children are allowed in the pool area unless accompanied by an adult.
* No pets permitted in recreation room.
* No glass containers or food allowed.

3. A series of checkmarks:

Career Steps
✔ Evaluate yourself.
✔ Establish goals.

✔ Write to professional organizations in your field.

✔ Be aggressive.

✔ Maintain a positive attitude.

✔ Get experience.

✔ Enter the job market.

A Final Word

This book has shown you a number of things about paragraph structures. The diagrams accompanying each pattern have provided a visual stimulus for framing ideas. From them you can create paragraphs that follow a highly self-conscious pattern. The book has detailed a writing process and a systematic sequence that beginning writers can follow to produce a specific paragraph form. More-experienced writers already use these patterns almost instinctively; they do not begin by saying to themselves, "I'm going to write a question-to-answer paragraph." Instead, they trust their subconscious judgment, developed over many years through reading, writing, and evaluating well-written prose. They have unconsciously absorbed elements of style and patterning. As less-experienced writers practice writing from these patterns, they too will develop the beginnings of their own sense of style.

Another point you have learned is to add variety to your writing by presenting ideas in different structures. No longer are you simply committed to a monotonous series of general-to-particular paragraphs. Instead, you now have a variety of different ways to work *within* the same general-to-particular structure.

You've also learned how particular structures give emphasis to your ideas and make your presentations dramatic. The patterns have taught you how to make particular points stand out. They have also helped you learn how to be economical with words and less aimless in presenting ideas. With practice, you will learn to omit or shorten steps in the sequence for each pattern. Instead of writing in a straightforward, linear way, you will learn to become more recursive in your composing process, often trying to loop back to previous ideas, to reconsider, and possibly to alter or rearrange steps in presenting them.

Additionally, you have learned to respect your readers

and to be concerned about their needs. You have learned to become sensitive to, among other things, their backgrounds, values, skills, and knowledges. You have become more conscious of order and logical relationships, because if you're not sensitive to your readers, then they will become bewildered and confused. But discriminating readers will recognize the patterns inherent in your paragraphs.

Still another skill you have developed is the ability to make discriminating choices among various types of supporting material. You have developed sensitivity to selecting appropriate types for the particular occasion. And you have discovered how to use the most persuasive and most vivid supporting materials.

Yet the whole idea of writing a single developmental paragraph is artificial. Even as you learn these patterns, you must recognize their artificiality. Writers seldom write only a single paragraph! Once outside a basic composition class, you will write sequential paragraphs in letters or longer papers. Imitating models is thus only a beginning, a starting point. From experimenting with these patterns, you will develop a style that expresses your own individuality. You should practice until these patterns become second nature to you.

Familiarity with these paragraph structures has helped sharpen your analytical skills. That is, you have learned to be more sensitive to structure, to logical connections, and to the appropriateness of particular patterns for presenting specific ideas. You can now recognize techniques experienced writers use, account for their choice of one structure over another, and recognize the inappropriateness of some structures. Clearly, work with these patterns should have helped sharpen your critical skills as a writer and an evaluator of well-written prose.

<table>
<tr><td>

From Paragraph to Theme

</td><td>

CHAPTER
9

</td></tr>
</table>

Many years ago an author of a composition text called the developing paragraph a "theme in miniature." The many similarities between paragraph and theme become evident when you study them globally. The most important thing to remember is that a paragraph is only a part of a theme, one unit that develops a single idea. A *theme* is a multi-paragraph composition that develops a subject. It may take the form of a personal essay, an article in a periodical, a book, film criticism, some business reports, or a composition assignment. Imagine that a paragraph is but one building block, and that several of these blocks in sequence construct a theme.

Definition

So far, you have been learning only about paragraphs. But writing single paragraphs is not a task regularly required in your college courses. Possibly when you were applying for college, some of the application forms asked you to write a brief essay that would be used in assessing your eligibility for the school. That may have been your first "real-life" writing task beyond high school. In college you will be writing short essays on your history exams, longer ones for your sociology and English classes, and reports of various lengths in many of your science and engineering classes. Knowing paragraph structure will guarantee your success in writing essay exams, but you need to know how to put paragraphs into sequence to write longer papers.

Let's take that step, now, from paragraph to theme. The major parts of a theme are:

Introduction
Body
Conclusion

You'll want to review some of the strategies for both introductory and concluding paragraphs covered in Chapter 7 before you go further. Chapters 5, 6, and 7 have explained various formats for "body" paragraphs. But how does a writer tie all of the major divisions of a paper together?

Begin with a Title

An alluring title of a Barbara Cartland romance or a Sidney Sheldon novel often determines whether you will pick up or ignore the book. Right, you may make a mistake and ignore a really worthwhile book by simply focusing on title. But titles do grab the attention of book buyers. Your theme title should also arouse the reader's interest. It should echo the main idea of the whole theme so that you can refer to it in your paper. Keep titles short and catchy, preferably under four or five words. Get to the point quickly. Also, they are seldom a whole sentence long. Create a title that is consistent with the tone of your essay: it should be clever or witty only if the paper is. For more serious papers, titles should reflect that intent. Be careful to avoid trite titles; a cliché, for example, may turn off your reader. You may decide to delay writing it until you are well into your first draft. Regardless of when you write your title, make it a useful one. And be sure every theme you turn in for evaluation has one.

Establish a Thesis

Let's assume that you have already completed many of the prewriting strategies you learned in Chapter 1, including brainstorming, listing, and note-taking activities. But instead of writing a topic sentence for a single paragraph, it's time now to formulate a *thesis statement* that covers the entire essay. A thesis answers this question: what's the big idea of this theme?

Let's imagine that your subject is America's passion for the automobile. You have done some research in recent issues of *Newsweek* and *Time*, learning the subject is controversial, with some believing it foolish for Americans to buy high-speed, gas-guzzling automobiles even though fuel seems to be abundant and speed limits have increased. You have read that the American Automobile Association has increased its membership and that the percentage of Americans traveling on interstate highways is growing. Car makers are excited, as their sales continue to increase. Yet some critics are alarmed that American priorities seem to have changed. No longer are car buyers primarily concerned about gas mileage or safety. The big words now are *passing power* and *performance*. Americans seem also to derive their personal image and status from their automobiles. Advertising promotes automobiles that stir the emotions of buyers who seek a car with a special flair, not merely one that is fuel-efficient or economical. Speed is now an essential, as buyers no longer worry about the 55-mile-per-hour speed limit. Most buyers seem to have forgotten that in 1970, two years before the introduction of the 55 limit, there were over 56,000 deaths on American highways. In 1987, there were over 48,000 deaths on American roads.

By now you should have an idea of what you plan to do. Your next step is to formulate a thesis statement. A thesis is similar to a topic sentence in that it states the idea that the whole paper will develop, whereas a topic sentence merely identifies the subject of a single paragraph. A *thesis statement* has two distinct parts: a statement of general idea and a series of points the writer will use to develop this idea. Working with the subject of Americans' passion for the automobile, you might formulate several thesis statements for a short paper of 500 to 1,000 words:

Thesis statement

Lowered speed limits have encouraged Americans to buy faster, more powerful cars and ignore important safety considerations.

Car and truck enthusiasts derive personal satisfaction from the image their vehicles provide.

American car buyers are motivated by unwise priorities when buying a car solely because of its power and status.

Construct an Outline

Topic outline

Once your thesis is established, you need to think about the ordering of ideas. For this an outline is essential. Begin with the simplest format, the *topic outline*, listing topics and subtopics in an orderly way. Using single words and phrases, jot down the main points for major sections in Roman numerals.

    I.

    II.

    III.

Subtopics, indicating divisions of these major sections, are listed in capital letters. A topic outline might look like this:

    I.   Introduction
    II. First major idea (developed)
         A. Primary support
             1. Supporting material
             2. Supporting material
         B. Primary support
             1. Supporting material
             2. Supporting material
    III. Second major idea (developed)
         A. Primary support
             1. Supporting material
             2. Supporting material
         B. Primary support
             1. Supporting material
                a. Supporting material
                b. Supporting material
             2. Supporting material

Roman numerals IV, V, and others that follow indicate additional development.

    VI. Conclusion

Working outline

The topic outline becomes a reasonable *working outline* when you use it in the library to do research. Without a working outline you are likely to write in a haphazard way, lacking a clear direction and sense of order. It breaks down your thesis into its parts and spells out some of the supporting materials you will need. Each division, whether a Roman numeral or a capital letter, will "develop" your thesis. You will need supporting materials to explain the major points of the thesis.

A more sophisticated format is the *sentence outline*. It is the final revised version of a working outline with each entry expressed in sentence form. For lengthy formal reports in business or science a table of contents often replaces the sentence outline.

Sentence outline

A Multiparagraph Essay Pattern

The essay itself, based on a finished outline, looks like the following chart:

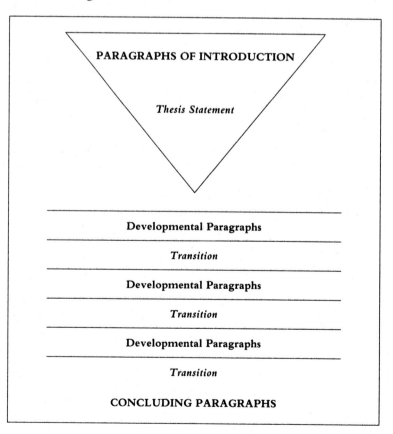

An essay may have several paragraphs of introduction or conclusion, depending on the length of the whole paper. Multiparagraph essays may have three or four paragraphs developing one major point, or a single paragraph may be adequate. A shorter paper may have only a couple of paragraphs, possibly with the introduction and conclusion in the first and last sentences of the paper. The pattern for a shorter paper might look like this:

PARAGRAPH I
Introduction and Part I of Thesis Statement

Transition

PARAGRAPH II
Part II of Thesis Statement and Concluding Sentence

Setting the Stage: The Introduction

For a very short paper a single sentence will serve as the introduction. (See the model for the two-paragraph theme.) You might even use this type of introduction in an essay examination answer. But for most of your writing, you will write at least one full paragraph of introduction. Longer introductory paragraphs—sometimes two or three—are appropriate for papers of several thousand words. Let's review the requirements for introductory paragraphs, more fully discussed in Chapter 8.

Try first to arouse your reader's interest. Grabbing that interest ensures that you will have a reader who at least will listen. It is important, too, to try to make yourself acceptable to the audience you are addressing. That means that you are considerate of their needs and have completed at least an elementary audience analysis. For introductions there are so many strategies that were discussed in Chapter 8 available that you may find difficulty selecting just the right one. Also, appropriateness may again dictate the choice; you would not want to use a fable or a bold jest in papers for science courses, where less personal approaches to subject matter are expected.

Your reader wants to know at once what your paper is about. For this reason, it's important to phrase your thesis (generally verbatim from your outline) in your introductory paragraph. Some instructors insist that thesis statements should be the last sentence of an introduction, pointing directly to paragraphs that develop each point. You may place the thesis in alternate positions that you believe appropriate, as arrangement should be a writer's decision, not an instructor's.

As you learned earlier, it is important to establish rapport with your audience, taking every precaution to avoid alienation. Your sincerity about the subject matter is vital to establish rapport. Your awareness of the audience is crucial. A topic as controversial as the use of fetal tissue transplants in the treatment of Parkinson's disease really tests you as a writer when you are analyzing the audience. Will the audience have a peculiar religious bias? Is the audience a group of medical practitioners? Is the audience likely to be gender-specific or a mixed group? These and other considerations about audience are crucial when you compose your introduction and help establish needed rapport.

Linking Words and Phrases

There is a special chapter (Chapter 4) that you have already studied that focuses on how to link ideas together *within* a paragraph. But coherence must also be evident *among* paragraphs. The whole paper must fit together. To help link paragraphs, try using some of these "echo strategies."

Devices That Repeat

1. Repeat a key word or phrase among several paragraphs. The form of the word may vary (*employ, employer, employee, employment*); or you may use a very close synonym (*citizen, resident, native, national, patriot; or flame, fire, flare, light, flash, spark*).

2. Repeat a significant word from the title. Gail Mortimer's article titled "The Smooth, Suave Shape of Desire: Paradox in Faulknerian Imagery of Women" has a number of rich, suggestive words to echo: *smooth, suave, desire, paradox, imagery.*

On the lines provided list words in the following titles that lend themselves to echoing.

"The Sad Lament of Pecos Bill on the Eve of Killing His Wife"

_____

_____

"Holy Ghosts: The Mythic Cowboy in the Plays of Sam Shepard"

_____

_____

3. Repeat an example, illustration, or event from a previous paragraph.
4. Repeat significant thoughts or opinions among several paragraphs.
5. Repeat an analogy if you've used one.
6. Repeat the pattern of a highly stylized, eye-catching sentence.

Devices That Enumerate

1. Use count words or phrases in the first sentence of a paragraph—like *one, first, first of all, to begin with.*
2. Toward the conclusion, use *last, the final point, finally, last of all.*
   Selecting appropriate enumerative words will forecast what is to come, give direction to the paper, and act as signposts.

Other Linking Devices

1. Echo the same subject through several paragraphs. (Repeated reference to "watermelons" will keep the idea of their size, color, pleasing taste, and annoying seeds in the reader's mind.)

2. Restate the thesis in a modified form, using different words or perhaps several sentences.

3. End most developmental paragraphs with a "clincher" that recalls the title or perhaps synthesizes and concludes one main unit.

Aaron Copland employs a number of these linking devices to give coherence to his essay about musical composers. Analyze his remarks, looking specifically for the linking devices he has chosen.

I can see three different types of composers in musical history, each of whom conceives music in a somewhat different fashion.

The type that has fired public imagination most is that of the spontaneously inspired composer — the Franz Schubert type, in other words. All composers are inspired, of course, but this type is more spontaneously inspired. Music simply wells out of him. He can't get it down on paper fast enough. You can almost tell this type of composer by his prolific output. In certain months Schubert wrote a song a day. Hugo Wolf did the same.

In a sense, men of this kind begin not so much with a musical theme as with a completed composition. They invariably work best in the shorter forms. It is much easier to improvise a song than it is to improvise a symphony. It isn't easy to be inspired in that spontaneous way for long periods at a stretch. Even Schubert was more successful in handling the shorter forms of music. The spontaneously inspired man is only one type of composer, with his own limitations.

Beethoven symbolizes the second type — the constructive type, one might call it. This type exemplifies my theory of the creative process in music better than any other, because in this case the composer really does begin with a musical theme. In Beethoven's case there is no doubt about it, for we have the notebooks in which he put the themes down. We can see from his notebooks how he worked over his themes — how he would not let them be until they were as perfect as he could make them. Beethoven was not a spontaneously inspired composer in the Schubert sense at all. He was the type that begins with a theme; makes it a germinal idea; and upon that constructs a musical work, day after day, in painstaking fashion. Most composers since Beethoven's day belong to this second type.

The third type of creator I can only call, for lack of a better name, the traditionalist type. Men like Palestrina and Bach belong in this category. They both exemplify the kind of composer who is born in a particular period of musical history, when a certain musical style is about to reach its fullest development. It is a question at such a time of creating music in a well-known and accepted style and doing it in a way that is better than anyone has done it before you.

Beethoven and Schubert started from a different premise. They both had serious pretensions to originality: After all, Schubert practically created the song form singlehanded; and the whole face of music changed after Beethoven lived. But Bach and Palestrina simply improved on what had gone before them.

The traditionalist type of composer begins with a pattern rather than with a theme. The creative act with Palestrina is not the thematic conception so much as the personal treatment of a well-established pattern. And even Bach, who conceived forty-eight of the most varied and inspired themes in his *Well Tempered Clavichord,* knew in advance the general formal mold that they were to fill. It goes without saying that we are not living in a traditionalist period nowadays.

One might add, for the sake of completeness, a fourth type of composer—the pioneer type: men like Gesualdo in the seventeenth century, Moussorgsky and Berlioz in the nineteenth, Debussy and Edgar Varese in the twentieth. It is difficult to summarize the composing methods of so variegated a group. One can safely say that their approach to composition is the opposite of the traditionalist type. They clearly oppose conventional solutions of musical problems. In many ways, their attitude is experimental—they seek to add new harmonies, new sonorities, new formal principles. The pioneer type was the characteristic one at the turn of the seventeenth century and also at the beginning of the twentieth century, but it is much less evident today.

Aaron Copland, "Different Types of Composers"

Analysis Questions

1. How often does Copland repeat the word *type*?
2. What different forms of the word *spontaneous* does he use?
3. What echoes of previous ideas do you find?
4. Where do you see devices that enumerate?
5. Which paragraphs end with clincher sentences?
6. What other linking devices do you find?

Wrapping Up: The Conclusion

See Chapter 8 for a full discussion of concluding paragraphs. Use the following checklist to evaluate early drafts of your conclusion:

CHECKLIST

1. Have you merely stopped, or does your paper have a graceful finish?
2. Have you digressed into new issues that are inappropriate to your subject?
3. Have you restated your thesis, perhaps in different words?
4. Have you echoed the title?
5. Have you referred to important points or outstanding examples developed in the body of the paper?
6. Does your conclusion forecast the future?
7. Does your last sentence have *punch*?

Final Overview

Step One   Select and limit the subject.
Do preliminary notetaking, brainstorming, and listing.

Step Two   Create a thesis statement, considering audience and purpose.
Check thesis for general idea and specific points.
Identify the controlling idea.
Continue to narrow the subject.

Step Three   Organize by outlining.
Begin with major divisions.
Fill in primary support materials.
Establish the major method of development.
Develop a topic, working, and sentence outline.

Step Four   Compose the major developing paragraphs.
Create a topic sentence for each.
Link topic sentences to the thesis statement.
Provide adequate supporting material.
Check for clarity, single focus, and completeness.
Check for transition within the paragraph and among paragraphs.

Step Five   Write an effective introduction, involving the reader and capturing reader interest.
Introduce the major divisions of the thesis.
Try to echo the title.

Step Six   Write a logical, appropriate conclusion.
Echo title, restate the thesis in a modified way.
Avoid digressions and contradictions.
Recall in summary main divisions of paper.
End gracefully.

Step Seven   Check for stylistic energy and emphasis.
Check for consistency in tone and voice.
Check for variety in sentence and paragraph structure.
Check for precise vocabulary.

Step Eight   Read aloud for sentence rhythm.
Listen for awkward structures, choppiness, and wordiness.
Let others read and advise.

Step Nine   Proofread carefully for surface errors in punctuation, mechanics, spelling, and grammar.

Step Ten   Make it look good!

Themes to Analyze

What follows is a series of papers, beginning with one written by a high school student. The middle papers are by college freshmen, and one includes all of the prewriting activities and peer evaluation sheets that preceded the final paper. Finally, a short essay by a professional writer illustrates the goals a beginning writer should aim for.

The Flighty Fairy

This is it. I finally have the opportunity to fulfill my long-awaited dream. I can hardly believe it, but tonight I will finally meet the infamous flying Tooth Fairy. I chose to meet with the Tooth Fairy because I have a few important questions that I must simply have answered. I cannot bear to live without the information any longer. I can remember way back to when I lost my first tooth. It was just before inflation hit. The night I lost my tooth I told my parents, and they instructed me to place my treasure next to my bedstand just before I went to bed. I did this, and in the morning, I found a shiny quarter. Boy, was I ever elated and full of glory that day! Every time after that, when I lost a tooth, I followed the above procedure. Sometimes, I even went as far as pulling my tooth before it was ready. One day, I had lost a tooth while at my friend's house. I told her of the shining quarters, and she replied, "A quarter, one quarter? I get four gleaming quarters every time!" Well, with that, I was steamed! The next tooth I lost, I received my solemn quarter, and was less than joyed. Here raises my first question to the Tooth Fairy. Why did everyone else receive more money after inflation hit but me? The way I calculate it, you owe me big!! The next question involves the Tooth Fairy's priorities. One night when I lost a molar, I failed to tell my parents but did place it on my bedstand. Where was the Tooth Fairy? I still have my tooth!! I recently had my wisdom teeth extracted, and just for fun tried the old routine.

What's up? Are you dead?

My Phase with Short Nails

My phase with short nails lasted many years. I don't
even remember when it all started, but I do remember
when, how, and why it ended. It ended three months ago
when I was asked to be part of a friend's wedding court.
Although I wasn't aware of it, the participation in that
wedding would change the situation. When I realized I
couldn't go through the whole wedding with short, stubby
fingers, I, for the first time ever, decided to have some fake
nails adjusted to my fingers. When I saw those huge, long
nails on me I almost cried with joy. I was very excited.
So excited I actually made my mom take pictures of my
hands. To me, it seemed that the nails enhanced the
beauty, shine, and sparkle of my rings. I felt my hands
should be in a hand cream or diamond ring commercial. I
was as excited as, I imagine, a child is when it gets that
rag doll or choo-choo train it asked Santa for. My eyes
glared with happiness as they saw how the long, shiny,
silky nails made my hands look so soft and seductive. So
alluring! That's what did it, and convinced me that I would
never again bite my nails. I thought, "Wow! Now you know
how nice your hands can look. You'd be a fool to continue
that stupid urge or need to bite your nails. If you truly
must have something to chew on, chew gum, but give up
the nails." Yes, indeed, that's what I thought, and that's
what I did, which is why I no longer wear fake nails. Now
I feel I was able to accomplish a goal, a dream, and I feel a
sense of complete satisfaction. Before, although the nails
looked great, they were not really mine, and there wasn't
much satisfaction. They were fake and the only thing that
made them mine was that I paid for them. Now that my
nails are long, I can't help worrying how long they'll last
before they break, but it doesn't matter. I'd rather have
that worry time after time, than not have anything to
worry about. I even feel like a new person. I see my hands,
think of how long it took, think of how great it makes me
feel, and enjoy it. Finally!

My First Date with HIM

Clunk, there went my shoe. Not just any shoe, mind
you, but the beautiful, red leather Italian shoe that I wore
simply because it matched my new red sweater. Unfortunately, the shoe is two sizes too large and a bit difficult to
keep on my foot. Now, as I stare down at it, resting inno-
cently on the floor of the theater, my embarrassment gets
the best of me. Thank goodness it's dark in the movie theater, I'd hate for HIM to see how fire engine red my cheeks
have become. First dates ... how I hate first dates. I could
absolutely kick myself for going on another first date. Well,
except for the fact it's hard to kick yourself when you're
not even wearing a shoe. Its time to think strategy, I decide. While seductively reaching down for my popcorn, I'll
simply pick up my shoe and replace it in its proper place,
on my foot. All right, time for action. As my hand reaches
down for my target, my greatest horror is realized. The
Jumbo Deluxe Size Coke I've been sipping is knocked from
my arm-rest and is sent tumbling to the floor. KA-SPLASH.
Now, not only is my shoe still on the floor but it is effectively holding a 24 oz. cola. Just stay calm. What should I
say? However, my thoughts are quickly interrupted by the
raising of the house lights. The movie is over, and he turns
to me and says with a smile, "Not much plot, did you think
so?" "No," I reply, "but it certainly had a lot of action."

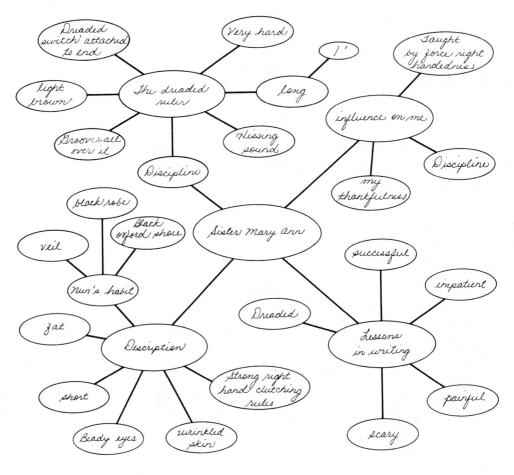

Tina

List outline

1. Give vivid description of Sister Mary Ann.
2. Next, tell what role parents played in it. (Once it)*
3. Influence she had on me.
4. Her discipline (Once it)
5. The dreaded ruler (Once it)

*Once it (reminds Tina to add an example).

6. The writing lessons (Once it)
7. Her influence on me

Tina

Audience Analysis

1. Who is my audience?
   My audience is other people who want to share their autobiographical sketches.

2. What does my audience already know about my subject?
   My audience at this moment knows nothing about my subject.

3. What do I want my audience to know about my subject?
   I want my audience to know how it feels to be in Sister Mary Ann's class. I also want them to know how she influenced me by changing me from a left-handed writer to a right-handed writer. I want them to feel like they are actually there in the class with her going thru the writing lessons.

Freewriting Draft #1

" Not with your left hand," Sister
Mary Ann would say sternly. I
remember that saying all to
well. She was a typical looking nun,
She wore a long black robe with a
black veil that ~~was trimmed with~~ swayed as she walked.
~~white.~~ Her strong right hand always
swung by her side, Carring the
dreaded ruler like it was an extension of her & own arm.
          I ~~rember~~ remember once
during writing lessons, I
wrote with my left hand. I
sat there in horror knowing
that soon I would ~~her~~ hear
Sister Mary Ann saying "Not with
you left hand" and then I'd say
"I guess I forgot, that can happen,
can't it?" I knew the next thing
to come would be the dreaded ruler. ⎯⎯⎯→
          The dreaded ruler was ~~about~~ a light
brown ~~with~~ about a foot long
with little grooves all over it.
~~It hurt like hell when it hit you~~
~~knuckles.~~ I knew the time
had come and all I remember was
hearing her say ~~was~~ " Put out
your hands and don't say a
word." ~~You didn't dare flitch~~
~~when the ruler I she pulled~~
~~up her arm like a gun and~~
~~like a gun about to fire and flung~~
~~stuck my knuckles and made~~
~~a loud "snap".~~ Inside I could hear
myself saying " Oh shit that hurt"
I could see tiny little pink welts
rising where the ruler had been.
          My parents decided for my
own good that I should be rightharded.
Once I heard them talking and

you know like the ones
you see in church all
the time.

She was also
my third
grade
teacher

a hissing
sound ⎯⎯→

my dad said "Being lefthanded is a "sign of ignorance" and ~~I would~~ ~~hear my~~ ~~momita~~ my ~~she~~ ~~mom~~ would say "Honey, she's only a child, and that's only a myth)" And my dad would say "My child will not be lefthanded." That was the end of ~~that between~~ that discussion.

    Sister Mary Ann's discipline was not a practice but a well known fact. She was a strict old lady but she was fair.

She pulled her arm back and like a gun about to fire flung the ruler through the air which made a distinct hissing sound. ~~When~~ it struck my knuckles it made a loud "snap."

~~Inside I~~ ~~pa was say, felt like screaming~~ ~~because~~

I was so nervous I felt like I was ~~up~~ ~~old~~ about to lose my lunch. ~~I~~ ~~a~~ Goosepimples popped up all over my skin like weeds in a garden. And I knew it was time for the dreaded ruler.

    I'm very grateful ~~thankful~~ for being taught by Sister Mary Ann although back then I thought of it as ~~torture~~ a punishment. Sometimes when I think about her I can still hear her monoton stern voice saying
    "not with you left hand"

My lessons in writing were always like a nightmare ~~I couldn't~~

Draft #2

" Sister Mary Ann "

"Not with you left hand!" Sister Mary Ann would say sternly.

I remember that saying all to well. my third grade year in Catholic private school is a good example of why there is a fear of going to school. We studied the usual things: reading, writing, and arithmetic. The only difference between a regular third grade class and this class was that we had a nun for a teacher. Now this was no ordinary nun but more like a direct messenger from God. Everything we said or did she knew, almost before we had even done it.

~~Once I~~ I remember once, I glued this girl's schoolbooks together with super glue. At the time I thought it was pretty funny. I said to myself silently:

"I hope I don't start laughing when she goes to open her books."

Somehow Sister Mary Ann found out and said

"not with you left hand!" Sister Mary Ann would say sternly.

I remember that paying all to well.
~~It was~~ My third grade year in
catholic private school was my
worst and best year. ~~My parents
decided that was.~~

Sister Mary Ann, a typical just like the ones you see in church all the time.
looking nun ~~just happened~~ to
be my third grade teacher. ~~Her~~ The
expression in her face ~~a~~
showed sincerity. Her deep
blue eyes were beaty round
objects that ~~could~~ would look right through.
The skin on her face was wrinkled
so much it looked like it made
her eyes droop. The outfit she
wore created ~~authority~~ a look of
authority that you didn't
question. She wore black, dull
oxford shoes which made
a dull thump when she walked
and could be heard from a distance.
Her strong right hand swung
by her side: carrying the
dreaded ruler ~~like~~ as if it
were an extension of her own
arm.

~~In her class there was, always an
exact amt. of time for, reading writing,~~
especially writing, and arithmetic. lessons in
Everyday we had * 1 hour writing ~~class~~
~~this class was always the wors.~~
which everyone practiced handwriting skills
~~The worst part of my third grade
year.~~
                                    were
The writing lessons ~~was~~ the
~~worst part of this class the w~~

entire year. In this class you were not allowed to write with your left hand. Unfortunately, I was one of the left-handed kids. Sister Mary Ann's rule was that if you wrote with you left hand you would be punished with the ruler.

I remember once during one of these writing lessons, I wrote with my left hand. I sat there quietly hopping that Sister Mary Ann would be busy with someone else and not notice what I had just done. It was to late, she saw me and said:

"Not with you left hand" — Tina

"I guess I forgot"; that can happen, can't it?" I said nervously.

I knew the next thing to come would be the dreaded ruler.

Peer Evaluation "Sister Mary Ann"

↗ dialogue and flashback - good!

Paragraph 1: Good beginning - first sentence, physical features could've been emphasized more.

Introduction shouldn't really contain the description yet. That same description would be better in a latter paragraph.

Paragraph 2: A little hard to follow at the beginning
Good use of flashback.
~~We don't understand what "star" is~~?
Good "cause & effect" — she uses her left hand and as a result she's going to get hit with the ruler.
A little more transitional words.
Could show a little more.

Paragraph 3: Real Good!!
Makes us imagine the dreaded ruler.
Good flow of material
Does not repeat words — good

Paragraph 4: Good paragraph
"oh shit — that hurt!"
Good description — very realistic — we actually felt it — it made us laugh.
Good wording

Paragraph 5 — Weak — Lack of description
Good flow, ~~but~~ of story but ending is weak.
use of more examples

"Sister Mary Ann"

"Not with your left hand!" Sister Mary Ann would say
sternly. I remember that saying all to well. My third grade
year in Catholic private school is a good example of why
there is a fear of going to school. We studied the usual
things; reading, writing, and arithmetic. The (oonly) difference between a regular third grade class and this class
was that we had a nun for a teacher. Now this was no
ordinary nun, she was more like a messenger from God.
Everything we said or did she knew about, almost before
we had even done it.
    I remember once, I glued this girl's schoolbooks to-
gether with super glue. At the time I thought it was pretty
funny. I said to myself:
    "I hope I don't start laughing when she goes to open
her books."
    Somehow Sister Mary Ann found out and said:
    "Tina, did you do this?"
    "Well ... no, I mean maybe"
    "Well did you?" "I'm waiting for an answer!" She replied.
    "I ... I guess I did" I suddenly blurted out.
    I found out just how funny it was when I got to sit in
the corner for a whole week. As (i) soon found out, Sister
Mary Ann's discipline turned out to be very strict and
never questioned. It was more like a well known fact.
    Sister Mary Ann looked like a typical nun, just like the
ones you see in church on Sunday. Her long black robe
created a sense of authority. She wore black, dull oxford
shoes which made a loud ("thump") when she walked and
could be heard from a distance. Her face was a large mass
of wrinkles and it seemed to make her eyes droop. Her
deep blue eyes were round beaty objects in the middle of
all these wrinkles. Her strong right hand swung by her
side(,) always carrying the dreaded ruler as if it were an
extention of her arm.
    Every day we had a certain amount of time we had to
splend on handwriting skills, this was called writing lessons. In this class you were not allowed to write with your
left hand. Unfortunately, I was one of the left-handed kids.
Sister Mary Ann's rule was that if you wrote with you left
hand you would be punished with the ruler.
    I remember once during one of these writing lessons, I
wrote with my left hand. I sat there quietly hoping that

she didn't see anything. It was to late, she saw me and said:

"Not with your left hand Tina"

I guess I forgot that can happen, can't it?" I said nervously.

I knew the next thing to come would be the dreaded ruler. Now this ruler, which extended a foot long with grooves all over it, was no ordinary ruler. Instead, I considered it a lethal weapon when put in the hand of Sister Mary Ann.

I sat there unable to move a muscle in my body. I was so nervous I almost threw up on the guy sitting next to me. My skin started to crawl and I could feel tiny goosepimples popping up all over by body, like weeds in a garden. I knew the time had come to face the dreaded ruler. Sister Mary Ann said:

"Put out your hands and don't say a word."
She pulled back her arm like a gun about to fire, and flung the ruler through the air, which made a distint hissing sound. When it struck my knuckles it made a loud "SNAP" which seemed to make it hurt that much worse. Inside I could hear myself saying:

"Oh shit that hurt!"
Tiny pink welts began rising where the ruler had been. A sharp streak of pain, like a lightning bolt struck, and all the nerves came to life.

Now when I think back on that time, I'm grateful for having Sister Mary Ann as my third grade teacher. The biggest reason is that now I'm right-handed and it makes things easier. She was the greatest influence on me throughout my childhood. I'll never forget Sister Mary Ann or her dreaded ruler.

The Way We Wrote

In my day, the back-to-school bell summoned us to, among other things, classes in "penmanship," but the Palmer Method never found a home in my small-muscle motions. So the reaction I received earlier this year to a letter I had penned to a friend in France came as a considerable surprise.

My correspondent, a thoroughgoing modern who is forced to communicate by letter these days because he has exhausted his credit with the French telephone company, embarrassed me with the effusiveness of his gratitude for my letter — gratitude not that I had written but that I had written by hand. Here I had thought I was burdening my friend with illegibility. Instead, I had unwittingly offered him a talisman.

A few weeks later I was breakfasting with a journalist colleague. A point I raised interested him, and he withdrew a pen from his pocket to make a note of it. I noticed him removing the pen's cap and suddenly realized that his tool was not the ubiquitous ball point or felt tip but a fountain pen. I hadn't held a fountain pen in my hand for years, but the esthesis of writing with one suddenly poured from my memory.

I remembered the faint hiss to be heard in a still room as the fingers and hand drew the nib across the paper, the dark line glistening wetly. I mused on the long-forgotten act of inserting the snout of my Shaeffer into the slanted well of a bottle of Skrip and gulping dark fluid into the instrument's innards.

But it's been a long time since this was the way we wrote. Much of the time, Americans don't write at all. We pick up the telephone and convert our thoughts into electronic impulses that flash briefly, into an ear or the magnetic tape of an answering machine. Even those of us who manipulate words by trade are increasingly estranged from putting ideas on paper by the direct action of our hands. Our fingers activate a machine that bangs printed letters onto paper — the typewriter — or, increasingly, we cause ghostly images to glow on a cathode-ray tube, images that cease to exist as soon as they scroll off the top of the screen.

Fortunately, others are less fickle than Americans. While we abandoned fountain pens for ball points and felt tips and then abandoned pens entirely except to fill out forms, write checks and jot down the occasional telephone number, Europeans by the hundreds of thousands went right on as if progress had never occurred. They learned the use of the fountain pen as schoolchildren, they carried their fountain pens to be tested for O-levels or their *bac-*

calaureat. Graduating to adulthood and the world of affairs, they continued to uncap and employ their Waterman, their Parker, their Montblanc, just as their parents and grandparents did.

So it came about that when Americans were ready to try fountain pens again—as it appears we are—the manufacturers were still out there, as though waiting for us. They'd been busy all these years selling pens in Europe.

The pen world of 1988 is strangely changed, though. European investors have bought heavily into fountain-pen companies, and Waterman—the oldest fountain-pen maker in the world—has left the United States entirely to take up residence in France. The passing years have also led to a massive rise in prices, especially for top-of-the-line fountain pens. At Fahrney's Pens, one of the nation's great pen emporiums, you can drop $500 on a sterling-silver Waterman Le Man or $400 on a Waterman Le Man whose barrel is turned from olive wood or briar. Much of the price of the expensive pens is in the nib, usually 14-karat or 18-karat gold tipped with iridium or rhodium. Pen people say the gold nib assures a steady, even flow of ink to the pen point and provides the flexibility needed for the ruffles and flourishes that adorn a bold, sweeping, confident hand. But clearly there's more going on here than high technology. With the exception of Lamy, which continues to market writing tools that look like a cross between thermometer cases and theodolite weights, a turn-of-the-century flavor dominates contemporary fountain-pen design. Mind you, that's the turn of the 19th century, not the 20th. The pens of the day may have space-age insides, but their shells are imposing personal jewels, many as big around as cigars, and no one could ever confuse them with the throwaway Bic you forget to return to the supermarket clerk.

A fountain pen is a personal, individual tool. To uncap it is to strike a blow for the importance of singularity. To apply it to paper, to convert your thought to permanent, distinctive black symbols by the motion of your own hand is to assert your enduring significance as a particular person in the midst of the sea of humanity. To send a handwritten letter to a friend is to say to that friend: These words are a part of me. I thought them with my own mind and made them permanent with my own hand. When you look at them, I am with you again and again.

William R. MacKaye, in *The Washington Post Magazine*

Writing Essay Exams | CHAPTER 10

What you have learned about writing paragraphs has direct application to your success in structuring answers on essay exams. There are any number of pitfalls in writing exams. The chief one is misreading the question, misinterpreting what the question asks you to do. Within each question is a set of instructions that you must interpret accurately. Read thoughtfully and carefully to get to the heart of the question. Precisely what does it ask you to do? Analyze it to determine what the question wants you to consider.

Here is a list of key terms that often appears on exams, key words that indicate what instructors expect in answers. Examine them carefully, as they will make reading an essay question more meaningful and easier to analyze.

Analyze   To break down an idea into its related parts and explain all of these parts in detail.

Compare   To explain points of similarity.

Contrast   To explain points of difference.

Criticize   To evaluate the merits of an item or a concept; to state an opinion on value or worth, giving the pro and con, approval and disapproval, and support with evidence.

Define   To give the meaning of a word, phrase, idea, or concept in positive terms.

Demonstrate   To explain or to show visually with specimens or examples.

Describe   To create an image, a word picture that appeals to the senses; to tell about an item.

Discuss   To explain fully in great detail; to consider various points of view or different sides of an issue.

Enumerate   To list and explain in numbered, concise form.

Evaluate   To appraise, giving opinions as to the value or worth of a concept, advantages and disadvantages, pro and con; to criticize the merits of an item.

Explain   To discuss fully, making plain and clear; to tell the how, what, and why of an item or concept.

Identify   To specify, name, or distinguish between similar items, objects, or persons so that only one is individualized explicitly.

Interpret   To translate the meaning of a concept or an item; to make clear and give meaning about what one thinks or believes about something, such as a line of poetry or the meaning behind a drama, story, or painting.

Justify   To give valid reasons for accepting an idea, issue, or item; to give evidence and facts to support your position; to take a stand and offer proof.

Outline Briefly   To use outline format to present an abbreviated analysis of an idea or concept.

Outline Fully   To use outlining to present a complete analysis.

Prove   To establish the truth, value, or worth of an item by presenting logical reasons and facts for believing something is true.

Summarize Briefly   To explain the main points only; to give the essence of an idea, but mentioning all facets.

Summarize Fully   To explain in detail the various parts of an item; to put the concept together in a unified format.

Synthesize   To put all of the parts of an analysis together into a concrete whole.

Trace   To explain the course or to follow the trail of (from beginning to end); to give a progression of points, possibly in chronological order.

Analyzing Exam Questions*

It will help if you read and mark the question, breaking it down into related parts. Use the following analysis of a test question from economics to guide you in analyzing questions:

Example: Compare and contrast the taxation policies of the Carter and Reagan administrations.
The question marked for analysis:

$$1 \quad\quad 2 \quad\quad\quad 3 \quad\quad 4$$
Compare / and contrast / the <u>taxation policies</u> of the
$$5$$
Carter / and Reagan administrations.

Note that you are asked to analyze five separate parts.

1. What is the main subject? — the taxation policies; underscore it.
2. What are your instructions? What are you to do with the subject? — to compare and contrast.
3. What does *compare* mean? — to show similarities.
4. What does *contrast* mean? — to show dissimilarities.
5. How will you structure your answer? You will need a minimum of two paragraphs. Why?
6. a. Introduce by explicitly defining your understanding of the term *taxation policies.*
   b. Then complete the first paragraph by stating the similarities, using enumerative structure to isolate the several, different aspects of the taxation policies.
   c. The second paragraph will enumerate the several dissimilarities.
   d. Then end your answer with a forceful conclusion.

The question is big and broad — possibly big enough for a book-length treatment, but you have only ten or fifteen

*We are indebted to Dr. Oliver Knight, late of the History Department of the University of Texas at El Paso, for this analyzing technique on essay examinations.

minutes to compose an answer. As a student you have no other choice. Should you narrow your answer to specific years, as the Carter administration lasted four years and the Reagan eight? Your answer might be stronger if you narrow it to the second half of the Reagan administration, for example, culminating in the Tax Reform Act of 1986.

The question invites enumeration of similarities and differences. But a simple listing will not be adequate; you must organize your list within the context of a paragraph. You need introductory comments that will include a definition of *taxation policies*. One or two sentences might provide adequate introduction. You must be the judge of whether five or six (possibly fewer, possibly more) supporting points need to be the main part of your answer. At the end of your answer have a few strong sentences that forcefully restate key ideas and conclude the discussion.

Here is another example of reading, analyzing, and marking a test question from a history course. It asks for special treatment because of a single word in the question.

> **Example:**   Discuss critically the causes and the results of the French Revolution.
> The question marked for analysis:
>
>   1   2   3   4
> Discuss / critically / the causes / and the results of /
>   5
> the <u>French Revolution</u>.

Again, the question has five parts:

1. The main subject is the French Revolution. Underline it.
2. You are to *discuss* fully (tell everything relevant) the causes.
3. You are to *discuss* fully (tell everything relevant) the results.
4. Your analysis is to be judgmental, as *critical* means evaluate and judge.
5. *Discuss* means to write in great detail, giving many specifics.

For a minimal answer you will need to structure and outline for at least two paragraphs — one for causes, one for results. However, the term *discuss critically* possibly indicates an answer of several paragraphs, perhaps one on each cause and one on each result. You'll need to sketch a brief outline to help you gather your thoughts before writing.

You probably have studied at least five major causes and six or seven major results. Among these, you need to decide which are the major ones to cover; this decision will reflect your critical judgment and evaluation, but your comments should reflect more than memorized facts. You'll need to limit yourself to what you believe are the four or five major causes and results, devoting probably several sentences to each. The word *critically* in the question invites subjective responses. That is, state your opinions, but be careful: not all essay questions permit this flexibility. It does not invite you to begin every sentence with "I think" or "I believe"; instead, it asks you to reflect, to evaluate, to judge.

Let's shift our perspective a bit, looking at a student's answer in response to this test question: Compare and contrast the different attitudes toward work of Margaret in "Finishing School" and the company man in Ellen Goodman's essay.

Although the company man and Margaret were workers they had several differences in certain respects, especially in their attitude toward working. The company man had a very important position in his company. He was the vice president; he wanted to be president. Therefore he had been working so hard to earn as much profit and prestige as he could. Margaret, however, was a servant to a white woman, Viola Cullinan. If Margaret had not been in poverty, she would have never worked with Mrs. Cullinan. Therefore, both these people have different targets towards working. One was working to become a successful man, whereas the poor black girl was working for survival. The most significant aspect of their jobs were the company man was really a workaholic. He had been working overtime. In contrast, as a servant Margaret had a working schedule. She worked every day from morning to evening. Compared to the company man, she had enough time to rest at night while he felt compelled to continue working, even on Sunday, supposedly his holiday.

What do you notice about this answer? It has some detail from each selection. Can you locate the two or three points of contrast the student tried to make? It is definitely a comparison–contrast answer, as the question required. Many of the transition markers are here, such as *whereas* and *compared to*. The student comments about both selections and there is some sentence variety; but clearly the student is in a hurry, as some of the sentences break down grammatically and mechanically. There is no clincher sentence; the answer merely stops in mid-air. Perhaps the addition of one summary sentence might have convinced the grader that the student had done serious thinking about both the selections and the question, and might have earned the student a grade higher than C.

Undoubtedly, the most important principle about writing essay exams is this: YOU HAVE TIME FOR ONLY ONE DRAFT. You have no time to revise and rewrite; your first try must count. For this reason, before you begin writing, take one minute to list (or outline) the points you must discuss. At the same time try to internalize all of the principles of the writing process you have already learned — topic sentences, introductions, supporting details, transitions, conclusions, and clincher sentences.

Once you have finished writing your answer, save at least two or three minutes to reread. Check for omission of key points or important concepts, and correct what omissions or mistakes you can, generally by striking out the error and inserting the correction above it, using a carat mark to indicate the addition:

Check spelling, grammar, and neatness. Legibility is vital.

Analyzing Your Exam Grade

Let's assume now that you have the exam back from your instructor, and you're upset, unhappy, and puzzled by your low grade and want to figure out why you didn't do better. Not all low grades are the result of inadequate knowledge. Occasionally, grades are low because students are not adept at test-taking techniques. Doing well on exams is a learned activity; success comes with practice and know-how. It might be wise to discuss your answers with your instructor, a grading assistant, or a member of a study skills staff, asking for advice and help. Perhaps a tutoring session might be wise.

Four common reasons for low grades on essay exams are:

1. Failure to read the test question correctly or to interpret the question accurately.

2. Failure to write complete answers with specific details, illustrations, statistics, appropriate examples, or other important details; the answer is superficial, incomplete, or inadequate.

3. Failure to define concepts, telling what a concept *does* rather than what it *is*; telling what a concept *is not* rather than what it *is*.

4. Failure to present a legible paper free of basic errors in grammar, punctuation, spelling. These are barriers to communication. And on an exam communication is vital.

Exercise 10–1

Examine the answers students have written for their Shakespeare exams. Try to find the strengths and weaknesses of each answer, following this model.

Question: Identify the quotation; name the play, the speaker, and the context. Then in one or two sentences explain the significance of the passage "I am more sinned against than sinning."

The speaker is King Lear in the play King Lear. He is talking to Kent, after being rejected and foully treated by his two daughters, Regan and Goneril. Lear admits that he has sinned, but his errors are nothing compared to the unjust treatment given him by these two ungrateful females. Has Lear been "more sinned against than sinning"? He has been blind to the faults of his daughters. Nevertheless he has divided the kingdom and abdicated his power to Regan and Goneril, a situation bound to end in disaster, since Lear still wanted to retain some authority and prestige. But Lear has all ready bred a lust for even more power in the hearts of the already too greedy Regan and Goneril.

Evaluation:

— good use of detail (Kent named; reference to blinding, abdication, greed, power grabbing)
— careless language (*all ready* instead of *already*)
— too general at times (refers generally to Regan and Goneril's treatment of Lear but mentions no specific action)

1.   This line comes from King Lear by William Shakespeare. Lear speaks. Regan and Goneril have been bad to him. This has upset him. Lear feels he does not deserve this since he has been good to them and given them everything he owned. What he doesn't understand is that they have rejected him because he no longer has nothing to give them. All that remains is for them to flatter him.

Evaluation: _____

_____

_____

Exercise 10–2

Imagine that you are in a course, taking an essay examination on the following topics. Based upon what you have learned in this chapter, how would you go about answering these questions? Don't worry about content; in many cases you may be completely unfamiliar with the material referred to in the question. On a separate sheet of paper simply describe the strategies you'd use in developing an answer for one of the five questions:

Example: Explain the differences between a deductible and nondeductible IRA contribution.

1.   First of all, I would mark the question after reading it carefully.

2. I probably would begin by defining the differences between the two contributions so that the evaluator will know I understand the differences.

3. I would try to focus on three or four characteristics of each type of IRA contribution.

4. I would try to focus on some of the contrasts between the tax benefits of the two types of IRAs so that the two concepts of deductibility and nondeductibility would be clear.

5. I would include at least two specific examples, one of a deductible IRA and one of a nondeductible one.

6. My tasks are to define, focus, and make clear — to communicate.

Analyze one of the following questions.

1. Trace the steps in "A Rose for Emily" that show the aging of Emily Grierson.

2. Read the poem below and interpret the relationship between musical language and the theme Robert Frost is developing.

3. Select one of the key images in Seurat's painting, "The Circus," and analyze its relationship to the central idea of the whole work.

4. Briefly outline the major points of contention in the first Lincoln–Douglas debate.

5. Enumerate the parts of and evaluate the effectiveness of the battle plan for the defense of Manila Bay by Admiral Dewey.

A Final Word

The purpose of essay exams is more to help you learn than it is to measure how much you happen to recall on a particular day at a particular time. Learn to accept examinations as challenges to your thinking, organizing, and writing skills; as an opportunity to synthesize your knowledge, understanding, and interpretation of the course. Sit back and think about the class and the various topics and theories covered. Form conclusions based upon the various concepts and ideas expressed in the textbook and by your instructor. If you think about the course material and keep up with classroom assignments, then you should have no trouble writing essay exams.

Index